PERCEPTION AND ITS DEVELOPMENT:
A Tribute to Eleanor J. Gibson

Photograph by Hugh Coffman

PERCEPTION AND ITS DEVELOPMENT:
A Tribute to Eleanor J. Gibson

Edited by
ANNE D. PICK
University of Minnesota

 LAWRENCE ERLBAUM ASSOCIATES, PUBLISHERS
1979   Hillsdale, New Jersey

DISTRIBUTED BY THE HALSTED PRESS DIVISION OF
JOHN WILEY & SONS
New York   Toronto   London   Sydney

Lawrence Erlbaum Associates, Inc., Publishers
365 Broadway
Hillsdale, New Jersey 07642

Distributed solely by Halsted Press Division
John Wiley & Sons, Inc., New York

Library of Congress Catalog Card Number: 79-52999

Printed in the United States of America

Contents

Foreword:
A Note on E. J. G.
by J. J. G.

James J. Gibson

I first met Eleanor Jack at a polite afternoon reception for the parents of the graduating Seniors of Smith College. She was herself a Junior, whose office it was to pass the punch. I was a recently appointed member of the faculty, which was supposed to be in attendance. She was dazzling. I did not waste the opportunity. We neglected our duties. She agreed to go out with me in my Model T Ford the very next evening. We did not go to a garden party but to a place called Mountain Park where the roller coasters were considered to be the steepest in New England.

The following academic year she took Advanced Experimental Psychology. She and eight other Seniors carried out experiments on all kinds of new problems. It was a year course, meeting 6 hours a week. There were few published results on any of the problems, and you could make discoveries. Most of the students went on to careers in psychology. Her final grade was A plus. During that year she went to the best house parties, at Amherst and Princeton, for she was extremely attractive and an absolutely great dancer, but she also found a great deal of time for study. And she got fascinated by the possibility of controlling the conditions under which a person (or a rat) could learn. This was 1932, and the laws of learning were about to be established!

Eleanor Jack stayed on as a teaching assistant at Smith College, along with a couple of her friends, at what would now be a starvation wage but which was not bad in the Depression. We fell in love during that year, and when she went home to Peoria for the summer, it soon became clear that we could not stand to be separated. So I drove to Illinois and hung on until her parents agreed to a wedding. I had a Model A Ford by that time, a more luxurious car. We got married just 6 days before classes were to begin again at Smith. The expenses of a honeymoon had been calculated so tightly that a broken fan belt on the last leg of the trip required me to borrow money to get back.

Why would a girl with all the attractions of the heroines of F. Scott Fitzgerald marry a college teacher instead of a millionaire? Because the academic life appealed to her, and she wanted an academic career. Going to parties was all very well, but the intellectual life was even better. The Smith College faculty was actually a lively society at that time. There was a serious Marxist study group, for example, but every now and then the members also did square dancing. So the academic life was fine, but the academic career, as she was to discover, was not so easily achieved by a woman.

The first step was a master's degree. She needed a thesis problem, so her new husband lovingly presented her with the best idea he had ever had for an experiment, one he had been saving up just for her. She turned it down. She worked on retroactive inhibition instead, a problem of less cosmic importance but more elegant procedure. The first name on the resulting paper was Eleanor J. Gibson, although 2 years before she had coauthored a paper as Eleanor G. Jack. No married women kept her own name in those days. A wife's career was identified with her husband's. A woman who rejected her husband's name joined the Lucy Stone League and was a bit peculiar.

She became an instructor at Smith and went regularly to Kurt Koffka's seminar, attended by the postdoctoral students of his laboratory and the faculty. She did not care much for Gestalt theory, however, nor for such questions as why things look as they do. She wanted to study hard science, the science of behavior. She would have to go away for a Ph.D., but how was it to be managed? Not until 1936, when her husband got his first sabbatical leave, could it be done. She went to Yale where Clark Hull was developing the first systematic theory of behavior, a hypothetico-deductive system based on conditioning. She had only 1 year off, so all the requirements for the degree except the thesis had to be met in a short period. But she got on famously with Hull and sailed through the examinations. She chose a thesis problem that fitted into his program of research but, characteristically, one she thought of herself, a problem on the neglected side of the conditioned reflex—the perceptual aspect of it—the phenomena called stimulus generalization and differentiation. She was the first woman to get an experimental degree with Hull, and he never forgot her. In those days, if women got Ph.D's at all, they were expected to do so in child psychology or mental testing. Yale was suspicious of women who wanted to do what men did.

Back at Smith, where the faculty was half male and half female, the unconscious prejudice against women was scarcely noticeable. She might have had an academic career there, since the supposedly insidious danger of nepotism was not sternly prohibited, as it was at the universities. But the War interfered. In 1940 she was an assistant professor with a full schedule, a fine old house to live in, a housekeeper with standards, a male baby, and an admiring husband. But she gave it all up except for the last two. The husband was sent to Texas where flying training for the Air Corps was concentrated, and she took the baby and went along without question, for she liked her family as much as her profession, and she never saw any reason why she should not have both. She had published her doctoral research by that time, and it had made a stir, so that she was beginning to be known in her discipline if not established in her profession.

In 1940 there was a science of psychology and a profession of teaching. The so-called profession of psychology was almost unheard of until after the War. She never had the slightest interest in it nor any inclination to join it.

So, for 6 long years she had a household, another baby, and a stay-at-home life, with food and gas rationing to cope with. The community at Forth Worth, Texas, was not stimulating, and that in Santa Ana, California, near the Air Base, was so reactionary as to be stifling. Whereas her husband was doing psychological research that, luckily for him, was full of interest, she could only mark time. She was good at housekeeping and family management, but it was not enough. So she was delighted to go back to Smith and resume teaching in 1946 at the end of the War.

She and her husband shared an enthusiasm for making experiments; it had brought them together, and they were addicted to it. (The passion for theorizing that was to seize him later had not fully developed.) It annoyed her, therefore, that the Psychological Round Table, a group of experimentalists who met often in Northampton, never dreamed of inviting a female psychologist to their argumentative sessions. If asked, they would have given the same pious reasons that Titchener gave for excluding women from his Society of Experimental Psychologists: The smoking and drinking would not suit them. The members of the Round Table, moreover, told dirty stories and tended to go on the town at night.

She was a full-fledged faculty member. But the doing of research was not as much honored at a college, even one like Smith, as it would be at a university. So, once again, she abandoned a teaching career when her husband got an offer from Cornell. There was no job for her, but she would have the title of Research Associate and could do experiments. It sounded promising.

The era of grants and contracts for research was just beginning in 1950. But Cornell did not at first allow her to apply for support on her own behalf and for her own project. The Office of the Coordinator of Research considered her to be a faculty wife. She had to get research money through a member of the faculty, usually her husband. "Just a formality," said the administrators. For years, she had no status and little local recognition, although her contributions to psychology were mounting up. Graduate students worked under her direction, but appointment to the faculty was not to be thought of, for the Gibsons would have two votes in meetings of the department. Her husband was in a double bind, for the slightest tendency to argue the injustice of the nepotism rule in the faculty code was taken to be an expression of that very evil. She herself never protested; she just kept working. Salary was less important than satisfaction. But the situation was unfair, and it was sometimes hard on the family tie.

The results of her experiments were often striking. She worked on learning and conditioning, but with a difference. She worked on perception, with her husband, but perception outdoors under the sky instead of perception of points in a darkroom. Notably, she worked on learning to perceive, a new field of study in 1956, and certain quite radical implications began to emerge. She worked with animals and infants. She collaborated with anyone who wanted to try out something new. She helped to invent the "visual cliff." She worked on the effect of early visual experience. Narrow specialties did not tempt her (although American psychology was moving toward them more and more). Her work ranged over the whole of the basic discipline. She worked with her husband on the kinds of perception induced by optical motions and transformations. She finally wrote a book on perceptual learning and development, the first of its kind. She took part in a large research project on how children learn to read, picking up psycholinguistics on the way. She coauthored a book on reading. She began to acquire honors. She became a Professor perforce, having earned that status long before she got it.

* * *

How did it come about that she made it to the top where so few women psychologists arrive, and in spite of all the discouraging obstacles? I am a poor judge, perhaps, being personally involved, but on the other hand, I ought to be in a position to know. It took a lot of stubborn persistence. But she had to collaborate with me, and with many others, especially at first, so she had to be tactfully stubborn—or mildly, or sweetly, perhaps—but not *plain* stubborn. She was bound to be a threat to her male collaborators, of course, including me, and she had to cope with it by never seeming to threaten. She didn't worry too much about who got the credit in these collaborations, for it was the idea that counted. And she had plenty of good ideas, enough to give away. She had a feeling for when an experiment was going to work, as I had myself, and she could smell a bad experiment a mile off. She admired the experimenters in psychology as compared to pure theorists or philosophers. The scientific formula of the 1930s—that a theory had to be vulnerable to disproof—was one of her convictions. Above all, she had a sense of the directions in which scientific psychology ought to move, and she moved in those directions.

What is the relationship between her work and mine over all these years? My judgment is even less to be trusted on that score, one would suppose, and yet it is a fair question. She has a separate but related body of research and publication, and she began it under the influence of Hull. We have collaborated on occasion but not as a regular thing. And when we did, we were not a husband-and-wife "team," God knows, for we argued endlessly. The popular concept of a married pair of scientists working harmoniously together is a sentimental stereotype in which the wife is a "helper." We have been influenced by somewhat different trends in psychology and somewhat different people, but not different enough to make us go in separate ways. We have always read the same books even if we did not agree about them, and thus each of us has always influenced the other more than anyone else did. But there are great differences in temperament and style. I have become a theorist. I enjoy arguing and she does not. I am uncompromising, whereas she dislikes dogmatic positions. She prefers literary art and I prefer visual art. She does not care about epistemology, but I am addicted to it. She prefers running rats to studying binocular disparity, whereas for me, it is the other way round. Despite all this, however, we seem to have the same deep convictions. We have the same moral commitments. We admire the same people, and when it comes to dislike, we dislike the same people—the glib and pretentious.

I simply do not know, therefore, whether we have the same theoretical position or not, and neither does she. When it is assumed that whatever one Gibson says, the other will agree to, we are annoyed, for it isn't so. On the other hand, if anyone should try to refute one of us by quoting the other, we should get even more annoyed. That may not be logical, but that is a fact.

Introduction

Anne D. Pick
University of Minnesota

We have acquired important new knowledge about the nature and development of perception in recent years, and the insights of Eleanor Jack Gibson have had a prominent role in guiding the search for that knowledge. The purpose of this volume is to honor her continuing contribution to our understanding of perception. The book is organized around five topics, each of which reflects the influence of her own thinking. Part I covers learning and generalization, which was the subject of her own doctoral dissertation at Yale University. Contributors to that topic in this volume are Donald A. Riley and Marvin R. Lamb, and Louise and Thomas Tighe. In both chapters there is emphasis on the need to analyze the relevant aspects of the stimulus and the task from the perspective of the subject. The stimulus as conceptualized by the experimenter is not necessarily the functional stimulus, and this theme is elaborated in other chapters in the volume as well. Two other themes occur first in these chapters, at least implicitly, and are elaborated in later chapters. The first is that pattern and structure are concepts important for our understanding of the basis for complex perception, and the second is that the relevant information for perception is given over time as well as space.

The topic of Part II is the development of spatial perception, and the contributors are Richard Walk, who collaborated with Eleanor Gibson in the original studies with the "visual cliff," and Albert Yonas. Both writers emphasize the importance of using natural, nonarbitrary behaviors to index perceptual functioning, and the need to consider the setting in which the relevant behavior occurs. A consideration of the adaptive significance of various aspects of perception is useful for understanding its phylogeny, ontogeny, and variability.

Part III deals wtih the perception of pattern and structure, and the contributors to this topic are Wendell Garner, and Anne Pick. One of these chapters is about perceiving letters, and the other is about perceiving melodies; in both, the need for a careful description of the structural properties that are relevant for perception is made explicit. It is also clear that in both cases, those properties are not simple elements but are complex relational properties.

Part IV covers the perception of meaning. Here, too, the contributors, Harry Levin, and T. G. R. Bower, write about meaning in quite different contexts, although there are important common ideas in both chapters. Harry Levin, a long-time collaborator of Eleanor Gibson's in the study of basic processes of reading, has reviewed the relation between oral and silent reading. He considers reading to be the extraction of meaning from the text, and he suggests that the processes of perception and comprehension are similar for reading aloud and reading silently. Bower writes about the acquisition of meaning by infant perceivers, and the course of their development as their perception of meaning becomes more detailed and precise.

The topic of Part V is exploration and selectivity, and Ulric Neisser, a Cornell colleague of Eleanor Gibson, and Elizabeth Spelke have contributed chapters about the perception of ongoing events. Both emphasize the relevance of the perceiver's own knowledge in guiding the perceptual exploration of events that results in the acquisition of new knowledge. Neisser is concerned explicitly with how knowledge of the structure of a visible event guides one's continued tracking of it. Spelke writes about the development during infancy of the perception of events that are both seen and heard.

A unique perspective on Eleanor Gibson's own career is provided by James J. Gibson in his Foreword to the book. In addition, Jackie herself, as she is known to many of us, has the last word at the end of the book where the text of an interview with her by Harry Levin provides her own perspective on the evolution of the science of psychology during the last few decades, as well as her judgment about the directions it is taking now.

Throughout all of the chapters there is a focus always on understanding the nature of what is perceived, and this is an appropriate focus for it has always been central to Jackie's own thinking. Other ideas, too, cut across the five topics and occupy prominent places in her work as well. Some examples are: (1) the idea that attention is the selective aspect of perception; (2) the assumption that what are perceived are patterns, objects, and events rather than stimuli; and (3) the belief that differentiation is a central concept for understanding perceptual learning and perceptual development.

Half of the contributors to this volume—Louise and Tom Tighe, Al Yonas, Anne Pick, Tom Bower, and Liz Spelke—are students of Jackie's, and this is eminently appropriate, for she excites the curiosity of her students, and she entices them to be her collaborators in the quest for new knowledge right from the start. She is well-known for taking a student's nascent, half-formed idea for an experiment, mulling it overnight, and returning it the next day— clarified, elaborated, and made precise in the form of an elegant plan for a study. She also always gives back rather than takes the credit for the idea and its significance.

The plan of this book was developed jointly by the editor and by Al Yonas, Dick Neisser, and Herb Pick. The chapter contributors were enthusiastic and agreed immediately to adhere to a rigid deadline so that the book would be ready for the occasion of its presentation. Larry Erlbaum and Ros Herion, of Lawrence Erlbaum Associates, have facilitated the project from the start, and Judy Allen took a major share of the responsibility for editing the manuscripts. I am grateful to all of these persons for their assistance, and I know also that they join me in acknowledging that the most important influence on the volume is provided by Jackie Gibson herself, in whose honor it has been written.

I LEARNING AND GENERALIZATION

1 Stimulus Generalization

Donald A. Riley
Marvin R. Lamb
University of California, Berkeley

For years psychologists studying learning have focused on the formation of associations via operant and classical conditioning procedures. The precise nature of these associations has been an important, and often elusive, issue. One way of addressing this question is to ask about the parameters of the stimuli that enter into associations. What stimuli present on a conditioning trial become associated? In what ways might these stimuli be represented internally? How might these internal representations get translated into responses? We may begin to answer questions of this sort by examining how the effects of training on one stimulus transfer to other stimuli.

In classical conditioning, for example, one stimulus (the US) occurs often in the presence of another stimulus (the CS) and rarely in its absence. When a change in behavior is observed upon the establishment of this predictive relationship, it is inferred that an association has been formed between the CS and the US. If, however, a stimulus similar to the CS is presented, the newly learned response is likely to occur. This effect has been called stimulus generalization. Such generalized responses rarely occur with as high a probability or as rapidly or vigorously as responses to the training stimulus, however. Instead, stimulus generalization tends to decrease as the similarity between the test stimulus and the CS decreases, resulting in what is called a gradient of stimulus generalization. These relations between training and test stimuli are of interest because they are central to our conceptions of learning.

In the history of thinking about stimulus generalization, two explanations have emerged: strength theory and stimulus classification theory. Strength theory assumes that as training proceeds, associations increase in strength. When, after some training, a test with stimuli other than those used in training reveals a tendency to respond, the associative strength is said to have generalized. That is, the excitatory strength gained by the training stimulus is thought to have spread to other stimuli as well. In stimulus classification theory, learning is conceptualized as the progressive identification of the defining properties of the stimulus that predicts reinforcement. As training progresses, the organism becomes more effective at this task, and the probability, speed, and vigor of the response increase. When tested with other stimuli, the organism may make mistakes for a variety of reasons. That is, the subject may incorrectly classify the test stimulus as a member of the class, "training stimulus." In this chapter we describe the development of these two conceptions of stimulus generalization from their inception to their present state and examine a small set of experiments that seem to bear critically on the relative merits of these two alternative views.

THE DEVELOPMENT OF STRENGTH THEORY

Strength theory began with Pavlov's development of a behaviorally based account of the formation of an association resulting from the contiguous presentation of two stimuli. In the course of his investigations, Pavlov found that other stimuli were also affected by this associative process, and it is from the analysis of this fact that the topic of stimulus generalization developed.

Pavlov's analysis of transfer of training along dimensions has been discussed at length in a number of different volumes and need not be described in detail here (see Mackintosh, 1974; Pavlov, 1927; Riley, 1968). Briefly, Pavlov observed that when an animal was trained in a classical conditioning task to salivate to a conditioned stimulus of a given brightness, size, or frequency, then other stimuli on the same dimension also tended to elicit the same response. The magnitude of the response, however, varied with the distance on the appropriate dimension from the conditioned stimulus. Pavlov designated this phenomenon "generalization of stimuli," and others later referred to the orderly change in responding as a function of similarity of the test stimulus to the CS as a "gradient of stimulus generalization." Conditioning, according to Pavlov, consisted of the development of an excitatory event traveling from the locus in the cortex corresponding to the CS to the locus corresponding to the US. With repeated pairings of the CS and US, the excitatory strength of the CS increased. In addition, the excitatory strength thus accruing to the CS was thought to spread to other nearby points in the cortex, with increasingly distant points receiving increasingly less excitatory strength. Thus, when a stimulus similar but not identical to the CS was presented, excitation from that stimulus would spread to the locus of the CS, arousing in turn that location; and as a consequence, it would also arouse the location of the US, evoking the conditioned response. Pavlov assumed that for each observed gradient of stimulus generalization, there was an isomorphic gradient of excitation in the cerebral cortex. This scheme, assuming spatial isomorphism between sensory events and cortical events, fell into disfavor as a result of a substantial amount of research reviewed elsewhere (see Riley, 1968), but the notion of generalization as an active process persisted.

When Hull (1943) took the facts of conditioning as a source of postulates from which to deduce more complex phenomena of performance and learning, one of the central facts of conditioning was that of stimulus generalization. Hull accepted as a fact of habit formation that the response associated with the CS would also be elicited by other similar stimuli according to a law of similarity. Although Hull did not follow Pavlov in assuming that generalization reflected the spread of excitation across the cerebral cortex, his writings and those of his students viewed generalization as a process associated with conditioning. As excitatory strength (or habit strength) developed in accord with the laws of conditioning, this excitation was said to "generalize" from the CS to other stimuli sharing common dimensions with it. Thus Spence (1937), in his analysis of transposition in terms of generalization of excitation and inhibition, wrote: "We shall assume there is a generalization of this acquired excitation tendency to stimulus objects of similar size and that this generalization follows a gradient [p. 433]."

One implication of the notion of generalization as an active process is that the spread of excitation can be to points that are known to be discriminable from the CS. Pavlov demonstrated that test stimuli were, in fact, discriminated from the CS early in the generalization test; only after the first few test trials were there any indication that excitation had accrued to stimuli other than the CS. Hovland (1937) ran a series of auditory conditioning experiments with human subjects. Following training, the subjects were tested wtih stimuli that were 25, 50, or 75 just noticeable differences (JND) from the CS. The fact that these increasingly remote test stimuli elicited increasingly smaller conditioned responses was taken to mean that the generalization of excitation was progressively smaller as distance from the CS along the sensory dimension increased. Although the point was not made explicitly, it should be clear that the method by which these points were selected implied that all test stimuli were highly discriminable. These precautions suggest that these investigators recognized that the stimulus generalization gradient could occur, not because of the spread of an excitatory process, but because of discriminatory failures. Experiments such as Hovland's and an earlier one by Bass and Hull (1934), also with humans and in which vibrotactile stimuli were used at four different points on the body surface from the shoulder to the calf of the leg, seemed to preclude the possibility that generalized responses were confusion errors.

Another early distinction provided by students of Hull was the distinction between primary and secondary stimulus generalization. Primary stimulus generalization was used to describe generalization in situations where there was no obvious reason to assume that the response to the different test stimuli was based on learned stimulus equivalence. Secondary stimulus generalization was intended to apply in situations where learned stimulus equivalence had either been demonstrated or was the most reasonable assumption. One of the earliest demonstrations of secondary stimulus generalization by Shipley (1935), working in Hull's laboratory, showed (Hull, 1943):

> a flash of light followed by a tap of a padded hammer against the cheek below the eye, thus conditioning lid closure to the light flash. Next the same subject was repeatedly given an electric shock on the finger. This evoked not only a sharp finger withdrawal from the electrode but lid closure as well. Finally the flash of light was delivered alone. It was found in considerable proportion of the subjects of both experiments that during this latter maneuver the light evoked finger retraction, *even though the former had never been associated with either the shock or the finger retraction.* The interpretation is that light evoked the lid closure and proprioceptive stimulation produced by this act (or some other less conspicuous act conditioned at the same time) evoked the finger retraction [p. 192].

The important point in this description lies in its assumption of a presumed second type of stimulus generalization—this one based on learned equivalence. Again, the assumption is clear that the subjects responded to two different stimuli in a similar way, not because they confuse them, but because of some other process. In this case, both stimuli activate a second process that controls the final output.

Thus, in the Hullian tradition, both primary generalization and secondary generalization were assumed to be processes by which response strength spread to test stimuli recognizably different from the training stimulus according to the similarity, physical or learned, between the test and training stimuli. The greater interest in primary stimulus generalization was at least in part because of the ready-made ordinal scales that separated several points from the training stimulus along a sensory dimension.

Both phenomena—primary and secondary generalization—were used as explanatory principles to account for more complex effects. Among these was Gibson's (1940) extension of stimulus generalization from classical conditioning paradigms to voluntary response tasks in humans, Spence's (1937) analysis of transposition in terms of interacting gradients of excitation and inhibition, and Hull's (1943) assumption of the summation of generalized positive habits to explain how stimulus–response associations increase in strength even though the same stimulus is never experienced twice (the stimulus learning paradox). The use of stimulus generalization as an explanatory principle had also been informally invoked by Pavlov (1927) to account for the facilitating effects of performing an easy discrimination on the ability subsequently to perform a difficult discrimination on the same dimension. This list of phenomena have in common the fact that all the behaviors described are in some sense under the control of stimuli that differ from the nominal training stimulus, and for all, there is an explanation that assumes generalization of excitation. It is interesting that the assumption that primary stimulus generalization results from the spread of a habit has been regularly questioned during the past 20 years, and today it is not taken very seriously, even by former proponents.

During the past 10 years, strength theory has undergone transformation largely because of the development of the Rescorla–Wagner (1972) model of conditioning. Like Hull's theory of learning, this model assumes that excitatory strength approaches a maximum exponentially, but the model also specifies that the conditionability of a stimulus that is part of a compound is determined by the strength of the entire compound and not by the current associative strength of the stimulus itself. A number of consequences of this assumption have been explored by Rescorla, Wagner, and their students. Of particular interest to us, however, is the implication of this assumption for phenomena of stimulus generalization. In particular, if the overall strength of a stimulus compound is low, then an increase in excitatory strength of the compound will increase the strength of all the members of the compound regardless of the initial strength of the individual members. As we shall see, these assumptions about the role of the compound in determining the conditionability of the components of the compound result in some interesting predictions. Another facet, however, of this thinking has been a new interest in considering a "stimulus" as an aggregate of elements, each of which may have its own excitatory strength.

THE DEVELOPMENT OF STIMULUS CLASSIFICATION THEORY

The assault on the "neo-Pavlovian" view of stimulus generalization was launched by Lashley and Wade in 1946. They argued, and variations were subsequently introduced by Prokasy and Hall (1963), that a process of stimulus generalization was unnecessary to account for what, under other circumstances, would be called errors. An animal that has been trained to respond positively to a certain stimulus is shown another stimulus and asked if it is the same one. If the animal responds affirmatively, it is an error. Errors, according to this view of stimulus generalization, occur for a variety of reasons. One is that the animal has not associated different stimulus values with different outcomes. Generalization gradients, Lashley and Wade argued, arise only after the animal has learned a discrimination on the dimension in question. They provided evidence for this position by showing that rats did not show a generalization gradient in a choice test following single stimulus training. But this amounted to an assertion that all previous demonstrations of stimulus generalization were in some way the product of inadvertent discrimination procedures, and other investigators quickly produced evidence that test procedures that did not permit such an interpretation would indeed produce generalization gradients (Grice, 1948). One might also argue that when generalization gradients are observed, they are the result of associations formed prior to the experiment itself. Several experiments conducted with pigeons reared and trained with monochromatic light have found evidence for generalization gradients even under these conditions and so have not supported this speculation (see Riley, 1977). Thus, stimulus generalization gradients seem to occur even in the absence of an opportunity for secondary generalization to develop.

There was, however, more to the attack on the Hullian interpretation of stimulus generalization gradients. Lashley and Wade also suggested that monotonically declining gradients could reflect variable stimulus difference thresholds. This argument assumes that an animal recognizes a class of stimuli to which it responds with an appropriate learned response and another class not associated with that response. If the threshold shifts from trial to trial, then a gradient should emerge. Prokasy and Hall (1963) argued similarly that even in cases of generalization gradients extending across highly discriminable differences, the gradient might be due to insensitive testing procedures that would result in the animal's failing to detect these stimulus differences. Thus, these interpretations of generalization gradients assume that the gradient occurs, not because of a gradient of habit strength, but because of variations by the subject in the classification of stimulus events.

Modern versions of stimulus classification theory assume that the animal, on the basis of different outcomes such as different reinforcement schedules, classifies stimuli into different categories and responds appropriately. Thus in a simple case, a pigeon might be required to peck at a key on the left in the presence of one stimulus and at a key on the right in the presence of another stimulus. The advantage, in this analysis, of having two clearly defined alternative responses lies in knowing precisely what response is to be given to each stimulus. If, as is often the case, the response alternatives are "respond" (e.g., peck) and "don't respond," the second class is unspecified. It consists of everything except pecking the key. Nevertheless, both procedures have been used.

The only quantitative analyses of stimulus generalization in terms of stimulus classification theory have used ideas from the theory of signal detection. A signal detection model of stimulus generalization assumes that there is random variability, or noise, associated with the presentation and processing of physical stimuli, so that each physical stimulus will, over time or after repeated presentations, activate a range of internal events. Thus, each physical stimulus gives rise to what some investigators (Boneau & Cole, 1967) have referred to as a discriminal distribution. This distribution represents the probability with which a given physical stimulus will activate various internal events and is usually assumed to be Gaussian in form. Stimuli that lie along a continuum, such as intensity, give rise to overlapping discriminal distributions. Thus, not only does the same physical stimulus activate different neural elements at different times, but different physical stimuli also often activate the same internal representation. Under these conditions, it is impossible for the organism to make decisions about external events with certainty.

Green and Swets (1966) have shown that the optimal decision rule in such cases is based on the likelihood ratio. This is the ratio of the probability that the activated internal event was produced, in signal detection terms, by a signal to the probability that it was activated by noise. If the likelihood ratio exceeds some criterion value, the organism decides that the internal event was activated by one class of stimuli (e.g., reinforced stimuli, or signals) and behaves in the manner appropriate to that class. Internal events associated with likelihood ratios below the criterion value result in behavior appropriate to some other class (e.g., nonreinforced stimuli, or noise). The particular criterion value chosen will depend on such things as the costs and benefits associated with incorrect and correct responses in the situation in question.

More specifically, a signal detection model assumes that the generalization gradient emerges as a result of the following processes. First, each stimulus along a continuum (e.g., intensity) gives rise to a discriminal distribution. The means of these distributions are monotonically related to the intensity values of each stimulus along the continuum. In addition, the distributions overlap. A criterion is established at some point in order to maximize payoffs. Each time a stimulus activates an internal event that lies to one side of the criterion, a response appropriate to that class of stimuli (e.g., a peck) is emitted (see Fig. 1.1A). Thus, the probability that a given response will be emitted in the presence of a given stimulus is proportional to that part of its discriminal distribution that lies to the side of the criterion associated with that response (see Fig. 1.1B).

The application of the theory of signal detection to problems of discriminative behavior in animals requires additional considerations that are often ignored. First, the animal must learn the appropriate response or pattern of responses required by the task. That is, in distinction to the case with human subjects, animals receive all their instructions from the reinforcement contingencies. Payoffs not only determine the criterion, they also determine what response is required of the animal on either side of the criterion line.

Second, Boneau and Cole (1967) have suggested that the type of model just described is inadequate, because the animal must know the form of its own discriminal distributions in order to form the likelihood ratios. They assert

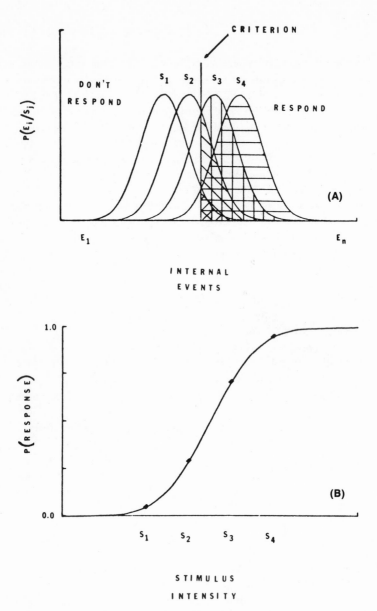

FIG. 1.1. This figure shows how a signal detection analysis can generate gradients of responding. (A) Four discriminal distributions corresponding to four stimulus intensities (see text). The different stimulus intensities are designated by a subscripted S and the internal events by a subscripted E. The criterion line represents the animal's classification of internal events into response and nonresponse regions. Given a particular stimulus, the greater the area of its discriminal distribution lying in the response region, the more likely it is to generate a response. This relationship can be seen by comparing the shaded areas of the discriminal distributions of the various stimuli (A) to the points on the response probability gradient corresponding to those stimuli (B).

that animals such as pigeons have access to this information only under very special conditions, if at all. To overcome this difficulty, Boneau and Cole proposed a signal detection model in which animals make decisions based on the probability of reinforcement associated with the different internal events. Such a model generates decision rules that are monotonic with likelihood ratio decisions.

Finally, stimulus generalization gradients for nonintensive dimensions such as wavelength, angular orientation, auditory frequency, and stimulus location typically show symmetrical gradients on the physical dimension in question. Thus, for example, training a bird to peck at a light of a certain frequency results in a symmetrical generalization gradient around that particular frequency. Such a distribution suggests that in the course of conditioning, two criteria develop—one for stimulus values at some point below S+ and the other for stimulus values at a corresponding point above S+.

The situation may well be different for intensive dimensions that show stimulus intensity dynamism effects. Heinemann and Chase (1975), for example, have argued that postdiscrimination gradients in intensity show no reduction in response strength for extreme values. Such a finding in signal detection terms can only mean that the response is determined by a single criterion. One problem for the development of an adequate signal detection analysis of stimulus generalization is to specify the conditions under which a subject develops two criteria or to describe some alternative mechanism for restricting responses on either side of S+.

As the reader may have already noted, interpretations of stimulus generalization have (at least) three components: The first deals with the nature of the effective stimulus, the second with the internal events that code that stimulus, and the third with the response. In the sections that follow we elaborate on these three components and consider evidence helpful to our comparison of the different models of stimulus generalization.

ALTERNATIVE CONCEPTIONS OF
THE EFFECTIVE STIMULUS IN
THE ANALYSIS OF STIMULUS GENERALIZATION

An implicit assumption in many conditioning experiments is that the stimulus selected by the experimenter as the CS is the only stimulus that gains associative strength during a conditioning trial. It is clear, however, that many other stimuli are present at the time of reinforcement and may gain associative strength. If they do, then it is possible that it is the presence of these other stimuli that maintains responding during the generalization test, even though the CS is not present. Investigators as early as Hull (1943) suggested that such occurrences would affect the slope of the generalization gradient. Jenkins and Harrison (1960) later showed that conditioning pigeons to peck at a lighted key in the presence of a tone resulted in a flat generalization gradient to auditory frequency if no time-out occurred. Silent time-outs with all else constant produced steep gradients, presumably because responses to background stimuli extinguished during this period. Mackintosh (1974) has described fully the subsequent research that shows that more salient stimuli (e.g., the lighted key, etc.) will completely overshadow the less salient (the tone) when both are equally predictive of reinforcement. When, however, the less salient stimulus is correlated with (predictive of) reinforcement and the more salient is not, then the slope of the gradient around the predictive stimulus will become steeper with training. An important limitation of this analysis of generalization is that it does not account for the similarity relation in the stimulus generalization gradient. It merely predicts that changes that tend to increase the relative predictiveness of S+ will reduce stimulus control by other stimulus elements present but not correlated with reinforcement. It must be the case, then, that some feature of the S+ stimulus itself is responsible for the gradients of responding along dimensions in generalization tests.

CONCEPTIONS OF THE INTERNAL REPRESENTATION OF EXTERNAL EVENTS

In all analyses of stimulus generalization, some assumptions, explicit or not, must be made about the relation between the nominal stimulus as described by the experimenter and the functional stimulus as reflected in some corresponding set of events within the organism. In Table 1.1 three alternative conceptions of this relation are shown. Each is consistent with the commonly observed gradient of stimulus generalization following single stimulus training.

The Spread of Excitation Hypothesis

The Pavlov/Hull hypothesis has already been discussed and needs little elaboration. It asserts that there is an event, directly corresponding to the nominal (i.e., designated by the experimenter) stimulus, that acquires control of behavior as a result of reinforcement. Habit spreads out from the event corresponding to the reinforced stimulus to the events corresponding to other stimuli, proportional to the similarity between those other stimuli and S+. Although the generalization of excitation to adjacent corresponding points, or events, is governed by the discriminal distance between them, variations in the amount of generalization also depend on other processes that affect the spread of excitation.

TABLE 1.1

A Comparison of Three Alternative Interpretations of
the Relationship Between the Nominal Stimulus and the Corresponding Internal Event
(Example in Wavelength of Light)

	Spread of Excitation *(Pavlov, 1927; Hull, 1943)*	*Random Trial-to-Trial Element Sampling (Boneau & Cole, 1967)*	*Within Trial Element Distributions (Blough, 1975)*
Nominal stimulus	550 nm	550 nm	550 nm
Corresponding internal event	Coded event corresponding to nominal stimulus present at time of response and reinforcement resulting in an increment in excitation (habit) to this corresponding event. Excitatory strength spreads to other similar internal events that code other stimuli. For Pavlov, these events are spatially proximal neural units. For Hull, they are undefined.	Trial-to-trial variations resulting from variations both in stimulus events and their internal representations result in a random distribution of corresponding events. On each trial one such event will be associated with response and outcome.	Stimulus produces a Gaussian distribution of excitation to elements corresponding to nominal stimulus and neighboring stimuli. All excited elements are associated with response and outcome.

17

The Stimulus Sampling Hypothesis

The stimulus sampling hypothesis developed by Estes (e.g., 1959) and his associates, and studied later by Boneau and Cole (1967) in their analysis of stimulus generalization in animals, assumes that the event corresponding to the nominal stimulus has a mean at the value of the nominal stimulus and a variance determined by some random noise process or uncertainty in the signal. This uncertainty in the event corresponding to the nominal stimulus might be due in part to external variations in the stimulus and the relation between the stimulus and the subject (e.g., variations in the orientation of the subject) and might be in part internal. Whatever its source, the result is a randomly varying effective stimulus. Some value of this stimulus, on the basis of contiguity with a terminal event, is selected on each trial as the event that is associated with the outcome.

The Corresponding Event Conceived of
As a Set of Normally Distributed Elements
Along a Stimulus Dimension

The spread of irradiation across a part of the brain was, as we have pointed out, discredited many years ago, largely on the basis of physiological evidence. The idea of some kind of spread has persisted, however, because the facts, especially those related to peak shift effects following discrimination training, seemed to demand some such assumption.

In addition to the physiological evidence against irradiation, three other factors have reduced the popularity of the concept of generalization as used by Hull and Spence. One was the force of Lashley and Wade's (1946) arguments that the disproof of Pavlov's theory of irradiation left the concept of generalization of excitation without a theoretical basis. A second factor was the development of stimulus sampling theory by Estes and others. The assumption that the specific element selected from the set of elements corresponding to the nominal stimulus changes from moment to moment allows the development of generalization without an assumed generalization process. By this we mean that stimulus generalization can occur in the absence of any spread of excitation. Rather, it is assumed to occur as a consequence of random trial-to-trial fluctuations in the effective stimulus. A third factor has been the success of the theory of signal detection in dealing with a wide range of problems that are similar to the problems raised in the study of stimulus generalization. As we have already indicated, the discriminal distribution assumed by Boneau and Cole (1967) corresponds to assumptions about the stimulus found both in the theory of signal detection and in stimulus sampling theory.

Recently, Blough (1975) has proposed another variant of the element model, which assumes that the internal event corresponding to the nominal stimulus is a set of elements corresponding to values on the physical dimension. The element gaining most excitatory strength following reinforcement is that directly corresponding to the physical stimulus value. Other elements also gain excitatory strength in proportion to their physical similarity to the nominal stimulus. The function relating excitatory strength to similarity is assumed to be Gaussian. Thus, as in earlier strength models such as Spence's (1937), excitation is distributed along a portion of the stimulus dimension on each reinforced trial. The assumptions about the mechanism responsible for the spread are different, however.

Whereas Spence assumed that the excitation spread in some fashion, Blough's model has elements corresponding to points on the dimension excited by stimulation and then increased in strength by reinforcement. Whether or not these different assumptions have any testable consequences remains to be seen. More important perhaps is the difference between this model and the stimulus sampling model described by Boneau and Cole (1967). In their model, the effects of reinforcement are peculiar to the element occurring on that trial. In Blough's model, all elements similar to S+ are simultaneously associated.

THE RESPONSE RULE

For present purposes, two rules of response determination can be discriminated: strength theory and classification theory. Strength theorists assert that the probability or magnitude of a response is directly determined by the associative strength of the effective stimulus. Stimuli that do not elicit responses have either zero associative strength, negative associative strength (that is, they are inhibitory), or they are for some reason ignored (see Mackintosh, 1974). Although it is the case that strength theory can use a threshold (see Spence, 1937) or a decision criterion set at some level below which the habit is not strong enough to control behavior, decision criteria along the dimension of generalization are not invoked to account for the shape of the generalization gradient. Rather, the slope is assumed to reflect differences in associative strength. Any of the three descriptions of the stimulus given in the previous section can be consistent with strength theory, and combined with the strength assumption, all make the same predictions about the slope of the generalization gradient.

Classification theory asserts that stimulus events are grouped into categories that are associated with different responses. To the extent that stimulus events associated with a particular response are presented, the response will occur. This requires, as we have already indicated, that response outcomes serve two functions. First they provide feedback as to the appropriate response required upon presentation of a member of a given class of stimuli. In addition, these outcomes provide feedback as to whether the stimulus just responded to in a given manner was indeed a member of a class associated with that response (i.e., they help to determine the placement of the decision criterion). Thus, it would seem, in order for two stimuli to be classified into different categories, different responses must be reinforced in their presence. This restriction would seem to limit the application of classification theory in many demonstrations of stimulus generalization. In a typical operant conditioning experiment using pigeons (e.g., Kalish & Guttman, 1957), the only differential reinforcement is between those stimuli present during S+ presentation and those present during the intertrial interval. Consequently, the criterion would presumably be set on a dimension related to the relevant stimuli present during the reinforcement period (such as the properties of the light stimulus) and the relevant stimuli present during the intertrial interval (such as the darkened box). The most likely dimension in this case would be brightness, with the criterion set at an intensity value somewhere between that of S+ and that of the intensity of the chamber during the intertrial interval.

Heinemann and Chase (1975) have suggested that the brightness of the chamber wall might also be a factor in determining the value of the decision criterion, because responses to the wall are not reinforced whereas those to the key are. They further suggest that such a criterion dividing the visual intensity dimension might also appropriately divide the color dimension. There is no direct evidence from work on brightness and color bearing on this interesting suggestion, but research by Hearst (1969) provides evidence directly opposed to it. He trained pigeons to discriminate between a bright stimulus with a line on it and a key devoid of features. Following this training, he found perfectly conventional generalization gradients with lines of different angular orientation, even though he also demonstrated that the training dimension was orthogonal to the test dimension. Therefore, Heinemann and Chase's analysis could not apply.

The critical point we wish to make is that in many of the experiments that have used dimensions such as wavelength or line tilt on a visual display, the most reasonable assumption is that the criterion is set on the intensity dimension and not on the dimension on which the generalization test occurs. Furthermore, such a criterion cannot divide the test dimension in a way required by a simple direct application of classification theory. This stricture does not apply to the maintained discrimination tasks that Blough (1967, 1969, 1975) has used nor to any work in which there has been a discrimination along the relevant dimension. For many of the best known studies of generalization, however, the relevance of the criterion to the generalization gradient is not obvious.

In contrast, for those studies where the decision criterion is on the dimension of generalization, the fact of generalization is a direct outcome of the theory. If the signal and nonsignal distributions overlap and are divided by a criterion, then the stimulus values in between the nominal signal and nominal nonsignal values will fall on either side of the criterion in a probabilistic manner, and a generalization gradient will result. Because a description of the generalization gradient in terms of stimulus classification theory depends on uncertainty in the effective stimulus, it is not clear how any assumption concerning the effective stimulus—except that which assumes a stimulus randomly fluctuating from trial to trial—can be applied. If this is so, then any evidence supporting a signal detection analysis of generalization would also support stimulus sampling theory.

EVIDENCE FOR CLASSIFICATION OF STIMULI

The strength hypothesis accounts for the decline in response probability by the assumption that there is a direct relation between associative strength and response strength or probability. The stimulus classification hypothesis assumes that the subject finds some basis for classifying the stimulus—for example, its brightness—and then responds according to the payoffs produced by those responses. Thus, in a typical conditioning task, the subject experiences S+ periods of some specified intensity in the presence of which a response is likely to be reinforced and "time-outs" that are different—perhaps a blackout—during which reinforcement following a response does not occur. In this task the two interpretations make the same predictions: responding during the presence of S+ and nonresponding during the blackout. When test stimuli between S+ and dark are presented, the strength hypothesis predicts an intermediate level of responding. The stimulus classification hypothesis predicts that the intermediate test stimuli should produce a mixture of the two reactions of responding and not responding—in this case an intermediate level of responding. Thus, both hypotheses would predict the same outcome.

One possible way to distinguish between the two hypotheses would be to use two distinctive responses that allow for the possibility of graded responses intermediate between them. Such an experiment has been done several times, most recently—and with the fewest ambiguities, for our purposes—by Cumming and Eckerman (1965). They trained pigeons to peck for food at one end of an illuminated bar when the bar was brightly illuminated and at the other end when it was dimly illuminated.

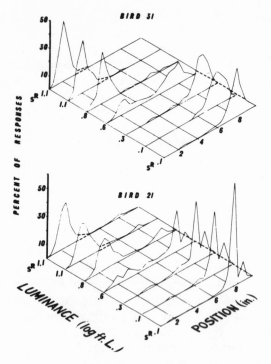

FIG. 1.2. Stimulus classification by two pigeons. The curves represent the distribution of key pecks along a 10-inch key. Original training required responding near the left end when the key was illuminated at .1 ft. L. and near the right end when illumination was 1.1 ft. L. The results of tests at these and intermediate luminance values are shown. (From Cumming & Eckerman, 1965.)

The question was, what would the birds do when the bar was illuminated at an intermediate level—peck in the center or distribute pecks between the two ends? The answer, shown in Fig. 1.2 for two birds, is clear. For intermediate stimulus values, the birds distribute their pecks at the two ends—an outcome consistent with the classification hypothesis and possibly opposed to the strength hypothesis. However, an advocate of the strength hypothesis could appropriately argue that the birds were trained to peck at the two ends and not to peck at the center. Consequently, an intermediate illumination level produces weak and conflicting responses consistent with the available response categories.

The Cumming and Eckerman experiment, interesting as it is, is only a demonstration. Further research using this paradigm but pitting these two hypotheses against each other is needed. Certainly, on the basis of this study, however, the classification hypothesis is plausible. The facts are consistent with the assumption that when given stimuli intermediate between the signal for "respond" and the signal for "do not respond," sometimes the animal classifies the signal one way and gives the response appropriate to the signal, and sometimes the animal classifies the signal the other way and gives the response appropriate to that signal. This study is consistent with the signal detection analysis and suggests that at intermediate levels of illumination, variable internal representations of the same physical stimulus result in that stimulus being classified in different ways on different occasions.

In developing the application of signal detection theory to animal research, Boneau and Cole (1967) analyzed data from an experiment in which pigeons were reinforced for pecking a key illuminated by any of 5 wavelengths from 535 to 539 nm (nanometers) and not reinforced when any of 5 wavelengths from 530 to 534 nm were presented. All 10 wavelengths were presented equally often, and positive stimuli were reinforced with $p = .06$. After the birds were trained, a series of trials were run during which response probability to each stimulus was obtained during extreme hunger, and under some degree of satiety. The results from these observations are consistent with the assumptions of signal detection theory. The effect of a motivational change is to shift the criterion but to leave the precision of the discrimination undisturbed.

The application of signal detection theory to a discrimination problem such as that used by Boneau and Cole made good sense, for the experimenters provided the animals with a reasonable basis for establishing a criterion for "peck stimuli" versus "don't peck stimuli." But can the theory be as readily applied to the results of single stimulus training of the type frequently found in generalization experiments? Blough (1967) has suggested that it can be and has argued that the conventional stimulus generalization gradient is too crude an analysis of the discriminative activity of the bird, in that it confuses the discrimination and criterion components of the detection task. He conducted an experiment in which pigeons were trained to pect at S+ (582 nm) on a partial reinforcement schedule and not to peck at any of the other wavelength values, all of which were presented on extinction schedules, in a maintained discrimination.

The results of this procedure (Fig. 1.3A) are typical of the results of generalization tests except that they are quite steep, as might be anticipated given the discrimination training procedure. Each obtained data point in this figure is an average, the individual values of which can be treated as confidence ratings of the bird's certainty that stimulus λ is (or as Blough has treated the data, is not) a member of the class S+. Thus we can define a "yes" response of very high confidence that a non-S+ signal has occurred as a low peck rate (e.g., 10 pecks or less) given that the mean rate of pecking to S+ is substantially higher than this value.

An application of this reasoning to the same data summarized in Fig. 1.3A is shown in Fig. 1.3B in which normalized receiver operating characteristic (ROC) curves (see Green & Swets, 1966) are plotted for each wavelength value. The line fixed on the diagonal shows the data for S+, each point representing a redefined rating: Thus, the leftmost point might be 10 or fewer responses, the next, 11 or fewer, etc. The probability of each of these events during a trial is shown on the abscissa (and also by definition on the ordinate).

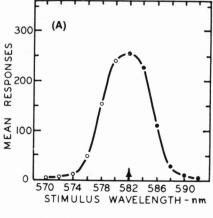

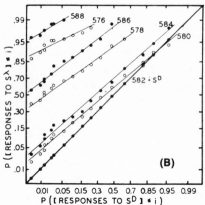

FIG. 1.3. An illustration of an application of signal detection analysis to stimulus generalization data. (A) A typical generalization gradient following training in a maintained discrimination with 582 nm the positive stimulus and all other stimulus values negative. (B) A breakdown of the same data with the range of response rates for each wavelength plotted as normalized iso-sensitivity contours (ROC curves). See text for further description. (From Blough, 1967. © 1967 by the American Association for the Advancement of Science.)

For S+, 10 or fewer is a highly improbable event, and 24 or fewer is highly probable. When this same set of operations is performed on a wavelength such as 588 nm, the probability of responding 10 or fewer times exceeds $p = .95$, and if the criterion for "yes" is set at 14 or fewer responses, the bird always responds "yes."

This analysis aids us in understanding generalization gradients in that it distinguishes between the possible contributions of discriminability and predisposition to respond on the generalization function. The linearity of the normalized ROC curves indicates that the discriminal distributions from which they arise are Gaussian, in accord with the assumptions of signal detection theory. The data points are not independent, however, with the consequence that the changes in probability on the two sides of the midpoint of any curve do not mean the same thing. Also, as Blough pointed out, the functions are not parallel to the diagonal, which is to say that the distributions along the two axes have unequal variance. One possible interpretation of this effect is that high response rates are controlled less by the test stimuli than are low response rates. Thus both the problems raised by the lack of independence between the various "ratings" and the likely lack of stimulus control at the right-hand end of the distributions raise questions about the meaning of these curves. Nevertheless, these problems do not negate the method but do indicate the need for further research.

Yet another question raised by this experiment is the generality of the assumption that a generalization gradient reflects the establishment of a criterion between the signal and nonsignal distributions that determines the classification of stimuli by the animal. In Blough's experiment, such an assumption makes good sense, for the basis by which the animal could establish such a criterion is present in the relation existing between the various stimuli and their respective reinforcement schedules (see Boneau & Cole, 1967). Under more typical single stimulus training, however, no such basis exists for establishing decision criteria along the relevant dimension (i.e., wavelength in the present case).

A number of other findings consistent with signal detection theory have been reported by Heinemann and his associates in discrimination tasks explicitly designed to allow a signal detection analysis. Thus, for example, Heinemann, Avin, Sullivan, and Chase (1969) trained pigeons to discriminate between two intensities of white noise by associating one with a left key and the other with a right key. The difference in intensity of the two training stimuli was systematically varied between groups. Following training, the animals were tested on a series of auditory intensities that included the training stimuli. Sigmoid psychophysical functions of the proportion of time spent pecking one of the keys varied in steepness as a function of the similarity of the two auditory intensities in the manner one would expect from signal detection theory. Signal detection theory also predicts that the tails of these distributions should be flat. This is because at some distance removed from S+, stimuli will generate discriminal distributions that lie almost entirely to one side or the other of the criterion. Thus these stimuli will nearly always be responded to in the same way (i.e., will be categorized into the same class). Strength theory, on the other hand, predicts that the tails of the distribution should curve back toward chance, as stimulus values become increasingly remote from maximum excitatory strengths. Hull (1943) recognized that intensity continua such as loudness and brightness raise special problems for a simple treatment of stimulus generalization, because intensity generalization gradients, rather than being symmetrical around the conditioned stimulus, are tilted upward toward the intense end—an effect he called stimulus intensity dynamism. Since this dynamism effect would, in qualitative terms at least, have the same result as that described by Heinemann et al., this result does not seem to create a major problem for strength theory.

STIMULUS GENERALIZATION AND
THE PROBLEM OF HABIT SUMMATION

The simple fact of generalization seems to be explainable either by strength theory or by stimulus classification theory. As strength theory developed, however, some experiments involving reinforcement and nonreinforcement of more than one stimulus seemed particularly amenable to analysis by strength theory. In particular, the idea of the summation of generalized habits provided a way of dealing with outcomes somewhat more complex than the outcomes of simple conditioning experiments. In the sections that follow we examine how well these issues are handled by strength theory and stimulus classification theory.

Summation of Positive Habits

Two attempts have been made to examine the consequences of training pigeons to respond to more than one stimulus when the same schedule of reinforcement exists with respect to each training stimulus. Kalish and Guttman (1957) conducted a number of experiments in which pigeons were trained with two randomly alternated S+ wavelengths. Different groups experienced different wavelength separations between the two S+'s. Following training, all birds were tested in extinction with stimuli ranging in wavelength value from well below the lower S+ value to well above the upper one. In all cases, tests included the training stimuli and values between the two. On the basis of previous work, the authors generated single stimulus gradients that served as the basis for theoretical predictions. Three models were considered: simple summation, no summation, and exponential summation with an upper limit obtained from previous work. Simple summation was ruled out by inspection, and neither of the other hypotheses provided a rigorous qualitative fit to the data. Nevertheless, in the area between the two S+s, there was evidence of summation in all experiments. The investigators pointed out that because of the very small differences in the predictions between the nonsummation and exponential summation models, the data did not really allow any decision to be made with confidence. Rather, they suggested that a study with three S+'s, rather than two, might provide definitive evidence of whether the summation fit an exponential function as proposed by Hull. With three S+'s appropriately separated, summation should result in a higher level of responding to the center S+ than to the two side ones. In a subsequent experiment, Kalish and Guttman (1959) performed the indicated experiment with three S+'s, each separated from the next by 10 nm. The results were quite unequivocal: No evidence of summation in the center was found either in the first extinction series on day 1 of testing or in a second series that was given the next day. The authors pointed out that the symmetrical curves are not characteristic of individual animals, most of which showed a distinct preference for one or two of the three equally reinforced stimuli. The reason for such a preference is not clear, but it suggested to the authors that the subjects were forming discriminations between the stimuli.

Blough (1969) reasoned that some of the ambiguities and complexities in Kalish and Guttman's results might be related to their measurement of the gradients during extinction. He proposed, instead, to measure the gradients around single S+'s and double S+'s in the course of maintained discriminations. Thus, rather than positive training at S+ only (or both S+'s only), extinction training at other test values was carried out on randomly alternated trials. Although the gradients resulting from such a procedure were steeper and more stable than those from S+ only training, the general picture that emerges was remarkably similar to that found by Kalish and Guttman. Rather than looking at the group means, however, as Kalish and Guttman had done, Blough examined the individual generalization functions of the three birds he used. Two such sets of gradients are shown in Fig. 1.4 for two of the birds along with a comparable average gradient from Kalish and Guttman (1957). The individual curves are based on single S+ functions generated for

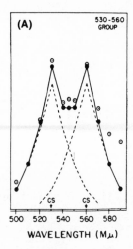

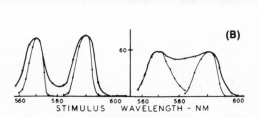

FIG. 1.4.   Two examples of generalization gradients in pigeons. (A) Training involved the two positive stimuli only. (From Kalish & Guttman, 1957.) Open circles are the mean empirical data; dotted lines are the theoretical single stimulus gradients; solid lines and circles are the theoretical values from exponential summation theory. (B) Data from two pigeons trained in maintained discriminations. (From Blough, 1969.) The single stimulus curves are theoretical. The double stimulus curves show marked similarity to Kalish and Guttman's despite differences in procedure. See text. (Kalish & Guttman, 1957. © 1957 by the American Psychological Association. Blough, 1969. © 1969 by the Society for the Experimental Analysis of Behavior, Inc. Reprinted by permission.)

each bird. Of the various theoretical possibilities already mentioned, we can rule out both the nonsummation hypothesis (the double S+ curves are too high) and simple summation (the double S+ curves are too high for the widely separated S+ values shown here, and they were too low for close combinations). The exponential summation hypothesis with an upper limit set at the height of the S+ values could account for the data from closely spaced double S+'s, but the predictions would be too low for those more widely spaced. Blough argues that the data are consistent with a signal detection analysis that assumes that the training procedure results in criteria being established on either side (along the wavelength dimension) of each S+. Both the locus and the variance of these criteria might differ from bird to bird depending on a number of factors having to do with the costs and benefits of responding or not responding in the presence or absence of reinforced stimuli. In the case of widely separated double S+ training, some stimulus values will fall in a nonresponse region zone above the criterion line for one S+ value and below the criterion line for the other. This condition would result in a dip in the empirical generalization curve. As the two S+'s are made closer together, this intermediate nonresponse zone will tend to disappear, resulting in a flattening of the generalization gradient between the two stimuli.

Such assumptions offer a reasonable account of Blough's data. Can they also be applied to Kalish and Guttman's similar results? We think not—at least not without making some additional assumptions for which there seems to be little justification. The problem that troubles us is the same as that mentioned before in a similar context. How are criteria established? It seems inescapable that different payoffs are required so that the subject will have a basis for classifying stimuli, but no such differences existed on the wavelength dimension in the Kalish and Guttman experiments. It would seem that we must either invent an argument about how criteria are established in the absence of explicit differential reinforcement, develop a different explanation for the shape of the generalization gradient following double S+ training, or recognize that the two apparently similar experimental outcomes may have different explanations.

Algebraic Summation of Excitatory and Inhibitory Tendencies

Many treatments of stimulus generalization have dealt with the fact that Spence's (1937) analysis of transposition predicts the facts of the peak shift quite well, even though it does not account as well for the facts of transposition following simultaneous discrimination learning (Riley 1968). Blough (1975) has introduced a modification of Spence's theory in which he predicts peak shifts and other phenomena specifically related to the maintained discrimination task.

Blough trained pigeons to respond to a large number of closely spaced wavelength values at an intermediate rate of responding by means of a moderate rate of reinforcement. Decreasing the rate of reinforcement at a single point reduced the rate of responding to the new S– and immediately adjacent stimuli and produced a peak in response rate to stimuli slightly further removed (see Fig. 1.5A). Increasing rate of reinforcement from the ambient level produced corresponding effects in the opposite direction. Introduction of a high reinforcement rate for a number of adjacent points and a lower reinforcement rate for a number of immediately adjacent stimulus values resulted in two different levels of response rate with an elevation on the high side of the transition point and a trough on the low side (Fig. 1.5B).

In Blough's account of these remarkable effects, he assumes that the excitatory strength of elements corresponding to the currently presented stimulus and other nearby stimuli is modified upward or downward depending on the occurrence of reinforcement. The magnitude of the change is an exponential function of the distance of the present excitatory level from the upper limit (in the case of reinforcement) or of zero strength (in the case of nonreinforcement). This aspect of the theory is a direct application of the

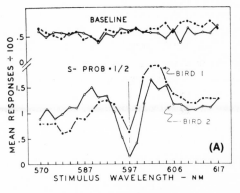

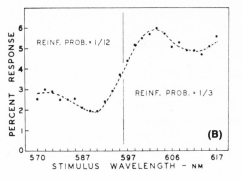

FIG. 1.5.   Data from pigeons in a maintained discrimination task. All stimuli were reinforced on some intermittent schedule so as to maintain an intermediate level of responding at all stimulus values. (A) The effect of lowering the rate of reinforcement at one stimulus value. Note the "peaks" on either side of S–. (B) The effect of associating different levels of reinforcement with adjacent sets of stimulus values. Note the "peak" and "trough" that emerge under these conditions. (From Blough, 1975. © 1975 by the American Psychological Association. Reprinted by permission.)

Rescorla–Wagner conditioning model and is a direct descendent of Hull's theory. Generalization of the change in excitation to adjacent elements follows a Gaussian function.

This set of assumptions is of interest in that it not only accounts for peak shift and the other effects already described but it also accounts for the size of the transition from the level of responding associated with one reinforcement density. That is, within the maintained discrimination paradigm, whatever behavioral contrast effects there are, are consistent with the quantitative predictions of the theory.

Perhaps one of the most remarkable aspects of this theory is that no mention is made of stimulus classification or decision criteria. It is quite simply a modern version of Pavlovian strength theory.

There are other recent data that provide additional support for Blough's theory. Rescorla (1976) has shown a number of interesting effects derived from the Rescorla–Wagner model. Because the difference between the two is that Blough's model makes specific quantitative assumptions about stimulus similarity and Rescorla's does not, qualitative predictions about similarity effects are consistent with both theories. Using conditioned suppression as an index of fear conditioning, Rescorla showed that discrimination training with two similar stimuli (A+, B–) followed by conditioning of the similar stimulus (B+) would produce greater conditioned suppression than further training on the original positive stimulus (A+). The account offered is the same as Blough's—A and B, because they are similar, share internal elements. Conditioning of B (low in excitatory strength because of the discrimination training) will result in greater excitatory strength accruing to the elements A shares with B than would occur from further conditioning of A itself (high in excitatory strength). Rescorla also demonstrated analogous effects following latent inhibition and conditioned inhibition.

Application of Summation Principles to Improvement in Discriminations

The third problem that has been explained by the assumption that generalized habits summate algebraically is the easy-to-hard effect, the history of which has been reviewed by Riley and Leith (1976). In the first research done on this problem, a dog was first trained in Pavlov's laboratory, in a differential conditioning experiment, with the lighter of two gray cards as the excitatory stimulus. After an extended period of training, during which no evidence of differential conditioning occurred, a new, much darker inhibitory stimulus was substituted for the original inhibitory stimulus. Now differential conditioning occurred within a few trials on this relatively easy problem. Training was then resumed on the original difficult discrimination, and within a few trials, this discrimination was also mastered. An interpretation of this effect that rests on assumed generalization gradients must assume generalization of inhibition extending from the easy S–to the hard S– but then falling rapidly. That is, the assumed gradients must be much the same shape as those assumed by Spence (1937) in his analysis of transposition, with one difference. Lawrence (1955) showed that an explanation of this effect that depended on assumed generalization gradients would require that the gradients become steeper with training, an assumption that at the time lacked the firm empirical support that it now has (see Hearst & Koresko, 1968). Indeed, it was in part this absence of support that led Lawrence to discount the generalization interpretation and instead to pursue an interpretation that assumed that easy training called the animal's attention to the relevant dimension.

These two interpretations—one the strength theory, the other an attentional hypothesis—have been the two principal interpretations of this effect. With some exceptions, the research strategy used to investigate the adequacy of these hypotheses has been to pit them against each other by finding situations in which the effect might occur in the absence of any reasonable application of a stimulus generalization explanation. The most persuasive demonstration of this is the experiment with pigeons by Mackintosh and Little (1970). They showed easy-to-hard facilitation with training on the hue dimension when the direction of the reinforcement values for the hard discrimination were reversed from the easy discrimination. The implications of this study are clear, as are those from other similar studies (see, for example, Singer, Zentall, & Riley, 1969). The study was not intended to test a hypothesis about stimulus generalization but to rule it out. One might find an easy-to-hard effect under such circumstances and conclude that the effect occurs for attentional reasons without ever determining whether or not transfer along the dimension might also be capable of producing the effect. So, in fact, there is very little evidence bearing on Pavlov's explanation.

Only one study, by Logan (1966), is directly related to this issue. Logan trained rats to discriminate between two tones by reinforcing responses in the presence of one tone but not the other. For different groups of rats, the difference between tones was either large or small. Trials were terminated by a single response or after 5 seconds if no response occurred. Those trained with a large difference learned more rapidly than those trained with a small difference, and furthermore, those same rats maintained their superiority when switched to the small tonal difference. That is, the rats demonstrated the easy-to-hard effect. Not only did the animals trained with the large difference learn more rapidly, but they learned with fewer errors. Logan assumed that the inhibition associated with S– was less for such animals and consequently, the stimulus generalization gradient around that S– was lower and flatter than the other gradients. This combination of assumptions and facts allowed Logan to predict that an easy-to-hard condition in which the change to hard was made by changing the value of S+ only would be more effective than

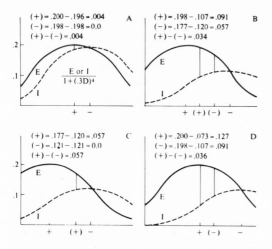

FIG. 1.6. Theoretical curves from Logan's analysis of the easy-to-hard effect. Maximum difficulty occurs with hard-only training (upper left), maximum facilitation when the transfer from the easy discrimination leaves the negative value undisturbed (lower left). (From Logan, 1966. © 1966 by the American Psychological Association. Reprinted by permission.)

groups in which either only S– was changed or in which both S+ and S– were changed. These assumptions are made explicit in Fig. 1.6, which shows predictions from the theory. The results supported the theory.

Furthermore, although the experiment seems suited to an analysis by signal detection, the results do not seem consistent with such an analysis. Unlike many of the experiments we have considered, this one involves a single response on each trial, and there is a clear S+ and S– on the relevant dimension. One could easily conclude from examination of the data that the easy discrimination facilitates discriminative performance of the hard task by insuring the establishment of a stable criterion. What is not clear from a signal detection analysis, however, is why moving S+ closer to S– would generate better performance than the other two easy-to-hard conditions.

One aspect of the experiment is disturbing. For some reason, subjects in the experiment have a strong disposition to respond. For the group trained on the hard discrimination throughout, learning the discrimination meant learning to suppress responding in the presence of S–. Given this bias in the data, the fact that the only group that showed no disruption when switched from easy to hard was the group in which S– was undisturbed may reflect peculiarities in this particular paradigm rather than evidence supporting a generalization interpretation of this effect.

SUMMARY

Thus far we have considered the effects of three variants of two stimulus training procedures: those experiments with two positive stimuli, those with positive and negative stimuli in which peak shift effects have been examined, and those with positive and negative stimuli in which the easy-to-hard effect has been examined.

The experiments involving two positive stimuli seemed to provide evidence for a stimulus classification theory (Blough, 1969). We pointed out, however, that an adequate account would have to explain how appropriate decision criteria become established in the absence of differential reinforcement: Kalish and Guttman's (1957) results were similar to Blough's after a training procedure that did not include any differential reinforcement on the dimension on which generalization tests were made. As we pointed out in the analysis of peak shift effects, Blough (1975) reported summation effects predicted from strength theory and not readily reconcilable with signal detection theory. No simple analysis that required the animal to classify internal events corresponding to stimuli along a dimension can easily predict or account for the peaks and troughs in Blough's data. Recent research by Rescorla (1976), also consistent with strength theory, may be consistent with a stimulus classification theory analysis as well. Recall that in this experiment, excitatory training on a stimulus similar to S+ but low in excitatory strength resulted in greater responding than additional training on S+ itself. This might occur because excitatory training on the previously nonreinforced S– permits a shift in the criterion toward S–. As a result, more of the discriminal distribution elicited by S+ would be classified as S+, and so the probability of responding to S+ would increase. Further training at S+, on the other hand, should have no effect on the criterion and thus no effect on responding.

Historically, with Spence's theory it was difficult to account for peak shift data from successive discrimination experiments: The subtraction of inhibition from excitation should have resulted in a peak shift, which it did, but it also should have resulted in a lowering of the gradient. The finding of behavioral contrast effects, an elevation of the gradient, thus presented a problem. Analysis of the results of a discrimination task by signal detection theory can also satisfactorily deal with the peak shift effect, for a stimulus removed from the S+ away from the criterion will produce a yes response with a higher probability than S+ if the criterion is appropriately set. As with Spence's theory, however, there is no explanation of behavioral contrast within the theory. Blough's model, on the other hand, explains both changes in the location and the elevation of generalization gradients when rate of responding is the behavioral measure. In this sense, then, Blough's model is superior both to the earlier Spence model and to the signal detection analysis of the peak shift effect.

The third area that we have briefly examined, the easy-to-hard effect, also provides evidence supporting a strength analysis. Logan's experiment showed the easy-to-hard effect both when the easy positive and negative values are symmetrically displaced out from the hard discrimination values and when only one value was displaced. It is clear that a signal detection analysis that accounts for the easy-to-hard effect by assuming that an easy discrimination allows for the reduction of criterion variance, thus increasing discriminability between the closely placed, hard discrimination stimuli, cannot account for these data. This follows because the criterion placed between the two hard stimuli in the symmetrical case would interfere with, rather than facilitate, transfer in the two asymmetrical cases. Whether some version of an attentional hypothesis might account for these results is unknown, but the usual assumptions cannot. An attentional analysis does not make differential predictions for the two asymmetric cases.

The foregoing discussion certainly points to the value of the strength hypothesis, but we would not advocate abandonment of classification theory in general or signal detection theory in particular as tools for consideration of the results of postdiscrimination generalization gradients. The facts just described, though indicating the plausibility of strength theory, are not unequivocal. Further, other facts seem to demand the application of classification theory. If decision criteria are established as a result of some experimental operations, then should we not assume that the same operations will establish criteria in other experiments such as Blough's (1975) in which comparable operations have been used? Conversely, if associative strength is established in some experiments as a result of reinforcement operations, shouldn't these same operations result in the development of associative strength in other experiments? These questions point to the possibility that the animal's behavior may be determined both by a stimulus classification principle and a strength principle.

Mandell and Nevin (1977) have made such a suggestion as a result of an experiment in which they found that changes in the reinforcement probabilities associated with two stimuli affected changes in decision probabilities and changes in rate of responding to the two keys in different ways. Whereas the change in the decision function occurred rapidly, the change in response rate was much slower and took place over a number of days. The implication of Mandell and Nevin's work is that choices, reflecting stimulus classification, are consistent with signal detection theory and different from response rate, although both may be determined by reinforcement rates. This solution to the analysis of stimulus generalization is attractive and merits consideration as an account of all generalization. Such an analysis might assume that initial choices are made on the basis of decision theory and subsequent rate on the basis of excitatory strength. At the present time, this proposition can only serve as a suggestion, for there are preliminary questions that require answers. For example, when an animal is presented with a stimulus that lasts perhaps for a minute, does the animal make only one decision or several? Is associative strength associated with the number of pecks in a burst, and are decisions made on the first peck of a burst? Probably this hypothesis is too simple, for as Gilbert (1958) and others have pointed out, a number of properties of an operant can be distinguished. Nevertheless, the general question seems to be the correct one.

A second question is whether this analysis will allow resolution of the apparent discrepancies in the literature. Can the habit summation effects in Blough's (1969) research be shown to be related in part to changes in criterion location and in part to changes in associative strength? We need more experiments like Mandell and Nevin's that allow comparison of first choice data with subsequent rate of responding. Can Logan's (1966) research be reconciled with a decision theory analysis? Because his results were all single response choice data, and because the procedure during easy training provided differential reinforcement on the test dimension, the necessary conditions for the establishment of a decision criterion seem to have been met. The data, however, strongly support a strength analysis. As we have pointed out, the results may reflect in part a ceiling effect that could explain why the asymmetric groups show different effects. But even explaining away the difference between these groups does not explain why the two asymmetric groups show an easy-to-hard effect. It is possible that Logan's results may be a selective attention effect. Learning to attend to the relevant dimension could increase discriminability of stimuli on the subsequent hard discrimination task and so be consistent with a signal detection analysis. Clearly, this problem is central to the analysis of these theories and deserves more consideration than it has received.

Finally, it might be argued that the assumptions we have attributed to signal detection theory in this paper are too restrictive. It is almost certainly the case that different and/or additional assumptions might enable the theory to handle some of the objections we have raised. We have chosen to restrict ourselves to this particular set of assumptions for two reasons. First, we believe we have accurately represented the theory as it has been applied to the problem of stimulus generalization. In addition, it has enabled us to contrast and compare strength theory and classification theory more clearly. We hope this has helped to clarify the issues involved. It is quite possible that as signal detection theory is expanded and refined, as it must be to account for the data, it will be indistinguishable from strength theories of the sort proposed by Blough (1975). The contribution of the theory, we believe, will be in clarifying the mechanisms responsible for behavior when task demands require a choice between two or more incompatible responses.

ACKNOWLEDGMENTS

The preparation of this paper was supported by National Institute of Mental Health Grant No. MH 22153 to Donald A. Riley. We wish to thank Herbert L. Roitblat and Robert G. Cook for their helpful comments on an earlier version of this manuscript.

REFERENCES

Bass, M. J., & Hull, C. L. The irradiation of a tactile conditioned reflex in man. *Journal of Comparative Psychology*, 1934, *17*, 47–65.

Blough D. S. Stimulus generalization as signal detection in pigeons. *Science*, 1967, *158*, 940–941.

Blough, D. S. Generalization gradient shape and summation in steady state tests. *Journal of the Experimental Analysis of Behavior*, 1969, *12*, 91–104.

Blough, D. S. Steady state data and a quantitative model of operant generalization and discrimination. *Journal of Experimental Psychology: Animal Behavior Processes*, 1975, *104*, 3–21.

Boneau, C. A., & Cole, J. L. Decision theory, the pigeon, and the psychophysical function. *Psychological Review*, 1967, *74*, 123–135.

Cumming, W. W., & Eckerman, D. A. Stimulus control of a differentiated operant. *Psychonomic Science*, 1965, *3*, 313–314.

Estes, W. K. The statistical approach to learning theory. In S. Koch (Ed.), *Psychology: A study of a science* (Vol. 2). New York: McGraw-Hill, 1959.

Gibson, E. J. A systematic application of the concepts of generalization and differentiation to verbal learning. *Psychological Review*, 1940, *47*, 196–229.

Gilbert, T. F. Fundamental dimensional properties of the operant. *Psychological Review*, 1958, *65*, 272–282.

Green, D. M., & Swets, J. A. *Signal detection theory and psychophysics*. New York: Wiley, 1966.

Grice, G. R. The acquisition of a visual discrimination habit following response to a single stimulus. *Journal of Experimental Psychology*, 1948, *38*, 633–642.

Hearst, E. Excitation, inhibition, and discrimination learning. In N. J. Mackintosh & W. K. Honig (Eds.), *Fundamental issues in associative learning*. Halifax: Dalhousie University Press, 1969.

Hearst, E., & Koresko, M. B. Stimulus generalization and amount of prior training on variable-interval reinforcement. *Journal of Comparative and Pyssiological Psychology*, 1968, *66*, 133–138.

Heinemann, E. G., Avin, E., Sullivan, M. A., & Chase, S. Analysis of stimulus generalization with a psychophysical method. *Journal of Experimental Psychology*, 1969, *80*, 215–224.

Heinemann, E. G., & Chase, S. Stimulus generalization. In W. K. Estes (Ed.), *Handbook of learning and cognitive processes* (Vol. 2), Conditioning and behavior theory. Hillsdale, N. J.: Lawrence Erlbaum Associates, 1975.

Hovland, C. I. The generalization of conditioned responses: I. The sensory generalization of conditioned responses to varying frequencies of tone. *Journal of General Psychology*, 1937, *17*, 125–148.

Hull, C. L. *Principles of behavior*. New York: Appleton-Century, 1943.

Jenkins, H. M., & Harrison, R. H. Effect of discrimination training on auditory generalization. *Journal of Experimental Psychology*, 1960, *59*, 246–253.

Kalish, H. I., & Guttman, N. Stimulus generalization after equal training on two stimuli. *Journal of Experimental Psychology*, 1957, *53*, 139–144.

Kalish, H. I., & Guttman, N. Stimulus generalization after training on three stimuli: A test of the summation hypothesis. *Journal of Experimental Psychology*, 1959, *57*, 268–272.

Lashley, K. S., & Wade, M. The Pavlovian theory of generalization. *Psychological Review*, 1946, *53*, 72–87.

Lawrence, D. H. The applicability of generalization gradients to the transfer of a discrimination. *Journal of General Psychology*, 1955, *52*, 37–48.

Logan, F. Transfer of discrimination. *Journal of Experimental Psychology*, 1966, *71*, 616–618.

Mackintosh, N. J. *The psychology of animal learning*. New York: Academic Press, 1974.

Mackintosh, N. J., & Little, L. An analysis of transfer along a continuum. *Canadian Journal of Psychology,* 1970, *24,* 362–369.

Mandell, C., & Nevin, J. A. Choice time allocation and response rate during stimulus generalization. *Journal of the Experimental Analysis of Behavior,* 1977, *28,* 47–57.

Pavlov, I. P. [*Conditioned reflexes*] (G. V. Anrep, trans.). London: Oxford University Press, 1927.

Prokasy, W. F., & Hall, J. F. Primary stimulus generalization. *Psychological Review,* 1963, *70,* 310–322.

Rescorla, R. A. Stimulus generalization: Some predictions from a model of Pavlovian conditioning. *Journal of Experimental Psychology: Animal Behavior Processes,* 1976, *2,* 88–96.

Rescorla, R. A., & Wagner, A. R. A theory of Pavlovian conditioning: variations in the effectiveness of reinforcement and non-reinforcement. In A. H. Black & W. F. Prokasy (Eds.), *Classical conditioning II.* New York: Appleton-Century-Crofts, 1972.

Riley, D. A. *Discrimination learning.* Boston: Allyn & Bacon, 1968.

Riley, D. A. Stimulus generalization. In M. H. Marx & M. E. Bunch (Eds.), *Fundamentals and applications of learning.* New York: MacMillan, 1977.

Riley, D. A., & Leith, C. R. Multidimensional psychophysics and selective attention in animals. *Psychological Bulletin,* 1976, *83,* 138–160.

Shipley, W. C. Indirect conditioning. *Journal of General Psychology,* 1935, *12,* 337–357.

Singer, B., Zentall, T., & Riley, D. A. Stimulus generalization and the easy-to-hard effect. *Journal of Comparative and Physiological Psychology,* 1969, *69,* 528–535.

Spence, K. W. The differential response in animals to stimuli varying within a single dimension. *Psychological Review,* 1937, *44,* 430–444.

2 The Unattended Dimension in Discrimination Learning

Louise S. Tighe
Thomas J. Tighe
Dartmouth College

Attention theories have dominated discrimination learning research for two decades (e.g., Lovejoy, 1965; Sutherland & Mackintosh, 1971; Trabasso & Bower, 1968; Zeaman & House, 1963). These theories, the lineal descendants of Lashley's theory, have in common the view that organisms are equipped with attentional responses that are specific to dimensions of stimulation. Discrimination learning is seen as a two-stage process whereby the organism first attends to one or more dimensions and then chooses a stimulus value (cue) on an attended dimension. The reward or nonreward outcome on each trial strengthens or weakens, respectively, both the dimension-attending response and the cue-choice response on that trial. Learning takes place only with respect to the dimension-attending and cue-choice response occurring on any trial. Thus, solution of a discrimination learning task can come about only by attending to the relevant dimension (that is, the dimension the experimenter has correlated with the presence/absence of reward) and then choosing the rewarded stimulus value of the relevant dimension. When the organsim has made this chain of appropriate responses with sufficient frequency that the relevant dimension-attending and cue-choice responses consistently outcompete other dimension- and cue-choice responses, the problem is mastered.

The attending responses that are at the heart of attention theory are made to dimensions or features of stimulation that can be apprehended within a given setting of the task, within what the Gibsons would call "a static array." Specifically, "dimension attention" is defined in terms of such properties of objects as size, brightness, form, color, orientation, position, and the like. Using such units of analysis, attention theory has had great success in explicating quantitatively a variety of effects of human and animal discrimination learning, effects that appear to strain a single-stage model of learning such as Spence's classic theory.

In this paper we take the position that general attention theory, whatever its successes, has nevertheless neglected a very important dimension in discrimination learning. The neglect stems, in turn, from a general conception of the stimulus that attention theory shares with the broader S–R theory from which it is derived. Our argument will be developed with reference to certain phenomena of discrimination learning that pose serious difficulties for attention theories but that can be accounted for by a formulation stemming from the Gibsons' conception of perceptual learning.

SETTING OR SUBPROBLEM ANALYSES

Let us begin our elaboration of these assertions by reference to an illustrative experimental situation. Figure 2.1 outlines a simultaneous discrimination task involving stimulus objects varing in size and brightness. The objects are presented in pairs, each pair presentation constituting a discrete trial on which the subject must choose one member of the pair. The figure shows the four possible settings within this task (i.e., the four pairings that exhaust the possible combinations of the size, brightness, and position features). Choice of an object containing a given stimulus aspect (e.g., "black") is rewarded in each pair, whereas choice of the stimulus object containing the opposing aspect is never rewarded. Over trials, the stimulus aspects that determine reward and nonreward are combined with the remaining stimulus aspects equally often but in a random order. Training continues until the subject consistently chooses the rewarded stimulus object.

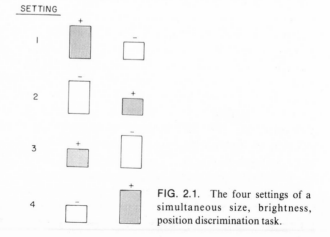

SETTING

FIG. 2.1.   The four settings of a simultaneous size, brightness, position discrimination task.

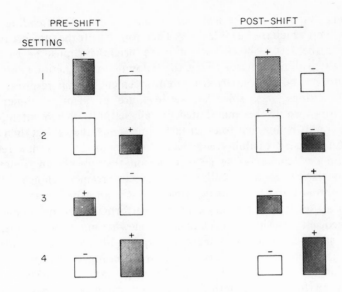

FIG. 2.2.   An extradimensional shift from brightness relevant to size relevant.

By the assumptions of the prototypical attention theory, just outlined, the stimulus presentation and reinforcement procedures of Fig. 2.1 would soon lead the typical subject to attend selectively to the brightness of the choice objects, to ignore the size and position of the objects, and to choose consistently the black objects.

Suppose, however, that after the subject has been strongly conditioned to attend to brightness and to choose "black" (i.e., after the subject has achieved a rigorous criterion of problem solution), the stimulus–reward relations of the task are suddenly changed, in the manner of Fig. 2.2, so that only choice of the large stimulus objects is now rewarded, and training is continued until the subject again attains solution. In the language of attention theorists, such a change in reinforcement contingencies would constitute an *extradimensional shift* and would be conceptualized as a change in the relevance of the task dimensions. The relevant dimension becomes irrelevant, and a formerly irrelevant dimension becomes relevant. But the operation can also be described less abstractly in terms of its specific effects within particular setttings of the task. Note that the reward shift affects only two of the four task settings. Specifically, it changes (reverses) the stimulus–reward relations within settings numbered 2 and 3 but leaves unchanged the stimulus–reward relations within setttings 1 and 4 (see Fig. 2.2).

The question considered here is: What expectations are generated by attention theory about performance on the changed and unchanged settings during postshift learning? Recall that the theory posits that before the correct cue-choice response can be learned, the subject must be attending to the dimension on which the cue is located. Therefore, before the subject can learn to choose the large objects, attention to brightness must be weakened sufficiently to allow attention to size to predominate. Extinction of attention to brightness would result from nonreinforcement of that response in the changed settings and, since all settings are of identical dimensional composition, would be manifested in all settings. When attention to brightness dips below that to other task dimensions, the subject then has in any setting some probability less than 1 of attending to the new relevant dimension and choosing the correct cue on that dimension. Finally, as attention to size becomes ascendant through reinforcement, choice of "large" would approach 100%. From this analysis, we can expect that errors will occur in all settings of the task and that performance in the changed and unchanged settings will be correlated. In somewhat more general terms, the analysis says that since shift learning requires abandoning a dimension-attending response that controls choice on all settings and acquiring a new controlling dimension-attending response, we can expect initial deterioration of correct performance in both changed and unchanged settings of the task followed by joint improvement in performance in changed and unchanged settings.

Experimental analyses of performance in the changed and unchanged settings of extradimensional shifts have been carried out with a variety of infrahuman species (Medin, 1973; Tighe, 1973) with results approximating those depicted in Fig. 2.3. The figure shows the group learning functions of animals in the unchanged and changed settings of an extradimensional shift carried out within a simultaneous hue and brightness discrimination in the manner shown in Fig. 2.2 The function labeled U (unchanged) shows the mean percent correct choice in the settings that maintained the stimulus–reward relations of the preshift phase, whereas C (changed) shows the mean performance in the settings in which stimulus–reward relations were reversed. As seen in Fig. 2.3, there was no decrement whatsoever in performance in the unchanged settings: All subjects continued at 100% correct choice in these settings throughout the shift phase. In contrast, performance in the changed settings begins near zero correct and improves gradually over trials. These functions provide no evidence that shift learning involved extinction and acquisition of dimension-attending responses common to and controlling the choices in task settings. Rather, the performances in the two types of settings appear totally unrelated. In this connection, it should be noted that in a recent experiment of this type that included analysis of choice times, Kulig and Tighe (1976) found that the subjects were learning to make a *more* rapid choice of the correct stimulus objects in the unchanged setttings *at the same time* they were extinguishing and relearning (reversing) their choice to the stimulus objects in the changed settings, even though the correct objects in the

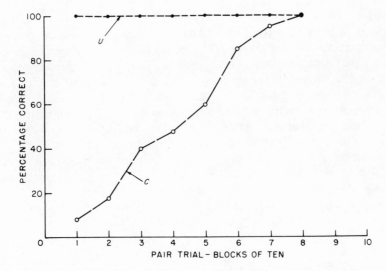

FIG. 2.3.   Percentage correct choice as a function of trials for the changed (C) and unchanged (U) settings of an extradimensional shift from brightness to hue. The data of this analysis are from V. Graf and T. J. Tighe (1971).

unchanged setting shared the dimension and cue value simultaneously undergoing extinction in the changed setting.

Similar setting or "subproblem" analyses have been made of extra-dimensional shift learning of children of different ages. Tighe (1973) conducted one such analysis on 4- and 10-year-old children who had been trained in a two-dimensional task (brightness and position) in precisely the manner shown in Fig. 2.2. Figure 2.4 shows the trial-by-trial group learning

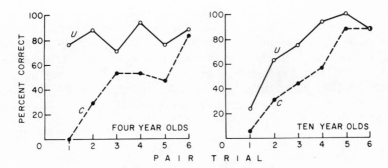

FIG. 2.4.   Group learning functions of 4- and 10-year-old children on changed (C) and unchanged (U) settings of an extradimensional shift within a two-dimensional task, collapsed across dimensions. [From T. Tighe, Subprob-lem analysis of discrimination learning. In G. H. Bower (Ed.), *The psychology of learning and motivation* (Vol. 7), New York: Academic Press, 1973.]

functions for each age level in the changed (*C*) and unchanged (*U*) settings of the shift phase. Considering, first, the curves of the 10-year-olds, note that these functions are consistent with the expectations of attention theory. Choice performance of the 10-year-olds is disrupted in both changed and unchanged settings, and the learning functions in the two types of settings are parallel throughout shift. These features indicate that performance was based on abstracted stimulus properties common to the different settings, as attention theory would maintain. In contrast, the curves of the 4-year-olds resemble the uncorrelated functions of the infrahuman subjects. The 4-year-olds exhibit a high proportion of correct choice in unchanged settings throughout shift but a gradual acquisition of correct choice in changed settings. Although the 4-year-olds exhibit some appreciable, albeit constant, error rate in the unchanged settings, analysis of individual learning revealed that approximately half the younger children tested solved the shift problem without making a single error in unchanged settings, whereas all the older children made one or more errors in unchanged settings.

The data of Figs. 2.3 and 2.4 are illustrative of a considerable number of similar observations on animals (see Tighe, 1973, for review of these data) and children (Cole, 1973; Tighe, 1973; Tighe, Glick & Cole, 1971) in a variety of training conditions. Considered together, these subproblem analyses establish that the discriminative performance of some subject populations differs in a fundamental way from the central expectations of attention theory.

Quantitative tests of the capacity of attention theory to accommodate the data from subproblem analyses of extradimensional shift learning have been made by Medin (1973). Essentially, Medin compared observed error rates on *U*-type functions with error rates mathematically predicted from the postulates of single-look and multiple-look attentional models when reasonable constraints are placed on the model parameters. He concluded that although attentional models could be made to fit some data from subproblem analyses of children's learning, these models must be rejected for the data of infrahuman subjects and, more generally, for subject populations whose error rates in *U* functions approach zero. Both Cole (1973) and Tighe (1973) report that a considerable number of 4-year-old children made no errors in unchanged settings of shift tasks, and thus the performance of younger children, at least under some test conditions, cannot be accounted for by attention theory.

AN ALTERNATIVE APPROACH

In this section we consider a formulation that does accommodate the subproblem data, a formulation that derives ultimately from the work of the Gibsons.

A number of ideas that are now well established run through the Gibsons' writings on perception: the ideas that perception is a matter of detecting information in stimulation; that stimuli are a rich source of information about objects and events in the world; and that organisms learn, in some significant sense, to extract information from stimulation. During the past decade, we have explored the implications of these ideas for analysis of traditional discrimination and concept learning paradigms. Our theorizing has been spelled out elsewhere (Tighe & Tighe, 1972, 1978) and so is conveyed here only briefly. Our indebtedness to the Gibsons, and in particular to Eleanor Gibson's perceptual learning theory, will be apparent to the reader.

Our basic premise is that individual, developmental, and species differences in traditional discrimination learning may reflect difference in the nature of the effective stimulus—that is, difference in the stimulus basis of correct choice responses. Implicit here is the assumption that learning tasks as ordinarily constructed afford more potential effective stimuli than is generally recognized by learning investigators. By this view, a first step in understanding qualitative subject differences in discrimination learning should be a careful consideration of the possible ways of perceiving the stimulus–reward relations of the task.

In talking about ways of perceiving stimulus–reward relations we have of course already departed from the traditional language of the learning theorist. In that language, subjects do not perceive stimulus–reward relations but rather discrete choice and reward stimuli. More specifically, in attention formulations, the choice stimuli are analyzed perceptually in terms of dimensions and cues, whereas the reward and nonreward stimuli are perceived not as part of the input to be discriminated but as separate, motivationally significant events. Similarly, the subject's choice response is not made to stimulus–reward relations but to the momentary stimulus array or aspects of it. If choice response occurs during attention to a given dimension and cue, the reward or nonreward that ensues is said to strengthen or weaken an association between those stimulus aspects and the response. What is learned, then, are associations between momentary stimulus aspects and choice responses, associations that are contained within settings of the task but that are activated by all task settings by virtue of the common dimensional and cue composition of the settings.

Under the alternative conception that we have urged, the potentially effective task stimulation includes not only momentary aspects of the input but also relations that exist *within the temporal flow of task events,* notably relations between aspects of the choice stimuli and presence/absence of reward. In this conception, the presence/absence of reward is seen as part of the task stimulation, and relations between properties of the choice objects and presence/absence of the reward are features of the stimulus input to be discriminated. If, as Gibson has maintained (1959), early and later stimulation often simply constitutes stimulation, then choice stimulus–reward relations are properly seen as stimulus variables *in the task*. As discrimination tasks are usually constituted, choice stimulus–reward relations are as much invariant features of the task as are the dimensions and cues spoken of by learning theorists; stimulus–reward relations are physically definable, detectable patterns in the input.

An important feature of this analysis is that stimulus–reward relations include patterns that obtain both within and across task settings. To illustrate this point, consider Fig. 2.1 as an exemplar of traditional learning tasks. By slowly scanning the rows of that figure from top to bottom, the reader can mimic the temporal flow of events within the discrimination task. Note that as successive trials unfold, certain objects are regularly followed by reward or nonreward (e.g., "large black" objects are followed by reward), and certain components of dimensions are regularly related to reward or to nonreward. The object–reward regularities exist within settings (i.e., within the presentation arrays) and can be isolated or known within settings, but the dimension or component–reward relations exist only across settings and can be isolated or known only across settings. Thus, the fact that "black" *alone* is consistently followed by reward is given by the fact that other stimulus properties with which black is combined in different settings are not consistently related to reward. It is our contention that the subject may meet the primary task demand ("choose correctly every time") either by detecting and choosing on the basis of the object–reward relations or by detecting and choosing on the basis of the dimension–reward relations. Thus, with reference to Fig. 2.1, a subject could accomplish the task by learning to approach "large black" and "small black," or other stimulus aspects in combination with "black," or, alternatively, by learning to approach "black."

The terms *object–reward relations* and *dimension–reward relations* in this analysis should each be taken to indicate a class of possible discriminations. That is, it is assumed that object–reward learning might involve *any* combination of the cue values of a choice object or combination of object values with contextual cues and that subjects might learn some but not all dimensions and cue–reward relations within a task. It should also be noted that object–reward relations and dimension–reward relations are not mutually exclusive bases of task solution. Rather, we assume that these two basic aspects of the task are normally processed concurrently. Choice behavior may be guided both by object–reward relations and dimension–reward relations, but the degree of control associated with each can be expected to vary with a number of task conditions (discussed later) that affect their relative discriminabilities.

From the viewpoint of the present analysis, then, the typical multidimensional discrimation tasks afford multiple levels of abstraction that are consistent with correct choice performance, and these alternative perceptual modes (perceptual in the sense that they are expressible as stimulus variables in the task input) must be considered as potential effective stimuli.

The present analysis should not be equated with Tolman's classic conception of learning as a matter of acquiring cognitions of "what leads to what" in the environment. The critical difference lies in the fact that Tolman had the conventional S–R theorist's conception of the stimulus. The learned stimulus relations he spoke of resulted from the formation of associations between discrete stimulus aspects, a linking of momentary perceptions. The stimulus relations we speak of are not themselves associations, interpretations, constructions, or deductions. Object–reward and dimension–reward relations are simply facts of the learning episode that has been constructed for the subject, and they can be directly apprehended as such. Under this view, the critical change that takes place in discrimination learning is not the formation of an association between stimuli or between stimuli and responses but rather is the differentiation of stimulus–reward relations as invariants within the sequential flow of task stimulation. These stimulus invariants and, more particularly, their manifold forms are what the learning investigator has neglected. They comprise the unattended dimension in discrimination learning, and we know little about the factors that control differential sensitivity to alternative temporal patterns in the input or about possible species and developmental differences in the capacity to pick up invariants in stimulus sequences.

Returning now to the setting analyses with which we began, the curves of Figs. 2.3 and 2.4 suggest that different subject populations have different solution modes—one tied to task settings and one independent of task settings. Specifically, the markedly different U and C functions of the infrahuman subjects (Fig. 2.3) and of the 4-year-old children (Fig. 2.4) clearly indicate the operation of different controlling stimuli in the changed and unchanged settings. In contrast, the parallel U and C functions of the 10-year-old children (Fig. 2.4) indicate the operation of a common controlling stimulus across settings. These differing patterns of subproblem learning are consistent with the view that the infrahuman subjects and young children accomplished the preshift problem primarily on the basis of the object–reward relations (which obtain within task settings), whereas the older children discriminated on the basis of the relevant dimension–reward relation (which obtains across settings). As detailed earlier, an extradimensional shift affects object–reward relations within only half the task settings but invalidates the original cue–reward relation in all settings. Consequently, the performance of subjects who discriminated on the basis of object–reward relations would be disrupted only in the changed settings, whereas the performance of those who discriminated on the basis of cue–reward relations would be disrupted in both changed and unchanged settings. The different patterns of data in Figs. 2.3 and 2.4 fit nicely within the theory we have outlined here and provide support for the general proposition that species and developmental differences in discrimination performance may indeed reflect differences in the nature of the effective stimulus.

SOME RELATED PHENOMENA
OF DISCRIMINATION

Perceptual Pretraining

If our interpretation of the subproblem data is correct, then young children and infrahuman subjects are responding to the task dimensions (at least to those in studies to date) as features that are in some way combined in perception, whereas older subjects are perceiving the dimensions as separable. In a series of perceptual pretraining experiments that antedated the subproblem experiments, we found such developmental differences in children's ability to isolate and use independently the dimensions of standard discrimination tasks (Tighe, 1965; Tighe & Tighe, 1966a). The pretraining experiments were motivated by the observation (Kendler & Kendler, 1962) that young children accomplish a discrimination reversal shift (which requires reversal of choice of stimulus values on the relevant dimension) more slowly than they accomplish an extradimensional shift (which requires choice of stimulus values on a previously irrelevant dimension), whereas older children and adults perform in the opposite fashion. This data pattern was widely interpreted in terms of mediational theories of discrimination learning (Kendler & Kendler, 1962; Zeaman & House, 1963), but we saw it as evidence of an age difference in the nature of the effective stimulus. To the degree that the subject discriminates on the basis of the object–reward relations of the task, reversal shift should be relatively difficult, since all these relations are changed in a reversal shift whereas only half are changed in extradimensional shift. In contrast, when the subject learns on the basis of dimension–reward relations, there is a basis for positive transfer in reversal shift in the form of attention to the relevant dimension–reward relation, whereas such attention should hinder extradimensional shift learning. To test this argument, a perceptual pretraining procedure was designed to facilitate abstraction of the task dimensions by young children (Tighe, 1965). The pretraining required the children to make nonreinforced same–different judgments to stimulus objects varying along the task dimensions and by this means gave the subjects practice in discriminating along each task dimension independently of the other and in the context of covariation of dimensions. Consistent with the differentiation viewpoint, the perceptual pretraining procedure selectively facilitated reversal shift in a series of experiments in which various parameters of the pretraining and transfer tasks were examined. The perceptual pretraining also facilitated young children's transposition behavior within multidimensional tasks (for a review of these pretraining studies, see Tighe & Tighe, 1978). Our interpretation of these findings is (1) that both transposition and ease of reversal shift reflect control of choice response by dimensional properties of the task stimuli rather than by their absolute or object properties, and (2) that pretraining promotes dimensional control by promoting isolation of the task dimensions.

Considered together, the perceptual pretraining and subproblem experiments provide substantial support for the proposition that young children have difficulty using stimulus dimensions independently as the basis of problem solution in traditional discrimination tasks. However, this proposition appears to be in conflict with a variety of well-known observations which indicate that young children (and infrahuman subjects as well) *are* capable of selective response to most stimulus dimensions. These observations include children's marked preferences for classifying input on the basis of specific dimensions, the determination of children's learning rate by dimension preference, faster intradimensional than extradimensional shifts by young children, and the like. Indeed, recent research on habituation indicates that even the infant attends selectively to common visual dimensions (Cohen, 1976). How are these discrepant sets of observations to be reconciled?

The discrepancy, in our view, is more apparent than real and stems from the widespread tendency to view dimension-attending responses as basic units of perception operating in the same manner under all test conditions. From the differentiation viewpoint, it is more plausible to suppose that the degree to which a dimension is perceived separately instead of being integrated with other features may vary markedly with the task structure, procedure, and demands.

Evidence on Separability Versus Integrality of Dimensions

In regard to task structure, it is relevant to note that form and color (in combination) have been the modal test dimensions used by investigators of the attention theory persuasion, whereas size and brightness have usually comprised the test situation for theorists claiming nonselective learning by young children (e.g., Kendler & Kendler, 1962; Tighe & Tighe, 1972). As manipulated in the studies at issue, the size–brightness combinations have a more integral, "tied together" perceptual quality than do the color–form combinations. If this hypothesis is viable, then some of the differences between selective and nonselective theories of young children's learning reflect differences in the learning situations sampled. (This would not be the first such circumstance in the history of learning theory!) Evidence of the greater integrality of size and brightness combinations as compared to form and color combinations has recently come from the work of Garner and his associates.

It is to Garner (1970, 1974) that we owe the distinction between dimension combinations that are perceived as the conjunction of separable, component dimensions and those that are perceived as integral, unitary wholes. Garner has used several converging operations to define the integrality or separability of dimension sets, including multidimensional scaling measures, absolute judgment tasks, and speeded classification tasks. Using these procedures, Garner has established that certain dimension combinations, such as brightness and saturation, are integral and are apprehended as a primary perceptual unit by human adults. Thus, college students cannot rapidly sort stimuli on the basis of their brightness alone without being disrupted by orthogonal variation of the saturation of the stimuli, and vice versa, thus indicating that the orthogonal varying dimension cannot be perceptually filtered out. On the other hand, form and orientation combinations are separable for college students: Speeded sorting on either of these dimensions is not impaired by orthogonal variation of the other, indicating that selective attention to the sorting dimension is possible.

Garner's analyses of dimension combinations have been carried out with adults, but Smith and Kemler (1977) have recently applied similar techniques in a developmental study. In their study, kindergartners, second graders, and fifth graders were asked to classify sets of stimuli that varied in size and brightness. The stimulus sets were selected in such a way that subjects had the option of classifying on the basis of overall similarity between stimuli, on the basis of shared dimensional values, or on a haphazard basis. For example, in a set consisting of a small black form, a small white form, and a slightly larger, light gray form, a dimensional classification would consist of putting together the first two stimuli, those identical on the dimension of size. A similarity classification would consist of putting together the last two stimuli, those that are most similar overall, as measured by the similarity judgments of an independent sample of subjects. A haphazard classification would consist of putting two stimuli together that differed considerably on both dimensions. A dimensional classification would of course, indicate that the dimensions were perceived as separable by the subject, whereas a similarity classification would indicate perceived integrality of dimensions.

The results were straightforward: Kindergartners relied predominantly on similarity classifications, fifth graders used predominately dimensional classifications, and the performance of the second graders fell between those of the younger and older children. There were few haphazard classifications at any age level.

In some related observations, children from the same age levels were tested in similar fashion on combinations of form and color dimensions. As Smith and Kemler note, with such nominal dimensions, stimulus configurations that pit similarity against dimensions as a basis for classification cannot be arranged. However, it was possible to test children's reliance on the dimensional classification as opposed to the haphazard response mode. Children at all age levels displayed virtually complete use of dimensional classification of the form and color stimuli.

In sum, children at all age levels treated form and color combinations as separable dimensions, whereas size and brightness combinations were treated as integral dimensions by kindergartners but as separable dimensions by fifth graders.

Garner's work in conjunction with Smith and Kemler's provides rather striking corroboration of the previously discussed observations from subproblem learning and perceptual pretraining. These several lines of converging evidence support the view that the effective stimulus in multidimensional discrimination tasks is a function both of task structure (i.e., of the specific dimension combinations at issue) and of the developmental level of the subject.

Discrimination Across Settings

In the context of our formulation, the work of Garner and of Smith and Kemler indicates that "object–reward learning" rather than "dimension–reward learning" will result when the task dimensions have an integral combinatorial quality in the task settings. It is also possible that dimension combinations that are separable *within* settings (i.e., that permit selective response in a given presentation array) may not be treated as separable *across* task settings, thereby biasing the subject to object–reward learning. Some evidence for this idea comes from experiments in which children were required to learn single instances of a concept in succession (Caron, 1968; Tighe & Tighe, 1978).

In one condition of Caron's experiment, 3-year-olds were trained on five pairs of geometric figures comprising a common angularity–curvature discrimination (the five pairs labeled *A* in Fig. 2.5). The children were trained on one pair at a time, each pair being repeatedly presented (with left–right

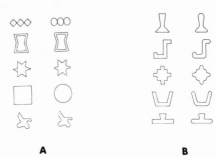

FIG. 2.5. (A) The five stimulus pairs used by Caron. (B) The five additional stimulus pairs.

A   **B**

position of its members varied from trial to trial) until the subject made three correct choices on four consecutive trials. Choice of the angular pair member was rewarded in all pairs. As seen in Fig. 2.5 the stimulus pairs consisted of simple black outline drawings on a white background with pair members equated on features other than angularity–curvature. Each pair discrimination, then, involved choice stimuli varying only on the nominal dimensions of form and position. Under these conditions, it might be expected that the children would quickly isolate the angularity–reward relation and demonstrate errorless performance with the latter pairs of the series. But Caron found that choices on the first presentation of each pair generally remained at chance level through the five pairs. On the first trial of the fifth stimulus pair, only 12 of the 28 children chose correctly. The failure to find transfer of learning across pairs is particularly suprising in view of the fact that as the children achieved criterion on each pair, they were required to respond further to that pair interspersed with re-presentations of previously learned pairs before progressing on to a new pair of the series. The subjects had little difficulty responding correctly on these review trials, but they nevertheless treated each newly introduced instance as an independent, to-be-learned discrimination. The children apparently discriminated each pair in isolation.

We were intrigued by this evidence of object–reward learning in the face of such a seemingly "separable" relevant dimension, so we extended Caron's test procedures to other stimulus samples and age levels (Tighe & Tighe, 1978). The five additional instances of the angularity–curvature concept labeled *B* in Fig. 2.5 were added to Caron's original stimulus pairs, and the resulting 10-item successive-instance task was administered to kindergarten, second-, fourth-, and sixth-grade children. The training procedures were identical in all essential respects to those of Caron except that four review trials were interspersed between each new instance of the task, each review series consisted of one presentation of the pair just mastered with three presentations of previously learned instances. The use of 10 stimulus pairs allowed the solution mode to be determined for the individual subject. Thus, correct first choice by a subject on each of pairs 6 through 10 in the learning series (an outcome that is beyond chance expectation) implicates solution on the basis of the relation common to the stimulus pairs, rather than by independent learning of the successive pairs.

The proportion of subjects displaying this choice pattern increased reliably from the kindergarten to sixth-grade levels. Specifically, these proportions were, from lowest to highest grade, 30%, 56%, 91%, and 88%. By this criterion, it can be concluded that most of the kindergartners failed to detect the common stimulus–reward relation across the stimulus pairs whereas most of the fourth- and sixth-grade children did detect and use this relation. These data, then, provide further evidence of strong control of young children's discrimination choice behavior by stimulus patterns unique to a given presentation array and progressive loss of such control with increasing age.

In an additional experiment, the hypothesis was tested that young children treat the task instances independently in this situation, not because they are unable to respond selectively to the angularity–curvature dimension, but because they fail to discriminate the dimension–reward relation as it occurs across settings. If this hypothesis is true, children would be more likely to display the more abstract solution mode with a training procedure that simply directs attention to the common feature across settings. Accordingly, a group of second-grade children were trained on the 10-pair task under a procedure whereby the first choice on each stimulus pair was made in the presence of the last learned pair and with the verbal prompt that the correct member of the newly introduced pair would be like the rewarded member of the last pair. This procedure was followed on the first trial only of each pair; on all other trials, previously learned pairs were not present to view. A control group of second graders were trained in the manner described for the previous successive-instance experiments.

The results were clear-cut: 88% of the children trained under the modified procedure chose correctly on the first presentation of stimulus pairs 6 through 10, whereas only 56% of the controls did so.

In sum, the successive-instance experiments provide further evidence of an age difference in the learning of object–reward vs. dimension–reward relations, and they indicate that young children may be prone to object–reward learning not only because of the integrality of certain dimension combinations within presentation arrays but also because of failure to respond selectively to task dimensions as they appear in relation to reward/nonreward across task settings. Hereafter we use the term *setting control* to refer to the failure to discriminate across settings on the basis of dimensions that are isolable within settings.

A GENERAL FRAMEWORK

To this point we have discussed the discrimination of stimulus–reward relations of traditional discrimination tasks in relation to three primary factors: subject population, combinatorial quality of the task dimensions, and setting control. These are, of course, general factors, each referring to a category of conditions or operations.

Subject Population

With reference to subject population, we have illustrated in Figs. 2.3 and 2.4 an apparent species difference in stimulus control of discriminative choice behavior. Independence in subproblem learning as seen in Fig. 2.3 has been found to characterize the extradimensional shift learning of a number of infrahuman species including rats, turtles, pigeons, and monkeys. None of the subproblem curves obtained to date with animal subjects has duplicated the pattern seen in the curves of the 10-year-old children in Fig. 2.4. Rather, the marked independence in subproblem learning by infrahuman subjects is generally observed even under testing conditions specifically designed to foster dimension selection and a dimensional basis of response (Tighe, 1973). The subproblem data thus provide strong support for the hypothesis that infrahuman subjects commonly accomplish discrimination problems on the basis of the object–reward relations of the task. Of course, a number of "dimension selection" effects are frequently reported in studies of animal discrimination learning (e.g., the dependence of learning rate on dimension assigned as relevent). But as Spence (1936) showed, and as computer simulations of Spence's model confirm (Wolford & Bower, 1969), such stimulus selection effects can be derived from a model that assumes response to combined properties of the choice objects.

With respect to the performance of human subjects, the age differences we have discussed are seen, from the perspective of differentiation theory, as reflecting primarily differences in perceptual learning experience with the stimulus variables of the task. What is at issue here is the detection of stimulus patterns within a temporal flow of stimulation, and it seems reasonable to hypothesize that opportunities for the kind and amount of perceptual experience conducive to such discrimination are correlated with age. The parameters of effective perceptual training (i.e., effective toward the detection of dimension–reward relations rather than of object–reward relations) are poorly understood as yet, although Gibson (1969) has offered a guiding theoretical analysis, and we have explored a number of conditions in relation to children's discrimination performance (Tighe & Tighe, 1966a, 1978). In this connection, the perceptual pretraining procedure discussed earlier can be seen as an efficient means of producing in young children, at least temporarily, the strong dimension separability and control of choice behavior that normally result from extended general discrimination experience.

A commentary on age differences in stimulus control of choice behavior should not ignore the existence of marked individual differences as well as developmental differences in stimulus control. Thus, by the criteria of our analyses, 30% of the kindergartners solved the successive-instance task in the same manner as the sixth graders, whereas 12% of the latter subjects fell in the performance category of the kindergartners. Such individual differences are presumably also a function primarily of differences in relevant perceptual learning experience.

Combinatorial Quality of Task Dimensions

Although little is yet known about the phenomenon of dimension integrality or separability, particularly in children, it seems likely that a number of operations will be shown to affect perceived integrality–separability. For example, how dimensions are combined in the presentation array may prove of critical importance. In this regard, we noted earlier that Smith and Kemler (1977) found that their kindergarten subjects relied almost exclusively on dimensional classifications when sorting color–form stimuli presented in what appeared to be the usual spatially overlapping manner (e.g., as colored forms), yet Shepp and Swartz (1976) found clear evidence of integral perception of color and form by first-grade children when the form stimuli were embedded within larger patches of color.

Another test condition affecting integrality–separability of dimensions is suggested by Smith and Kemler's (1977) observation that although their kindergarten subjects perceived size and brightness as integral dimensions by the criterion of classification behavior, these children nevertheless used dimensional terms in describing their classifications to the experimenter. As Smith and Kemler note, this observation indicates that size and brightness were perceived integrally at a primary perceptual level but were available to the children as separate categories of experience at a more derived mode of processing. This hypothesis, in turn, suggests that whether a given dimension combination will be treated in integral or separable fashion may depend on the degree to which the test conditions permit a reflective or analytical mode of response.

Finally, Shepp (1978) has pointed out that perception of dimension combinations may vary according to task demands. For example, he notes that the adult's reaction time to "same" in the same–different task is too fast to be accounted for by either serial or parallel processing of features, and that this has led some investigators to propose that same responses are made to wholistic properties of the stimuli. In such tasks, then, the subject could be basing same responses on integral perception and different responses on dimensional perception.

Setting Control

A number of variables are readily suggested as likely contributors to setting control of choice behavior; for example, intersetting (or intertrial) interval, number of task settings, relative salience of relevant as opposed to irrelevant dimensions, manner of stimulus presentation, "distracting" properties of the reward, perceptual and cognitive strategies the subject brings to the task. There is little evidence on this cateogry of conditions in relation to setting control, but several experimental observations fit the analysis sufficiently well to warrant mention.

The first observation is from the optional shift procedure, which allows the subject the option of learning the second of two consecutive discriminations by executing either a reversal or an extradimensional shift. Selection of optional reversal shift is a generally accepted index of the operation of dimensional control of choice behavior, whereas selection of optional extradimensional shift is taken to index control of choice by the specific stimulus items (Kendler & Kendler, 1962; Tighe & Tighe, 1966a; Zeaman & House, 1963). Tighe and Tighe (1966b) examined optional shift learning on dimensions that, from independent measures, were judged to be of unusually high and low relative salience for young children. The task stimuli consisted of horizontal versus vertical black stripes (H–V) placed on flat versus raised white squares (F–R)—that is, a two-dimensional versus a three-dimensional representation of form. Learning in the first discrimination was found to proceed rapidly when F–R was relevant (4 mean trials to criterion) but very slowly when H–V was relevant (73 mean trials to criterion), thus indicating the differential salience and presumably the separability of these dimensions. When F–R was the relevant dimension, 100% of the 3-year-olds exhibited optional reversal shift, an outcome that indicates strong dimensional control of choice behavior and that is characteristic of adult performance on the optional shift task. On the other hand, when H–V was the relevant dimension, 0% of the 3-year-olds elected a reversal shift. The question here is why, if the H–V and F–R features were perceptually separable, was there no evidence of dimensional control in the H–V-relevant condition? Our suggestion is that when H–V was relevant, the children could not sustain selective attention to that feature in the face of the salient but irrelevant F–R feature, and in consequence, these features became compounded in object control of choice behavior. Such compounding would not obtain when F–R is relevant, because there is then no need to overcome the competition of a highly salient irrelevant stimulus property. Consistent with this view, suproblem analyses of the cue compounds formed in object–reward learning by animal subjects suggest that cue compounding proceeds by compounding of the relevant cues with cues equally or more salient than the relevant cues, whereas less salient cues may be excluded from the compounds (Tighe, 1973). The foregoing interpretation of performance in the H–V condition is consistent with the view that dimensions that are separable as they appear in a static array may not be responded to selectively as they are manifested across changing arrays, particularly in competition with salient irrelevant features. Shepp (1978) has made the similar suggestion that children may attain a stage where they can perceive certain dimensions separably but yet cannot attend selectively to those dimensions for performance purposes.

A second observation pertinent to setting control comes from subproblem analysis of children's shift learning. As previously discussed, 4-year-olds display subproblem independence, and 10-year-olds display subproblem dependence in the learning of two- and three-dimensional shift tasks (e.g., see Fig. 2.4). However Tighe (1973) found that the pattern of young children's subproblem learning could be altered markedly by increasing the number of task dimensions. Four-year-olds learned an extradimensional shift in a task involving simultaneous variation in the brightness, height, form, and position of the choice objects. In this condition, the performance of the 4-year-olds was equally disrupted on changed and unchanged settings, and the learning functions on these elements were parallel throughout shift. This pattern is like the typical subproblem pattern of 10-year-olds. From the viewpoint of our formulation, this outcome means that the increase in task complexity led the 4-year-olds to shift from an object–reward to a dimension–reward basis of discrimination.

We suggest two hypotheses to account for increased dimensional control under higher task complexity. The first has to do with the relative ease of object–reward vs. dimension–reward learning under different degrees of task complexity. When irrelevant dimensions are added, the number of settings (and of object–reward relations) increase disproportionately. With one irrelevant dimension, two settings are required to represent the possible dimensional combinations in the choice stimuli. With two irrelevant dimensions, four settings are required; with three irrelevant dimensions, eight settings are required; and so on. An increase in task dimensions, then, would increase the relative difficulty of object–reward learning, and this may induce a shift to dimension–reward learning, assuming the capacity for such discrimination is present. The second hypothesis is that increasing the amount of irrelevant variation in the task may highlight the invariant dimension– and cue–reward relation. The notion that invariance emerges in the context of variance in stimulation is a central tenet of perceptual learning theory (Gibson, 1969). Both these hypotheses assume that increase in task complexity facilitates dimensional control by increasing the discriminability of dimension–reward relations relative to that of object–reward relations. The important point is that both hypotheses must assume that under the lower degrees of task complexity associated with object–reward learning, the dimensions were perceptually separable, but the discriminability of the relevant dimension–reward relation was poor relative to that of the object–reward relations.

Finally in regard to conditions influencing setting control, recall that young children solved the successive-instance discrimination task in the manner of older children when their attention was directed to the common feature-reward relation across settings. This outcome indicates that the relevant dimension was isolable by the younger children and raises the question of what accounts for the initial age difference in performance on this task. One possibility is that with increasing learning experience, children become more likely to actively search out invariants in stimulus sequences, and that the younger children had not yet developed the appropriate search processes, for example, backward scanning of the sequence in relation to present sequence elements.

In this section we have discussed the general factors of subject population, dimension quality, and setting control as if they were readily separable factors in operation, but it is more reasonable to suppose that these conditions ordinarily operate in interactive fashion to yield a continuum of relative discriminability of object–reward and dimension–reward relations of a task. If we are correct in the assumption that object–reward and dimension–reward relations function as stimulus variables in the task array and that perceptual learning is the primary factor in the detection of these stimulus patterns, then with sufficient extra- and intratask experience, all subjects should become sensitive to dimension–reward relations, within the limits of species-determined capacities for perceptual learning.

CONCLUDING COMMENT

We have contrasted the formulation presented here with attention theory basically for didactic purposes. Cognitively, as well as perceptually, contrast aids isolation and definition of distinguishing features. We do not see the differentiation and attention viewpoints as contradictory positions but rather as complementary viewpoints. The basic message of attention theory—namely, that organisms perceive stimulus input in terms of component features and respond selectively to those features—is wholly compatible with the formulation presented here. The primary difference between the two orientations lies in the conception of the perceptual units of analysis. Attention theorists have exhaustively considered the component dimensions that comprise the static array of discrimination tasks—that is, that exist within the array of choice and context stimuli present at the moment of choice. But they have ignored both lower-order units of perceptual analysis (object perception) and the units that result from perceptual analysis of the temporal flow of task stimulation. In the latter regard, they do not make provision for the regular relations that obtain between stimuli in the task sequence, relations that, we maintain, are themselves stimuli that the subject can attend to and learn about. More specifically, attention and learning theories have overlooked the possibility that stimulus–reward relations at different levels of abstractness afford alternative bases of task solution. Learning to perceive the stimulus patterns defined by dimension–reward relations as opposed to object–reward relations is neither learning in the classical sense nor perception in the classical sense, but it is perceptual learning in the Gibsonian sense of the registration of information *in* stimulation. The present analysis suggests that individual, developmental, and species differences in discrimination and concept learning may be due to differences in just this form of learning.

REFERENCES

Caron, A. J. Conceptual transfer in preverbal children as a consequence of dimensional training. *Journal of Experimental Child Psychology,* 1968, *6,* 522–542.

Cohen, L. B. Habituation of infant visual attention. In T. J. Tighe & R. N. Leaton (Eds.), *Habituation: Perspectives from child development, animal behavior, and neurophysiology.* Hillsdale, N.J.: Lawrence Erlbaum Associates, 1976.

Cole, M. A developmental study of factors influencing discrimination transfer. *Journal of Experimental Child Psychology,* 1973, *16,* 126–147.

Garner, W. R. The stimulus in information processing. *American Psychologist,* 1970, *25,* 350–358.

Garner, W. R. *The processing of information and structure.* Hillsdale, N.J.: Lawrence Erlbaum Associates, 1974.

Gibson, E. J. *Principles of perceptual learning and development.* Englewood Cliffs, N.J.: Prentice Hall, 1969.

Gibson, J. J. Perception as a function of stimulation. In S. Koch (Ed.), *Psychology: A study of a science* (Vol. 1). New York: McGraw-Hill, 1959.

Graf, V., & Tighe, T. Subproblem analysis of discrimination shift learning in the turtle (Chrysemys picta picta). *Psychonomic Science,* 1971, *25,* 257–259.

Kendler, H. H., & Kendler, T. S. Vertical and horizontal processes in problem-solving. *Psychological Review,* 1962, *69,* 1–16.

Kulig, J. W., & Tighe, T. J. Subproblem analysis of discrimination learning: Stimulus choice and response latency. *Bulletin of the Psychonomic Society,* 1976, *7,* 377–380.

Lovejoy, E. An attention theory of discrimination learning. *Journal of Mathematical Psychology,* 1965, *2,* 342–362.

Medin, D. L. Subproblem analysis of discrimination shift learning. *Behavior Research Methods and Instrumentation,* 1973, *5,* 332–336.

Shepp, B. E. From perceived similarity to dimensional structure: A new hypothesis about perceptual development. In E. Rosch & B. B. Lloyd (Eds.), *Cognition and categorization.* Hillsdale, N.J.: Lawrence Erlbaum Associates, 1978.

Shepp, B. E., & Swartz, K. B. Selective attention and the processing of integral and nonintegral dimensions: A developmental study. *Journal of Experimental Child Psychology,* 1976, *22,* 73–85.

Smith, L. B., & Kemler, D. G. Developmental trends in free classification: Evidence for a new conceptualization of perceptual development. *Journal of Experimental Child Psychology,* 1977, *24,* 279–298.

Spence, K. W. The nature of discrimination learning in animals. *Psychological Review,* 1936, *43,* 427–449.

Sutherland, N. S., & Mackintosh, N. J. *Mechanisms of animal discrimination learning.* New York: Academic Press, 1971.

Tighe, L. S. Effect of perceptual pretraining on reversal and nonreversal shifts. *Journal of Experimental Psychology,* 1965, *70,* 279–385.
Tighe, L. S., & Tighe, T. J. Discrimination learning: Two views in historical perspective. *Psychological Bulletin,* 1966, *66,* 353–370. (a)
Tighe, T. J. Subproblem analysis of discrimination learning. In G. H. Bower (Ed.), *The psychology of learning and motivation* (Vol. 7). New York: Academic Press, 1973.
Tighe, T. J., Glick, J., & Cole, M. Subproblem analysis of discrimination-shift learning. *Psychonomic Science,* 1971, *24,* 159–160.
Tighe, T. J., & Tighe, L. S. Overtraining and optional shift behavior in rats and children. *Journal of Comparative and Physiological psychology,* 1966, *62,* 49–54. (b)
Tighe, T. J., & Tighe, L. S. Stimulus control in children's learning. In A. D. Pick (Ed.), *Minnesota symposia on child psychology.* (Vol. 6). Minneapolis: University of Minnesota Press, 1972.
Tighe, T. J., & Tighe, L. S. A perceptual view of conceptual development. In R. D. Walk & H. L. Pick, Jr. (Eds.), *Perception and Experience.* New York: Plenum Press, 1978.
Trabasso, T., & Bower, G. H. *Attention in learning: Theory and research.* New York: Wiley, 1968.
Wolford, G., & Bower, G. H. Continuity theory revisited: Rejected for the wrong reasons? *Psychological Review,* 1969, *76,* 515–518.
Zeaman, D., & House, B. J. The role of attention in retardate discrimination learning. In N. R. Ellis (Ed.), *Handbook of mental deficiency.* New York: McGraw-Hill, 1963.

II DEVELOPMENT OF SPATIAL PERCEPTION

3 Depth Perception and a Laughing Heaven

Richard D. Walk
George Washington University

We stand
Measuring far depths and heights
Arched over by a laughing heaven
—George Santayana

The foregoing quotation from Santayana is an insightful comment on the study of depth perception. In fact, it has many meanings that apply to this situation. In the present chapter I describe a few triumphs and a great many frustrations in studying visual depth perception. First, however, I expand on what I mean by "a laughing heaven."

Every laboratory is afflicted with its set of gremlins, its own laughing heaven. Animals die, they get diseases at inappropriate times despite all our precautions, felines become infertile for long periods while time ticks on toward the termination of the grant, the subjects are indifferent to the task, babies howl, the lab is overheated, pipes freeze, workmen come and start banging on things just as you begin testing a crucial subject, the scheduled human subjects do not show up—the list goes on. This laughing heaven is illustrated in Fig. 3.1—a sculpture that states much of this metaphorically. It also states, this sculpture, that the principal investigator is indebted to the help received from governmental regulations, a helpful university administration, and cooperative subjects.

If you look even more closely at Fig. 3.1 you will see that the forces that hinder the researcher lie mainly within the self. The truth will out. No wonder heaven is laughing.

FIG. 3.1.   Athlete wrestling with a
Python. (Sculpture by Leighton,
1754.)(Courtesy of the Tate Gallery,
London.)

Heaven is also laughing as it gives us false answers, the ones that tempt and
seduce us, lead us to become complacent, and then prick the balloon of our
self-conceit. No sooner do we feel we have found an answer than nature gives
us a figurative boot in the seat of the pants. We are indeed arched over by a
laughing heaven that mocks us.

A discussion of some of the problems of depth perception will lead to a
better understanding of the Santayana quotation. The topics include: (1) a
consideration of just what depth perception is; (2) discussion of motion
parallax and the stimulus for depth perception, a particularly frustrating
topic; (3) a presentation of our notion of a "learned cue" for depth perception;
(4) a discussion of the distinction between the tunnel and the gorge, a
distinction that traditional perception does not recognize; (5) a discussion
based on some experiments with kittens (far from complete at the present
time) of the importance of attention as compared to active locomotion in a
visual environment for the development of depth perception; (6) a brief
investigation as to whether depth perception improves with experience. These
are, of course, only a few of the knotty problems in depth perception, but they
are chosen as representative of my own thinking at the present time.

The visual cliff is the apparatus for much of the research discussed in this
chapter. One version of it is illustrated in Fig. 3.2.

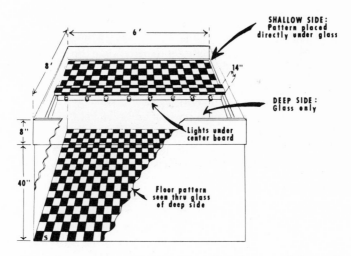

FIG. 3.2.   Diagram of the large visual cliff, used for testing human infants and some animals (goats, puppies, kittens). (From Walk, 1966.)

WHAT IS DEPTH PERCEPTION?

We discriminate depth in order to survive. The eyes are very efficient for the discrimination of visual depth in that they enable us to make a decision about a drop-off long before we reach it. At night we might feel the drop-off tactually or even sense a change in air pressure or temperature. Auditory cues are very efficient; they would be particularly so if we were bats, and they are used more by the blind than the sighted, though they are potentially available to the sighted. The point is that the discrimination of depth in the real world is multisensory. In real life, away from the laboratory, we may use vision as a main distance cue, but the other senses are available to us. Vestibular senses, for example, help right our body and maintain our balance. Taste seems to be the only sense we cannot use for distance perception.

The research discussed here is about visual depth discrimination. The rat has poor visual depth discrimination but good depth perception. This is because the rat feels its way down and seldom (except when it jumps) commits itself to a depth decision based solely on vision. The chick, on the other hand, hurls itself off an edge based solely on visual information.

We do not know the extent to which our senses have been modified by the requirements of the environment in our search for survival. Man appears able to survive in almost any environment where food is available, ranging from high mountains with treacherous cliffs to desert flatlands with few discernible irregularities in the terrain. It is possible that individuals reared in such different environments have marked differences in depth discrimination, but we have no evidence on this. Animal species reared in the presence of depths are more cautious and discriminate depth better than those reared in flatlands (for a review of those studies, see Walk, 1978).

An excellent review of the multisensory nature of depth perception is provided in a paper by Cullen (1957). The Kittiwake gull nests on high cliffs and can be compared to ground-nesting gulls. The cliff-nesting habitat has changed the way the Kittiwake behaves in many situations. For example, the young are not camouflaged, and predators are not attacked because predators are so rare. The Kittiwake has strong claws with which to cling to cliffs. The female lies down during copulation rather than standing up as ground nesters do. The young chicks remain immobile, they do not run. Because the chicks cannot get out of the deep nest, the parents have no food call, and the parents do not recognize their chicks among a group of strange chicks. McLannahan (1973) found that not only is the Kittiwake excellent on the visual cliff; it is also excellent on a tactual cliff—in the dark, other chicks fall off the tactual cliff whereas the Kittiwake chick stays immobile.

The gull studies also stress that some depth discrimination is genetic and some is modified by experience. The Kittiwake can be reared in the flatlands, and the chicks do not change their behavior—so strong is the adaptation to the cliff environment. This is not necessarily adaptive, since flatlands chicks must be prepared to flee the nest to avoid predators. The chicks of some species, such as the Iceland gull, adapt to the environment in which they are raised, becoming like cliff nesters in a cliff environment and like ground nesters in a ground environment.

The lesson, then, is that depth perception is multisensory. Our studies are visual depth discrimination studies, and it may be easy to overgeneralize from them, since a weakness in visual depth discrimination may or may not be of consequence to a species that uses many cues for depth perception.

MOTION PARALLAX AND
THE STIMULUS FOR DEPTH PERCEPTION

In our monograph (Walk & Gibson, 1961) we demonstrated the importance of both motion parallax and of texture. The usual visual cliff pattern confounds motion parallax and the texture as cues for depth. If a similar pattern is placed both near the animal and distant from it, the animal receives motion parallax as it moves its head, but the distant pattern also projects a smaller texture. See Fig. 3.3. If the distant texture is increased in size, it can project textured elements that are the same size as are the closer elements at the animal's eye. See Fig. 3.4. This condition is known as the "equal density"

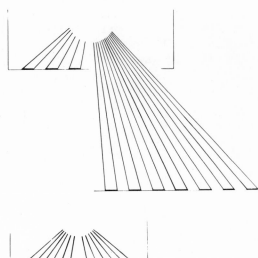

FIG. 3.3. Unequal density. A schematic diagram of the projection to the subject's eye of equal textures on the shallow side (left) and deep side (right). The distant pattern projects a finer pattern to the subject's eye.

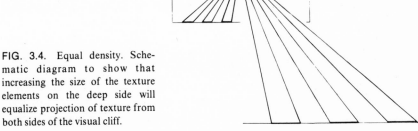

FIG. 3.4. Equal density. Schematic diagram to show that increasing the size of the texture elements on the deep side will equalize projection of texture from both sides of the visual cliff.

condition, and since the textured elements now project equally, the major cue remaining is motion parallax.

Experiments with equal density were carried out with rats, chicks, goats, and sheep (Walk & Gibson, 1961) and with human infants (Walk, 1966), and all species discriminated depth as well with the equal density situation as they did with the regular unequal density one. Other things being equal, then, we felt that motion parallax was, as we put it, "of critical importance as a stimulus for discrimination of depth" (Walk & Gibson, 1961, p. 30). Others have controlled for motion parallax in this way with similar results, too, but the important point to remember is that even though we thought at the time that we had eliminated all cues but motion parallax, the topic was far from closed.[1]

---

[1]Since the animal has two eyes, one could call on binocular cues like retinal disparity (unlikely for the rat but likely for the chick). With equal density, monocular rats (Trychin & Walk, 1964) and chicks (Schiffman & Walk, 1963) perform like binocular subjects in their overwhelming choice of the shallow side.

The importance of texture can be shown by placing gray on the shallow and deep sides. If a gray surface is 10 inches below the glass and also directly under the glass, hooded rats have no preference for either side (Walk & Gibson, 1961). Without texture, they cannot discriminate depth. Human infants were tested with a texture on the shallow side and gray on the deep side. The depth of the deep side below the glass varied from no depth at all to 40 inches (0 in., 10 in., 20 in., 40 in. below the glass). About 30% to 40% of the infants were coaxed to the mother under these conditions, and depth of the surface below the glass, so important for a textured pattern, made no difference (Walk, 1966). Obviously, pattern is important; without it, depth cannot be discriminated; yet again, the topic is far more complex than it appeared to be.

The DeHardt Effect

Doris DeHardt (1969) placed 3-inch checks 10 inches below the glass. This meant that they projected textured elements to the animal's eye similar to those from a 1-inch check size on the shallow side (allowing for the height of the center board and the rat). She put the same 3-inch checks directly under the glass. The animals now essentially disregarded the shallow side pattern and went overwhelmingly to the deep side.

The problem here was not the animals' apparent lack of preference for 3-inch checks on the shallow side. The problem is the preference for the deep side. In an experiment with a "one-sided cliff"—where the animal could only go toward the deep side—the percentage of animals descending was almost nil when the visual depth was 10 inches (Walk & Gibson, 1961, p. 12). We would have expected few descents to the deep side with the conflict situation of the DeHardt experiment; after all, the cue of motion parallax was still there. DeHardt explained her results as being a preference for an optimal retinal angle.

We repeated the experiment and secured results similar to hers (Walk & Walters, 1974). The rats preferred the deep side when a 3-inch pattern was on it, along with the 3-inch checks on the shallow side, with 78% choosing the deep side, whereas substitution of a ¾-inch checked pattern on the shallow side reversed the preference; in that case, 76% chose the shallow side. We also used a one-sided cliff in a partial replication of the Walk and Gibson (1961) study and varied textures on the deep side. The larger projected texture elicited significantly more deep descents.

Is it, then, "optimal retinal angle" and not motion parallax that determines the animal's behavior? If optimal retinal angle was the only factor, the condition we used to show the importance of motion parallax (equal projected densities) should be one where the animal would descend equally often to both sides, since retinal angle is the same on both sides.

To explore this further, Walk and Walters (1974) used chicks as well as rats and varied visual depths, keeping retinal angle constant. Increasing visual depth does tend to diminish the DeHardt effect for the rat. Whereas with the 10-inch visual depth 78% went to the deep side, the number dropped to about 50% for both the 20-inch and 40-inch visual depths. Of course, when a small pattern was on the shallow side, the choice overwhelmingly was to that side. Since choices did not change too much with increased visual depth, the conclusion would seem to be that for the rat, at least, the visual choice is made more by texture than by motion parallax.

The chick gave somewhat of a different story. The DeHardt effect was still there (more choices than expected of the deep side), but it was not as strong. We used two different retinal angles on the deep side to "attract" the animal—the 11° one she had used for the rats and a 4° one because of the chick's preference for smaller sized elements. For the chick, choices dropped off rapidly with an increase of visual depth. But at 25 inches of visual depth, 25% of the descents were to the deep side with the 4° retinal angle; whereas with the 11° pattern, which had some power at lower depths, there were practically no descents at 25 inches.

This is a complicated area. We know from studies of element size preferences with the chick (Karmel, 1969; Schiffman, 1968, 1969) that when patterns are just beneath the glass, the chick prefers 2°-sized patterns over 4°-sized ones. But the 2° pattern did not elicit many deep choices, whereas the slightly larger 4° one did. What this means is that we are not sure just how weak motion parallax is when it interacts with texture preferences because of the possibility that other unknown textures may elicit even more deep descents. We cannot tell how weak motion parallax is, because "optimal retinal angle" may also interact with visual depth.

Nevertheless, the chick seems to respond to both texture and motion parallax and to be much more responsive to motion parallax than is the rat. Considering the visual systems and the ecological habits of the two species, this is not surprising, though the research itself, downgrading the importance of motion parallax for these experimental conditions, was a surprise to us. We were, in fact, sure there was some experimental flaw in the DeHardt (1969) experiment and that it would not be replicated except under very special circumstances.

What of the human infant? The DeHardt effect can also be shown with human infants, but the relative importance of texture and motion parallax cannot be determined (Walk, Walters, and Rosner, 1978). Instead of using a large nonpreferred pattern on the shallow side for human infants, as we had with rats and chicks, we used a small one of ⅛-inch checks, since pretesting had shown that the large (9-inch) checks were ineffective in that the infants still had a firm allegiance to the shallow side. Davidson and Whitson (1973) had used small checks on the shallow side with chicks, and they had found more deep-side choices than with a regular-check-sized shallow pattern.

For human infants, we first used 2-inch checks on the deep side and ⅛-inch checks on the shallow side with a 10-inch visual depth and compared it with a more regular situation with 2-inch checks on both shallow and deep sides. The 10-inch visual depth is a good one with which to explore stimulus parameters, because a fairly large proportion (about a third) of the infants are coaxed to the mother at the deep side. It is easier to look for changes in a weak condition than in a strong one. We found the DeHardt effect for human infants in that 77% were coaxed to the mother at the deep side with the ⅛-inch checks on the shallow side, whereas only 33% were coaxed to her there when the shallow pattern was 2-inch checks—double the usual number and a highly significant difference.

One wonders how such an effect can work with infants. They seem to pay attention mainly to the mother, and she is at the deep side where the pattern, 2-inch checks, is the same for both groups. Yet the ⅛-inch checks do make a tremendous difference as one can see from the change in behavior.

We next decided to lower the deep-side pattern, keeping retinal angle constant at around 6°. As we went to 14 inches, 55% crossed to the mother at the deep side, and at 18 inches, only 34% crossed to her there. We thought the human infant was like the chick in showing a fairly strong sense of motion parallax, even though it was also influenced by some "optimal retinal angle." However, we found that our patterns (3-inch checks at 14 inches and 4-inch checks at 18 inches) had slightly increased retinal angle to 7° and 8° respectively. The 3-inch checks at 18 inches are around 6°, so we tested more children with this condition. To our surprise, 83% crossed to the mother at the deep side, significantly different from the 8° pattern at this depth. Would 2° really make this much difference?

One must mention that the ⅛-inch checks were not an aversive stimulus pattern. We placed ⅛-inch checks under the glass as compared to a gray surface directly under the glass and gave the children a "choice" of the two stimulus patterns. We found that 81% went to the ⅛-inch checks. Obviously, the infants could see the ⅛-inch checks, and they would prefer them under some circumstances.

In sum, the infant appeared to be relatively indifferent to the effects of motion parallax as long as a nonpreferred checked pattern was on the shallow side and some "optimal retinal angle" was projected from the deep side. But we were out of funds by this time and could not use greater visual depths, holding retinal angle constant, so this is just a strong inference. But whatever the result of such future experiments, motion parallax is weaker than we thought it was.

In other studies with human infants, a preference for certain textured elements has been found. The technique is to use much younger infants (about

1 to 4 months old) and to find which pattern they prefer. (See Karmel & Maisel, 1975, for a review of some of these studies.) The patterns preferred by the 4-month-olds, for example, subtend less than 1° of visual angle. The relation to the study just described in which the infants are much older and a 6° pattern was preferred is far from clear.

Continuous Contours (Stripes)

In some of the studies discussed previously the patterns may not have been very definite to the organism. The large patterns (rats, chicks) may have been outside the range of easily perceivable patterns. The 3-inch checks, for example, were not preferred over gray as one expects any ordinary pattern to be (Walk & Walters, 1974). The ⅛-inch checks were preferred over gray by human infants, but they still may have been somewhat indefinite. Stripes, however, are a very definite pattern. They are used to elicit "optokinetic nystagmus" or visual following because they are such definite patterns. The ones we used were red and white stripes of cloth about ⅞ inches wide.

The original interest of this experiment was to study whether performance differed for stripes perpendicular or parallel to the center board, since retinal disparity cues might be better for perpendicular stripes. Yet it turned out that the orientation of the stripes to the center board was not an important factor and can be disregarded.

The visual depth was 10 inches, and 78% of the infants crossed to the mother for the striped condition, whereas for checks of roughly equivalent contour, only 36% of the infants crossed the deep side to the mother. We then lowered the visual depth to 14 inches, and 84% crossed to the mother compared to 49% who crossed with the checks. We even took the striped pattern and cut it up by cutting along all the contour lines to produce long, red and white strips of cloth and then wove them into checks. The contour from the checks was now double that from the stripes rather than slightly less, but the results were the same; only 46% crossed to the mother. In all cases, then, significantly more infants crossed the deep side to the mother for the stripes than crossed for the checked patterns. At one time, at home, we had a bed sheet made of stripes, but fortunately, we had no crawling infants at the time.

The weakness of stripes or straight contours does have some touch points in research on infant and adult perception. Greenberg and O'Donnell (1972) found that very young infants preferred to look at checks over stripes. MacKay and Jeffreys (1973) had adults look at parallel lines as contrasted with lines that had corners or breaks in them. The visual evoked potential was marked for the checks or broken lines but was remarkably flat for the parallel lines. In tachistoscopic experiments, it has been found that the threshold is much lower for detecting contours that change in direction than it is for detecting those that do not (Mayzner & Habinek, 1976).

When the DeHardt effect experiments and the experiments using stripes are considered, it is clear that in order to have adequate depth discrimination, a stimulus pattern should be of adequate size, and it should have contours that change in direction. Species seem to differ along a dimension that might be defined as that of a choice of an "optimal retinal angle," and it is not yet clear how much such optimal elements can influence depth discrimination. But with this qualification and the possibility that there are some unknown ineffective stimulus properties, we can say that our ordinary environment with its pebbles, grasses, and roughly textured soils represents the type of texture that enables an organism best to discriminate depth. The shallow-side pattern, or the pattern that is close to the organism, seems to be more important than the pattern on the visual void.

But what of motion parallax? Its importance is far less clear. We are not even sure that it cannot be essentially negated by some unknown optimal distal pattern. One remembers the strong reaction to the deep side by an animal like the goat: It essentially collapses and is immobile until turned so that a near stimulus pattern is close to it. Would some optimal checked pattern make the goat prefer to remain standing on the deep side rather than going to the shallow side? This seems unlikely. Does the goat really respond to motion parallax in ways other species to not? If so, is it because of the goat's special eye, with its sloping ramp retina, or is it some marked reaction to depth based on unknown stimulus features?

One thinks of flying in an airplane where depth seems unreal, where people below look like ants, as compared to the fright in looking down from a tall building. Have experiments in which we have not controlled adequately for texture cues seduced us into thinking that motion parallax can operate adequately when just two textures are visible—a near one and a far one? Perhaps motion parallax really needs more intervening stimulation for its optimal effect (for example, in looking down from a building or looking into a gorge).

An obvious conclusion might be that the laboratory should give some clue to the more ecologically valid, yet more loosely controlled, visual cliff situation. Laboratory experiments are not at all like the present ones, so the relation between the laboratory and the studies discussed here cannot be specified precisely. Johansson (1973) found that motion parallax was a very accurate basis for estimating distance when the stimulus judged was four dim light bulbs. A study somewhat similar to the proposed ones is one in which subjects judged absolute distance with and without self-produced head movement motion parallax (Ferris, 1972). He had black targets at varying distances from a textured or white background. The motion parallax condition was always better, even without training. The general tendency was to underestimate the distance of the target, and accuracy improved markedly with training, particularly for the motion parallax condition. Judgments were somewhat more accurate with the textured field as a background.

How would one investigate some of the variables of the visual cliff situation in the laboratory? Perhaps the simplest method would be to have subjects estimate with and without head movement the distance of various stimulus patterns that differed in texture. A successful experiment, replicating some of the visual cliff results, would indicate that it is harder to estimate the distance of striped patterns than of checked patterns and that the distance of some "optimal retinal angle" patterns is also difficult to estimate. Such experiments then might be tried out with schoolchildren to see if there is a developmental trend for some patterns. The laboratory method would be particularly valuable in pinpointing patterns that might be used on the visual cliff. In any case, it is clear that despite years of research, motion parallax—taken for granted as a prime cue for depth perception—is far from understood.

A "LEARNED CUE"

In our original monograph (Walk & Gibson, 1961), we observed that rats would descend to a ¾-inch checked pattern in preference to a ¼-inch one. They would choose the ¼-inch checks over a plain gray surface, so they could see the ¼-inch checks well enough. Rats reared in the dark, however, had no preference for the ¾-inch checks, though on exposure to the light for 1 week, the dark-reared also preferred the large checks. A reasonable hypothesis based on these consistent findings is that the choice of the larger checks is based on learning. Larger objects tend to be closer. If an animal were confronted by two objects of different sizes, yet of equal distance, the choice of the larger would be a generalization from the experience of large objects being closer.

Subsequent research has generally disproved this generalization. In one experiment (Walk, 1965), the dark-reared rats chose the ¾-inch checks after only 24 hours in the light. This would seem to be a very short time for an animal such as the rat to learn to associate largeness with closeness. If the objects were not squares but circles, the rat had no preference, though it should be noted that the circles were somewhat larger than were the checks— ½-inch vs. 1½-inch ones (Walk, 1965).

The research that is relevant for this problem is that based on certain "pattern preferences" in the chick and the rat (Karmel, 1969; Schiffman, 1968, 1969). The animals will descend to some-sized checks of an "optimal" size for the species, rejecting checks of larger and smaller size. The chick prefers checks about ⅛ inch in size and the rat elements of about ½ to 1 inch in size. The preference of the chick for small, grain-sized elements had been demonstrated previously (Fantz, 1961). Such preferences are related to the "optimal retinal angle" discussed previously, and they weaken the "learned cue" hypothesis, since each species sometimes prefers the smaller checks, sometimes the larger ones, depending on the comparison stimulus.

What of the change in the animals' pattern preferences after they were reared in the dark? One hypothesis is that this is a temporary suppression based on a slight visual weakness; however, the research permits no definite answer to this question. Dark-reared rats have no difficulty discriminating visual depth with a ¼-inch pattern on the shallow side and a ¾-inch one on the deep side, but they apparently cannot discriminate two patterns of unequal size (¼ inch and ¾ inch) at equal distances until after some exposure to the light.

THE TUNNEL AND THE GORGE

A tunnel involves distance ahead and a gorge distance downward. In theory, at least, the tunnel and the gorge could be identical, so that the only difference between the two would be that the tunnel is in the horizontal plane and the gorge is in the vertical plane. An observer, if stationed appropriately, would get the same motion parallax from the tunnel as from the gorge. Yet it is reasonable to hypothesize that looking into the gorge would elicit intense fear whereas looking into the tunnel would not. How is the organism stimulated differently by the tunnel and the gorge? The visual stimulation is identical, but the gorge activates the vestibular (gravity) system in ways the tunnel does not. There are connections between the visual cortex and the pons (Baker, Gibson, Glickstein, & Stein, 1976; Glickstein & Gibson, 1976) and between the visual cortex and the cerebellum (Burne, Mihailoff, & Woodward, 1978). One presumes the limbic system would be involved in depth downward more than in depth ahead, other things being equal.

Ungulates, such as goats or lambs, have a strong reaction to depth downward—a stereotyped backing movement that effectively immobilizes the animal and prevents movement forward. But how could the ungulate be given the same visual stimulation for horizontal as for vertical depth? The animal looking into the tunnel would have to be strapped with its body vertical, so it could look through its legs at the tunnel, similar to looking through the legs at a gorge. It would be a hard procedure to construct.

The tunnel–gorge distinction emphasizes vestibular-proprioceptive-kinesthetic stimulation for depth perception, and this can lead to predictions that are somewhat impractical to assess at present. Let us suppose that kittens were raised in a weightless environment—in the space lab, for example. Then the visual–vestibular interactions of the normally raised kitten would be weakened by weightlessness (perhaps they only develop in a gravity environment, so that "weakened by weightlessness" is not the correct phrase). With the visual cliff it is assumed that animals avoid visual depth. Would an animal reared without normal vestibular stimulation also avoid depth? Would it show the same fear reactions on the deep side as the normally reared kitten? A visually deprived animal slowly recovers the discrimination of depth when placed in the light. Would an animal deprived of vestibular stimulation also slowly recover depth discrimination and recover the fear of visual depth? Answers to these questions might demonstrate the importance of visual-vestibular interaction for normal visual depth perception—an intersensory effect.

Figure 3.5 is a reproduction of a print by Escher that shows both distance downward and distance ahead. If the print is rotated, the distance downward becomes distance ahead and vice versa. For me, there is a slight emotional reaction for distance downward but not for distance ahead. This may be my imagination, and since the stimulus is a two-dimensional picture, it is not crucial for the distinction. On the other hand, one cannot help but ask whether the galvanic skin response (GSR) to depth downward in the Escher print, even if everything is obviously two-dimensional and not three-dimensional, might be different from the GSR to the horizontal picture.

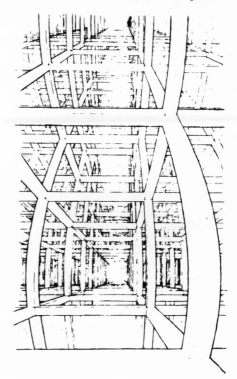

FIG. 3.5. Escher print that illustrates the tunnel–gorge distinction. Bottom (gorge) part of print, if turned to one side, looks like a tunnel. (M. C. Escher, Etude pour la lithographie Cage d'escalier, encre de Chine, 1968, cat. no 99b).

The concept—that the separability of depth downward and depth ahead necessitates the involvement of the vestibular system in order to make that distinction—is supported by an anecdote related by Kasdan (1978): "An amusement park attraction which spins people in a giant drum, then drops the floor several feet, is not frightening—the centrifugal force generated is stronger than gravity, so the wall of the drum to which people stick is experienced as the surface of support [p. 5]."

What are the cues for depth downward? What are the cues for depth downward that make us feel depth? More than the discrimination of depth is required; it also is necessary to have a feeling of looking down from a height. Such cues to depth are in both the three-dimensional and in the two-dimensional plane. Perhaps a better understanding of the two-dimensional plane will provide direction for research in the three-dimensional situation.

When Eleanor Gibson and I made a motion picture about the visual cliff (Walk & Gibson, 1959), we wanted to get such a scene on film. Cornell is full

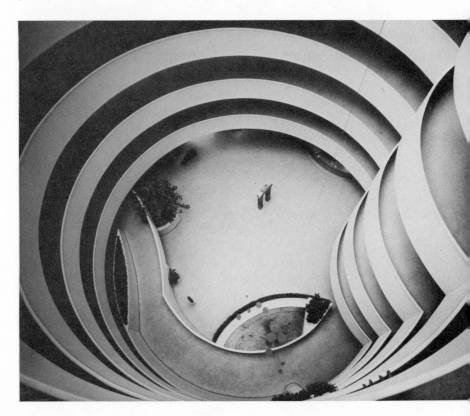

FIG. 3.6.   Depth downward. Interior view of the Solomon R. Guggenheim Museum. (Photo by Robert E. Mates.)

of gorges, an ideal location. I took the 16-mm motion picture camera and pointed it down various gorges, panned it back and forth—no luck. On one occasion, my eye glued to the eyepiece trying to get a good depth effect, I almost fell over the edge. I took the camera up various towers and pointed it downward—again no luck. Despite the fact that the pictures were all taken from a definite height, no scene was at all frightening. Finally, in desperation, we made a special trip to New York and went to a studio that stocked many kinds of footage. We selected a shot of a construction site taken from above, but the shot, though better than any of my own, was not as dramatic as we wished.[2]

If you look at photographs of depth downward, you will note that linear perspective seems to help, a continuous diminishing texture (see Fig. 3.6). A human being or animal as a reference point is also a help; this is often dramatic when the person is on a projecting surface, such as a girder, that extends out into space. But these are just guesses. No systematic study of depth downward has ever been undertaken in still photographs, paintings, or motion pictures. We also do not know if the "feeling" of depth has developmental aspects, if some or if all such cues develop with age, or if they are all there from the beginning. Fear of visual depth on the visual cliff develops gradually over the 1st year (Campos, Hiatt, Ramsay, Henderson, & Svejda, 1978; Scarr & Salapatek, 1970), but this does not mean that such apprehension would be present in pictures at this time (if we could find a way to test it).

In any event, I propose to make such a study of pictures—exploratory at first, becoming more systematic as the dimensions of the research become clearer. What of my vestibular–visual interaction study? This might have implications for the next generation, when babies are raised in a weightless or partially weightless environment for interplanetary space travel. The technical problem of keeping the kittens alive in a weightless environment has me stymied, even without thinking of asking a skeptical NASA for support.

ATTENTION OR ACTIVE LOCOMOTION?

The type of experience necessary for the development of space perception has been discussed in psychology for many years. William James (1890) discussed the case, cited by the philosopher Schopenhauer, of Eva Lauk, an Estonian girl who was born without arms and legs yet who still could discriminate depth and was of normal intelligence. I have discussed this case previously (Walk, 1978). Such a case is not crucial for modern theories of space

---

[2]The movie, *To Fly*, is an excellent source for fearsome depth effects. Sometimes one feels as if one were about to fall from a great height.

perception, because the child still could be fairly active, but the case does raise the issue of the role of sensorimotor experience in depth perception. It also raises the issue of the importance of sensorimotor experience for clinical populations such as the handicapped and the retarded. Note that Eva Lauk raises the issue of both cognitive as well as perceptual factors when normal sensorimotor experience is altered in some way.

The psychological experiment most relevant to the issue is the classical one by Held and Hein (1963) in which the importance of self-produced movement for depth perception was demonstrated. Held and Hein reared their kittens in the dark for 8 to 12 weeks and then assigned them either to an active group or to a passive one. They had an ingenious arrangement (see Fig. 3.7) where two kittens were exposed to the same visual environment under two conditions. One kitten actively pulled its counterpart around and around the circular environment while the second kitten sat passively in a small box that restricted both locomotion and the sight of its limbs. After about 10 days of such exposure, 3 hours a day, the active kitten began to show the visual placing response, extending its paws outward when it was brought toward a visual surface. Both kittens were then tested on the visual cliff. The active kittens discriminated visual depth, and the passive ones did not.

The M.I.T. group conducted many experiments with kittens (summarized in Hein, 1972), but two central questions remain: (1) Would the same results apply to very young kittens tested soon after the normal appearance of depth discrimination on the visual cliff at about 4 weeks of age? (2) Is active locomotion through the environment the only way for depth discrimination to appear in the deprived kitten?

To answer the first question, we tested kittens at 27 days of age. They were raised in the dark for 18 days and then either exposed to light in a holder that allowed no locomotion or sight of the paws (see Fig. 3.8), or they were exposed to the same environment and allowed to locomote through it for 3 hours a day (one should note, parenthetically, that the amount of locomotion

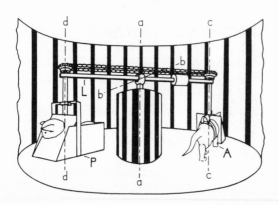

FIG. 3.7. An active (A) kitten (right) pulls its passive(P) littermate (left). The letters a–a, b–b, c–c, and d–d indicate the axes of rotation about which the animals move. (From Held & Hein, 1963. Reproduced by permission.)

FIG. 3.8. Passive kitten in our experiments, unable to see its body or its paws and unable to locomote. (Photo by Richard Walk.)

for the 18-day-old kitten is minimal and is for many days thereafter). In addition to the active and the passive groups, we had kittens reared in the lighted laboratory for the entire 27 days and dark-reared controls reared in the dark for the same period. This is our first experiment (Miller & Walk, 1975). We also wanted to repeat the original Held and Hein (1963) experiment, so we reared kittens in the dark for 8 weeks and then exposed them to the light for 3 hours a day for 10 days. The same controls were used as before (i.e., one group of kittens was reared in the lighted laboratory for the entire period, and another group of kittens was raised in the dark until given the depth discrimination tests). We used the same visual cliff test as was used by Held and Hein, and we repeated the tests until depth discrimination appeared, since after the first testing, all kittens were given 3 hours a day of active locomotory experience until their performance was adequate. We also instituted a "calling test" on the first day of testing, calling the kittens to come to the experimenter successively from the shallow and the deep sides of the visual cliff.

The results of the two experiments are shown in Fig. 3.9 and 3.10. At 27 days of age, active and passive kittens were different only on the first visual cliff test; from then on, the two groups were indistinguishable. On the calling test, all groups, including the dark-reared, averaged significantly longer latencies in descending toward the deep side than they did in descending toward the shallow side. A reasonable deduction from this first experiment is that depth discrimination is innate in the kitten; it is hindered but only slightly, by deprivation. Contrast these results with those from kittens reared in the dark for 8 weeks before exposure to the light began. The passive kittens behaved remarkably like the dark-reared, at least initially. Passive exposure appeared to be of little help for an animal visually deprived for a long time. This precise replication of the essentials of the Held and Hein (1963) study

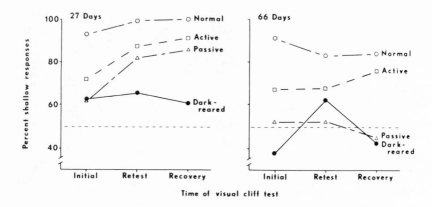

FIG. 3.9.   Shallow-side responses of kittens reared under various conditions (see text) and initially tested at 27 days of age or 66 days of age.

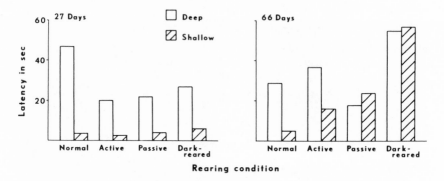

FIG. 3.10.   Latency of descent off center board toward the experimenter when called from the shallow side and the deep side for four groups of kittens. Tests were at 27 and at 66 days of age.

was heartwarming, but, considered along with the earlier Miller and Walk (1975) study, it still leaves the question as to whether active locomotion, which is not necessary for the initial appearance of depth discrimination, may be necessary to maintain it.

This question leads to yet another, posed earlier, as to whether active locomotion is the only way for depth discrimination to develop in the deprived kitten. If there are other ways to elicit depth discrimination, then we might question the role of active locomotion in the maintenance of depth discrimination. Some other process may be more important.

To answer this question, we used two additional types of passive exposure—one type we called "attention passive" and the other type we called "passive locomotion." The "attention passive" group (dubbed the "car watchers" by my assistant, Jane Shepherd) are placed in their passive restraining holders (see Fig. 3.11A) next to a toy roller coaster that has small cars that run continuously. The kittens watch the cars intently; in fact, they seem almost impelled to watch the cars. The "passive locomotion" group (or as Jane Shepherd calls them, the "go cart" group) are in a passive holder that they can move forward by lifting the head to close a microswitch. The "cart" then goes forward, round and around in a circle, up to 300 times in a 3-hour period for one animal. The apparatus is shown in Fig. 3.11B.

Although our results are only preliminary, they indicate that both "passive locomotion" and "passive attention" will help depth discrimination. The "car watchers" are particularly good; the "go cart" animals have a tendency to

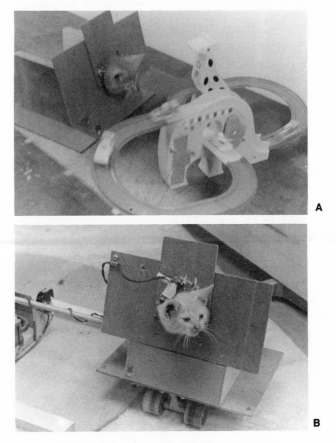

A

B

FIG. 3.11. (A) Passive kitten given extra attentional exposure to toy roller coaster with continually moving toy cars. (Photo by Richard Walk.) (B) Passive kitten in "go cart" that can be moved forward when kitten lifts head to close microswitch. (Photo by Richard Walk.)

dash forward on the visual cliff. These preliminary results indicate that attentional processes may prove to be important in depth discrimination. Active locomotion may simply be a method that ensures that the animal pays attention. Note that the active locomotion animal approaches and retreats from visual surfaces and so gets experience that is particularly appropriate for the discrimination of depth, whereas the "attention passive" or "car watching" animal simply moves its head back and forth—experience that is not at all like that required to discriminate depth on the visual cliff.

DOES DEPTH PERCEPTION
IMPROVE WITH EXPERIENCE?

The human infant's heart rate when placed on the visual cliff at 5 months of age is one of deceleration; the infant is apparently interested in the depth but is not fearful (Campos, Hiatt, Ramsay, Henderson, & Svejda, 1978). At 9 months of age, the infant's heart rate accelerates, indicative of fear. The 5-month-old does not crawl, but the 9-month-old does. Is it experience with depth that is responsible for this change? It could be maturation, or it could be experience.

The human infant does change with age, and these changes are tied to stimulus conditions. Infants 7–9 months old do not differ from infants 10–13 months old when the stimulus pattern is definite and the visual depth is great enough. For example, when the visual stimulus was 1–2-inch checks on the shallow and the deep sides and the deep side was 36 inches below the glass, about 10% of both the older and the younger groups crawled to the mother at the deep side.

A homogeneous gray placed on the deep side changed this. Under that condition, 52% of the infants 7–9 months of age crossed the deep side to the mother compared to 29% of the 10–13-month-old infants (Walk, 1966). When ¼-inch checks were placed on the shallow side, along with a definite deep-side pattern, 49% of the 7–9-month-olds and 20% of the 10–13-month-olds were coaxed to the mother. It may be that some visual acuity mechanisms in the younger crawling infants are not as well developed, or it may be that the younger infants were more willing to crawl forward to the mother in the face of uncertainty. We know from the research of Fantz, Ordy, and Udelf (1962) that the infant of this age has good visual acuity; but the visual cliff situation is "dynamic visual acuity" or acuity during visual motor behavior, and this type of visual acuity has not been measured in the young infant.

Younger infants often crawl off beds and a few weeks later refuse to get close to the edge. In our experimental situation, with definite patterns on both sides of the visual cliff, visual depth was varied by placing the deep side closer and closer to the glass. The same percentage of 7–9 and 10–13-month-old infants crawled to the mother at the deep side with 40 inches of visual depth, and only a few more of the younger group crawled to her with 20 inches; but with 10 inches of visual depth, 68% of the 7–9-month-old children crossed the deep side to the mother as compared to 23% of the 10–13-month-olds. Here we have a definite break or discontinuity. Apparently, the younger infants cannot discriminate visual depth as well as the older ones can, and this seems to be a weakness in motion parallax. The difference at this depth seems much like the difference for older and younger infants in crawling off beds.

There is additional evidence from studies of infants at the age when they begin to crawl. Infants who are crawling at 11 months may have started to crawl at 6 months of age or at 10 months of age and therefore have different amounts of crawling experience. We found that infants tested at the age of 10 to 13 months who had started crawling late behaved like 7–9-month-olds in the sense that the later crawlers were more likely to cross the deep side to the mother in the ambiguous stimulus situations just mentioned (indefinite patterns or close visual depths).

Does this mean that depth perception improves with experience? One can take either side of the issue. Maturation could be responsible for the changes. The infants who crawl late ("late crawlers") could simply be developing more slowly.

Animal studies permit more precise contol, but they also cannot answer the question. Bradley and Shea (1977) reared gerbils in cliff environments and in flat environments. The cliff environment animals were better than the flat environment animals at 30 days of age. This may indicate some improvement with experience, but many more such studies are necessary.

"Improvement with experience" is not the same thing as "influenced by experience." Improvement means that it either appears earlier as a result of experience or that it gets better and better as a result of experience. Influenced by experience simply means a change as a result of some kind of experience. Many studies have shown that depth perception is influenced by experience. Such studies are reviewed in Walk (1978). For example, as was indicated earlier, gulls can be raised in either a cliff environment or in a flat one. Gulls of similar genetic stock reared under these conditions show the effects of experience. Those gulls reared in the presence of depths are less likely to jump off platforms, less likely to exit from the nest, and less likely to go to the deep side of the visual cliff than are ground-reared gulls. An interaction of genetic and experiential factors is also demonstrated in that some species of gulls are practically unmodifiable by the experience whereas other species are more likely to adapt their behavior to the environment.

Does depth perception improve through experience? It is a reasonable supposition, but the evidence is not yet strong enough unless one counts long-term studies like the gull experiments.

CONCLUSION

I have reviewed a number of areas related to depth perception, trying to show some of the problems, many of them unexpected and frustrating, that at times give the researcher the feeling of being "arched over by a laughing heaven."

The study of visual depth perception with the visual cliff began as a study of light-reared and dark-reared rats, and within a year we had built a visual cliff for testing human infants. At George Washington University we are also slowly collecting data with a visual cliff for adults. Many, many species have been tested on the visual cliff by many different researchers, demonstrating the adaptability of the apparatus and that depth downward is an easy visual discrimination for any species with an adequate visual system.

In the present chapter, extension of research on depth downward to paintings and photographs was mentioned as was basic laboratory research with adults on the distance perception of different kinds of patterns to help us better understand the stimulus for depth perception. Yet the solution of many fundamental problems is elusive.

How did it all begin? For me, it began when I was studying fear with paratroopers (Walk, 1959) in a particularly personal way. Many years ago, in 1953, I stood on a training device at the Airborne Center in Fort Benning, Georgia, called the "mock tower." The "mock tower" is so named because it is a training device or mock-up, and the tower is used to help teach the trainees to exit from an aircraft. Trainees are taught to exit from the mock tower so as not to become entangled in their parachutes. They jump out of a door the same dimensions as those of their aircraft, wearing a parachute harness, helmet, and mock reserve parachute. They are hooked up so that when they leap from the 34-foot-high tower, straps snub their fall after a drop of 8 to 10 feet. The device is perfectly safe, but perceptually it is like a jump off a 34-foot cliff. Strong individuals stride up the tower, walk to the open door with confidence, look down, blanch, tremble, and refuse to go farther. Others have the same physiological reactions, but they go forward; and in exiting, their knees collapse under them, and they fall out the door like limp sacks of wheat; a few will go through the same stereotyped fearful responses as many as 30 times before they are mercifully stopped by the cadre and failed, their records marked, "not adaptable for airborne training." For some, such an experience—facing something within the self that had never been suspected— can be devastating. For a few, the mock tower was a guillotine of their hopes. For the rest, at some later time, there are other guillotines. Most, of course, master their fear and push on toward the ultimate reward of the training, parachute jumping. A few may never feel any fear at all and wonder at the trepidation of their peers. Figure 3.12 illustrates an enthusiastic but inept mock tower exit.

FIG. 3.12.   Awkward paratrooper trainee jumping from "mock tower" at Ft. Benning, Ga. Straps snub fall after 8–10 feet. Prescribed position: Legs should be together and straight, elbows by side with hands on ends of reserve chute, chin tucked in, body straight. (Photo by Richard Walk.)

For me, a PhD civilian who was studying the airborne training program, the perceptual and the cognitive were intertwined. If my knees were a little weak as I jumped, another part of me was fascinated and asked, "why?". I jumped many times from the mock tower, and I never failed to ask myself, "But why?"

Fortunately, I went to Cornell from Fort Benning, and got to know Eleanor and James Gibson. The pathway from "why" to the research described here was not a direct one. At one point I contemplated constructing a miniature mock tower and training rats to jump from it; it was an idle thought that, fortunately, was never carried out. The Gibsons, particularly James Gibson, knew about perception, and they had also thought about the perception of depth. Eventually, almost fortuitously, the visual cliff was started when we had rats in the dark to test for form discrimination but wished to get some measures that could be carried out as soon as the animals came out of the dark.

The first visual cliff paper was published in 1957 (Walk, Gibson, & Tighe, 1957), and Eleanor Gibson and I collaborated for a few years, laying the groundwork for many of the questions whose answers are still only partially available.

I have searched for the answer to the "why" I asked 25 years ago and never found it. Perhaps someone who reads this chapter will join the search and push my elementary research a little further into the unknown. Should you do this, dear reader, be warned, for you will be, as I was and still am, "arched over by a laughing heaven."

ACKNOWLEDGMENTS

The research reported here was supported, in part, by grants from the National Institute of Mental Health, the National Science Foundation, and an N. I. H. Biomedical support grant to George Washington University.

REFERENCES

Baker, J., Gibson, A., Glickstein, M., & Stein, J. Visual cells in the pontine nuclei of the cat. *Journal of Physiology*, 1976, *255*, 415–433.
Bradley, D. R., & Shea, S. L. The effect of environment on visual cliff performance in the Mongolian gerbil. *Perception & Psychophysics*, 1977, *21*, 171–179.
Burne, R. A., Mihailoff, G. A., & Woodward, D. J. Visual corticopontine input to the paraflocculus: A combined autoradiographic and horseradish peroxidase study. *Brain Research*, 1978, *143*, 139–146.
Campos, J. J., Hiatt, S., Ramsay, D., Henderson, C., & Svejda, M. The emergence of fear on the visual cliff. In M. Lewis & L. A. Rosenblum (Eds.), *The development of affect* (Vol. 1). New York: Plenum Press, 1978.
Cullen, E. Adaptations in the Kittiwake to cliff-nesting. *Ibis*, 1957, *99*, 272–302.
Davidson, P. W., & Whitson, T. T. Some effects of texture density on visual cliff behavior of the domestic chick. *Journal of Comparative and Physiological Psychology*, 1973, *84*, 522–526.
DeHardt, D. C. Visual cliff behavior of rats as a function of pattern size. *Psychonomic Science*, 1969, *15*, 268–269.
Fantz, R. L. The origin of form perception. *Scientific American*, 1961, *204*(5), 66–72.
Fantz, R. L., Ordy, J. M., & Udelf, M. S. Maturation of pattern vision in infants during the first six months. *Journal of Comparative and Physiological Psychology*, 1962, *55*, 907–917.
Ferris, S. H. Motion parallax and absolute distance. *Journal of Experimental Psychology*, 1972, *95*, 258–263.
Glickstein, M., & Gibson, A. R. Visual cells in the pons of the brain. *Scientific American*, 1976, *235*(5), 90–98.
Greenberg, D. J., & O'Donnell, W. J. Infancy and the optimal level of stimulation, *Child Development*, 1972, *43*, 639–645.
Hein, A. Acquiring components of visually guided behavior. In A. D. Pick (Ed.), *Minnesota symposia on child psychology* (Vol. 6). Minneapolis: University of Minnesota Press, 1972.
Held, R., & Hein, A. Movement-produced stimulation in the development of visually-guided behavior. *Journal of Comparative and Physiological Psychology*, 1963, *56*, 872–876.
James, W. *The principles of psychology* (Vol. II). New York: Holt, 1890.
Johansson, G. Monocular movement parallax and near-space perception. *Perception*, 1973, *2*, 135–146.
Karmel, B. Z. Complexity, amounts of contour and visually-dependent behavior in hooded rats, domestic chicks, and human infants. *Journal of Comparative and Physiological Psychology*, 1969, *69*, 649–657.

Karmel, B. Z., & Maisel, E. B. A neuronal activity model for infant visual attention. In L. B. Cohen & P. Salapatek (Eds.), *Infant perception: From sensation to cognition.* New York: Academic Press, 1975.

Kasdan, P. *The discrimination of similar horizontal and vertical visual environments.* Paper given for a seminar, George Washington University, 1978.

MacKay, D. M., & Jeffreys, D. A. Visually evoked potentials and visual perception in man. In R. Jung (Ed.), *Handbook of sensory physiology.* (Vol. VII/3). *Central processing of visual information* (Part B). Berlin: Springer-Verlag, 1973.

Mayzner, M. S., & Habinek, J. *Visual recognition of simple intersecting and parallel line patterns.* Paper presented at the meeting of the Psychonomic Society, St. Louis, Mo., November 12, 1976.

McLannahan, H. M. C. Some aspects of the ontogeny of cliff nesting behavior in the kittiwake (*Rissa trydactyla*) and the herring gull (*Larus argentatus*). *Behaviour,* 1973, *44,* 36–88.

Miller, D. R., & Walk, R. D. *Self-produced movement is unnecessary for the development of visually-guided depth discrimination.* Paper presented at the meetings of the Eastern Psychological Association, New York, April 1975.

Scarr, S., & Salapatek, P. Patterns of fear development during infancy. *Merrill-Palmer Quarterly,* 1970, *16,* 53–90.

Schiffman, H. R. Texture preference in the domestic chick. *Journal of Comparative and Physiological Psychology,* 1968, *66,* 540–541.

Schiffman, H. R. Texture preference and acuity in the domestic chick. *Journal of Comparative and Physiological Psychology,* 1969, *67,* 462–464.

Schiffman, H. R., & Walk, R. D. Behavior on the visual cliff of monocular as compared to binocular chicks. *Journal of Comparative and Physiological Psychology,* 1963, *56,* 1064–1068.

Trychin, S., Jr., & Walk, R. D. A study of the depth perception of monocular hooded rats on the visual cliff. *Psychonomic Science,* 1964, *1,* 53–54.

Walk, R. D. *Fear and courage: A psychological study.* On deposit at George Washington University Library, 1959. (Available through interlibrary loan.)

Walk, R. D. The study of visual depth and distance perception in animals. In D. S. Lehrman, R. A. Hinde, & E. Shaw (Eds.), *Advances in the study of behavior* (Vol. 1). New York: Academic Press, 1965.

Walk, R. D. The development of depth perception in animals and human infants. *Child Development Monograph,* 1966, *31*(107), 82–108.

Walk, R. D. Depth perception and experience. In R. D. Walk & H. L. Pick, Jr. (Eds.), *Perception and experience.* New York: Plenum Press, 1978.

Walk, R. D., & Gibson, E. J. *Behavior of animals and human infants in response to a visual cliff.* University Park, Pa., Psychological Cinema Register (PCR-2095), Pennsylvania State University, 1959. (Film)

Walk, R. D., & Gibson, E. J. A comparative and analytical study of visual depth perception. *Psychological Monographs,* 1961, *75,* (15, Whole No. 519).

Walk, R. D., Gibson, E. J., & Tighe, T. J. Behavior of light- and dark-reared rats on a visual cliff. *Science,* 1957, *126,* 80–81.

Walk, R. D., & Walters, C. P. Importance of texture-density preferences and motion parallax for visual depth discrimination by rats and chicks. *Journal of Comparative and Physiological Psychology,* 1974, *86,* 309–315.

Walk, R. D., Walters, C. P., & Rosner, W. *The DeHardt effect with human infants.* Paper presented at meetings of the Eastern Psychological Association, Washington, D. C., April 1978.

4 Studies of Spatial Perception in Infancy

Albert Yonas
University of Minnesota

When I arrived in Ithaca in the fall of 1964 to begin graduate school, I was assigned to be a research assistant to Eleanor Gibson. I had not intended to study perceptual development or even perception, but I soon found myself in an environment in which the study of perception was the most exciting intellectual activity I had ever witnessed. In this setting, an interest in the topic of infant spatial perception was assumed. Although the classic studies by Walk and Gibson (1961) with the visual cliff had been completed and my research at Cornell dealt with perceptual learning in older children and adults, I learned that perception of the layout of the environment and of spatial events is central to an understanding of perception.

During my graduate school years, Eleanor Gibson elaborated the differentiation theory of perceptual learning. She was preparing *Principles of Perceptual Learning and Development* (1969) for publication and doing experiments to reinforce the theory. The arguments and issues in that book were the core of my graduate education. The question of whether the infant enters the world experiencing only meaningless sensations or begins life with an undifferentiated but always three-dimensional world was clearly a central issue.

I can think of two methodological lessons learned from Eleanor Gibson that have strongly influenced my work on perceptual develpment. The first of these is a concern with what the typical environment of the infant is like and what natural behaviors are available to the infant at a particular point in development. The use of reaching to index the infant's spatial perception is an application of this ecological lesson. The second lesson, exemplified in Walk and Gibson's (1961) visual cliff research, directs us to discover the particular

89

visual information for depth that is detected by the infant. They systematically explored the importance of motion parallax, binocular vision, and texture density. I have followed a similar course in my own work.

In this chapter I describe research carried out at Minnesota over the last 7 years on three related aspects of the development of spatial sensitivity. In the first part of the chapter I review work on the development of sensitivity to binocular information. In the second part of the chapter I deal with sensitivity to information for the approach of an object and the development of avoidant responses, such as blinking and head withdrawal, that could reveal the presence of this sensitivity. In the third part of the chapter I describe work on the development in infants of sensitivity to static pictorial spatial information.

DEVELOPMENT OF
BINOCULAR DEPTH SENSITIVITY

Although perception may be the oldest field of psychology, and although speculation on the spatial perception of infants has had a very long history in philosophy, the actual empirical study of infant perception is a remarkably recent activity. In 1935, Carr reported the first evidence that children are sensitive to binocular information for depth. He presented 2- to 5-year-old children with three real objects that differed only in relief and three corresponding line drawings viewed through a stereoscope. Although the 2-year-olds were at chance in identifying which of the three real objects was represented by each line drawing, the older children reliably matched the stereograms to the objects. Given the complexity of the judgment required by the task, the poor performance of the 2-year-olds is not surprising.

Johnson and Beck (1941) were later able to demonstrate binocular sensitivity in six 2-year-old children by using the reaching response as an indicator of depth perception. Using polarized filters and a stereoscopic slide projector, slightly different images of a doll were presented to the left and right eyes of the subject. When both images were projected, the children reached for the doll at a distance of 10 inches (25.4 cm). When only one of the images was presented, the children reached for the image on the screen, 20 inches (50.8 cm) away. Spontaneous comments by older children indicated the unusual nature of their tactual experience with a virtual three-dimensional object. "Say it must be magic; I can't feel it [p. 252]," a 6-year-old exclaimed. Surprisingly, experimental work extending this method to infants did not begin until 25 years later.

In an article published in 1966, T. G. R. Bower summarized an extensive set of studies reporting evidence of size and shape constancy in infants. He briefly described a size constancy experiment in which three types of viewing conditions were contrasted: monocular viewing of an actual object, binocular viewing of a rear-projected photographic slide of the object, binocular viewing of a stereoscopically projected object. Using generalization of a conditioned head-turning response to index size constancy, Bower reported that the degree of size constancy for the group viewing the stereoscopic projection was somewhat less than for the group viewing the real object monocularly. The group viewing the rear-projected slide showed no evidence of size constancy. He concluded that binocular parallax was somewhat effective information for size but was less effective than motion parallax. Unfortunately, a full description of the study has not been published.

More recently, Bower, Broughton, and Moore (1970) concluded that infants as young as 7 days of age are sensitive to stereoscopic information for the location of an object. They reported that infants were emotionally upset when they reached out and failed to make contact with a virtual object. This report is surprising, given the finding by Aslin (1977) of very poor convergence in the new-born and the reports by Gesell and Thompson (1934); White, Castle, and Held (1964); and Dodwell, Muir, and DiFranco (1976) of slow development of visually directed reaching. It may be that the observed distress was due to the effects of darkness, the polarized goggles, or some aspect of the situation other than the mismatch of visual and tactual information.

In the first of a series of studies in our laboratory of infant sensitivity to binocular depth, Gordon and Yonas (1976) reasoned that if infants' reaches terminated at locations that varied systematically with the location of a stereoscopically projected virtual object, there would be convincing evidence of binocular depth perception. A stereoscopic shadow-caster was used to present the virtual object. Polarized filters were placed in front of two point-source lamps, and a second pair was placed over the infant's eyes. With this apparatus, a real object was positioned between the lamps and a rear projection screen. If an observer has binocular depth perception, he or she will see not a pair of shadows on the screen but a single object at a precise location in space. Using this method of presentation, a virtual object was positioned at three distances from 5½-month-old infants: 15 cm, 20 cm, and 30 cm. The first two locations were judged to be within reach, but 30 cm—the distance to the screen—was just beyond the reach of the infant. Two television cameras and a videotape machine were used to record the behavior of the infants.

While the study was in progress, it seemed to the experimenters that the infants were reaching for the virtual object. However, an analysis of the location of the reaches revealed that the end points of the reaches did not vary reliably with the location of the virtual object. There was considerable variability in response. As a preliminary phase of this study, the infants had been presented with a real object positioned 15 cm from them; only those infants who reached for the real object were presented with the virtual object. An analysis of the reaches to the real object had shown that the reaches of infants at 5½ months were rather inaccurate. Although the infants generally contacted the real object, the contact often appeared to be accidental. The infant generally closed his or her hand in front of, or to the side of, the object and frequently contacted the object first with the back of the hand. Thus, it appears that the location of the hand at the end of a reach provides little evidence of precise binocular depth sensitivity.

However, there were three other measures that indicated that 5½-month-olds were responsive to the apparent location of the virtual object. When the virtual object was located beyond reach rather than within reach, the infants tended to lean farther forward and place their heads closer to the screen. In addition, the infants reached more frequently and made more grasping responses when the virtual object was positioned within reach. Considered together, the leaning behavior, the frequency of reaching, and the frequency of grasping provide clear evidence that by 5½ months, infants are responsive to binocular information for depth. On the other hand, we can conclude very little about the precision of the depth information provided the infants by the binocular stimulation. We do know from these results that they can distinguish an object that is within reach from one that is out of reach.

It seems that reaching that is precisely localized provides an ideal index of the development of more fine-grained binocular spatial sensitivity. To investigate the development of such behavior, Gordon, Lamson, and Yonas (1978) tested infants of three ages in an experiment based on the earlier study by Gordon and Yonas (1976). Infants aged 5½, 7½ and 9½ months were presented a virtual object at three distances. Their reaches to the object were videotaped. For all three age groups, there were fewer reaches made to the virtual object when it was at its most distant position. In addition, infants in all three age groups leaned farther forward when the virtual object was in its most distant position than when it was at the intermediate position; they leaned even less when the object was in the position closest to them. It seems, then, that on the basis of binocular information, infants at 5½ months may be able to make a distinction finer than that of differentiating accessible and nonaccessible spatial locations.

The accuracy of the reaches increased reliably with age. The 5½-month-olds tended to place their hands a constant distance from their bodies, whereas the 7½- and 9½-month-olds reached out farther from themselves when the object was at a greater distance. Apparently, at 5½ months it is the trunk rather than the arms that responds with more precision to binocular depth information.

The 5-month-olds tested by Bower et al. (1970) and by Bower (1971) were reported to have shown "marked surprise [Bower, 1971, p. 31]" when they encountered a virtual object created by a stereoscopic shadow-caster. The behaviors they listed as indicating surprise were distinctive: staring at the hands, rubbing the hands together, and banging the hands on the chair. Perhaps the infant was testing the ability of the hands to produce tactual sensations after the unexpected experience of reaching for an object that evoked no tactual sensations. In contrast to Bower's report, Gordon and Yonas observed no behavior that indicated surprise or that touch was being tested. The responses that were observed, mainly patting or pinching, appeared to be continuing attempts by the infant to grasp the object.

In a similar study, Field (1976) reported that when 14- to 20-week-old infants reached for a virtual object, none of the infants showed either surprise or distress. Field suggested that fingering movements made around the location of the virtual object by 31-week-old infants indicated that these older infants may have expected a tactual outcome to their reaching attempts, but this response does not suggest that the infants were surprised or that they questioned the effectiveness of touch.

Even if 5½-month-olds do not express surprise or distress in this situation, one might expect that older infants, who reach with greater precision, would be upset to place their hands on the visual location of an object and experience no tactual sensations. However, Gordon et al. (1978) found little change in the responses of infants from 5½ to 9½ months of age. When the infant's hand reached the location of the virtual object, the most frequent response was a continuation of the reach or the instigation of another reach. On about 20% of the reaches, the initial reach was followed by waving the arm, suggesting that the infant was searching for the object. However, there were very few emotional responses or attempts to examine, visually or tactually, the insensitive hand. Since Johnson and Beck (1941) reported that several preschool children did express surprise when they could not touch a virtual object, it is likely that this response appears sometime between the 9th month and the preschool years. Given the difficulty that 5-month-olds have in successfully reaching for a small object, a visually directed reach that fails to produce tactual stimulation should not be so unusual. The absence of surprise in 7- and 9-month-old infants, who do reach with some precision, may be due to the late development of the ability to express surprise. On the other hand, the infant may develop (perhaps only after the 1st year) the cognitive abilities needed to reflect on a conflict between touch and vision and to appreciate the highly unusual nature of this experience.

Although it is clear that infants have some sensitivity to binocular depth information by 5½ months of age, we know little about the initial appearance of this sensitivity. Yonas, Oberg, and Norcia (1978) presented 14- and 20-week-old infants with binocular information for a slowly approaching object. The stereoscopic shadow-caster created a small virtual object that looks to a viewer with binocular vision as if it would collide with the bridge of the viewer's nose. To create a nonstereoscopic control condition, the polarized filters were removed from the point-source lamps. In this condition, instead of the approaching object, the viewer sees two shadows expanding and separating on the rear projection screen. The two objects appear to be approaching on a path that would miss (as opposed to colliding with) the viewer—one object veering off to the right, the other to the left. It thus provides the same visual experience as the stereoscopic condition would provide to a viewer who has diplopia rather than normal binocular vision.

The responses of the 20-week-olds were quite different in the two conditions. In the stereoscopic condition, they reached toward the screen three times more frequently than they did in the control condition. They also blinked and withdrew their heads more frequently in the stereoscopic condition, suggesting that the 20-week-olds were trying to avoid collision with the approaching virtual object. In contrast, the 14-week-olds provided us little evidence that they were responsive to binocular depth information. The frequency of forward arm movements, head withdrawal, and blinking did not differ in the two conditions for the younger infants. However, the conditions did differ on one measure for both age groups. That difference was more sustained orientation to the center of the display in the stereoscopic condition. This behavior indicates that the viewer's eyes are converging on the approaching object (without binocular depth perception, one would see two diverging shadows and would probably look from side to side). Although convergence is not a clear indication that binocular depth sensitivity is present, it seems a requisite to its appearance.

On the basis of the present evidence, it would be a mistake to conclude that binocular depth sensitivity is absent in infants under 20 weeks of age. In a preliminary study carried out by Rezba (1977) the latency of swiping arm movements was recorded for a group of 15-week-old infants. In this study, a stereoscopic virtual object evoked arm movements sooner when it was located close to the infant than when it was positioned out of reach. Although the arm movements of 3½-month-olds have little of the character of object-directed reaching, these infants do detect systematic variation in the stimulation. If the arm movements are actual attempts to contact the object, then the more rapid movements to the close virtual object imply that binocular depth sensitivity is present at 15 weeks. Clearly, more work is needed before we can describe the development of binocular sensitivity over the first 4 months of life.

The fact that we have two eyes provides us with two different types of depth information. One type of information is based on convergence of the eyes— referring to the angle between the two eyes. A second type of information is binocular disparity—the difference between the images in the two eyes that occurs when a three-dimensional scene is viewed. Although on one hand, no explicit attempt was made to separate the two types of information in the studies described previously; on the other hand, little disparity information is available when a stereoscopic shadow-caster is used to present a single virtual object. Unless the infant were detecting the spatial relation between the rather distant edge of the rear projection screen and the virtual object, only convergence information for depth should be available. Von Hofsten (1977) used a prism arrangement to modify the convergence angles for 5- to 8-month-old infants viewing a small object. He reported that the reaches observed were very frequently directed at the virtual object location, suggesting that sensitivity to convergence is present. Of the reaches that were observed in his study, 34 of 42 were judged to be directed at the virtual object. Unfortunately, the basis for those judgments was not described nor were any inferential statistics provided to support the reliability of the conclusions.

The random dot stereogram created by Julesz (1971) allows us to assess sensitivity to disparity, without providing any *monocular* information for convergence. In Julesz' diagrams, a rectangular region appears in front of a background only when viewed stereoscopically. If infants fixate the raised region when disparity is small and do not do so when disparity is very great, this strongly suggests that depth, rather than binocular rivalry, is directing the gaze. Fox, Shea, Aslin, and Dumais (1978) have used a kinetic version of the Julesz stereogram display to probe the beginning of depth sensitivity in infants who are too young to reach. It seems that, whereas 2½-month-old infants do not orient their eyes toward disparity information, infants at 3½ months of age do detect this information. The hypothesis that the spatial character of the binocularly generated contour (rather than some other property) is directing the infant's gaze will need to be examined in future studies. The transfer paradigm (Yonas & Pick, 1975) may be helpful here. If habituation to the shape of an object specified only by disparity information will transfer to a presentation of that object in which the three-dimensional shape is specified by motion parallax or other depth information, one could then argue that depth is detected. Such experiments seem possible, and with the growing number of investigators working on infant perception, we may soon have a more complete picture of the early development of binocular depth perception.

DEVELOPMENT OF RESPONSIVENESS TO INFORMATION FOR COLLISION

One of the most pressing problems in investigating the onset of sensitivity to depth information is to find a meaningful response available to the young infant that is a clear indicator of depth sensitivity. One reliable response may be blinking at an object that is about to collide with the infant's eyes. Although a blink response can readily be elicited in the neonate by blowing on or touching the face or by a loud noise (Gesell & Thompson, 1934; Jones,

1926; Kasahara & Inamatsu, 1931), newborns infrequently protect their eyes by closing the eyelids when an object approaches the face. Peiper (1963) has summarized the reports of several early investigators who reported that blinking to visual approach first appeared at approximately 2 months of age.

White (1971) studied the effects of enriching the stimulation available to infants on the development of a number of responses, one of which was the blink response. In his experiment, a target was dropped toward the infant from several distances. A sheet of Plexiglass shielded the infant from changes in air pressure. White reported that whereas a few 2- to 5-week-old infants blinked occasionally to the largest drop of the target, by 9 to 13 weeks of age, half the infants blinked on 70% to 80% of the trials. Thus, frequency of blinking at the display increased dramatically with age. Enrichment itself had no effect on the appearance of the response.

We found similar results in a series of studies carried out in our laboratory. Yonas, Bechtold, Frankel, Gordon, McRoberts, Norcia, and Sternfels (1977) found 4-month-old infants showed significantly more blinking to a symmetrically expanding shadow that specified collision than to an asymmetrically expanding shadow that specified an object approaching on a path that would miss the infant. Infants of 3 to 6 weeks of age made slightly more frequent blinking responses to the collision display, but the difference was not statistically significant.

If we accept the hypothesis that the blink is a clear indication that an infant perceives the event of impending collision, we are left with the problem of accounting for the large increase in the frequency of blinking at an approaching object over the first months of life. In 1926, Jones suggested three possible accounts of this increase: (1) Blinking to optical approach may be due to Pavlovian conditioning of an innate tactual blink reflex; (2) it may be due to maturation; or (3) it may be due to a combination of both factors. Schiff (1965) ruled out the effects of learning for a presocial species of birds when he found that chicks reared in the dark for several weeks after hatching behaved defensively when presented with an optical looming display. If one can extrapolate from chicks to humans, a maturational account is suggested.

Although of course we cannot rear human infants in the dark in order to assess the effects of experience on the development of blinking at an approaching object, we can compare the performance of infants of the same age who had gestational periods longer or shorter than the normal 40 weeks. In other words, we can evaluate the effects of the duration of experience in the visual world and the effects of age since conception. In a study carried out by Pettersen, Yonas, and Fisch (1979), three groups of 10-week-old infants were tested: a group of preterm infants born 3 to 4 weeks before due date, a group of full-term infants born within 1 week of due date, and a group of postterm infants born 3 to 4 weeks after due date. A dark triangle of a porus material was moved for 1 second from a position 30 cm from the infant to the infant's eyes. This looming event was repeated approximately 40 times, and the proportion of trials on which a blink occurred was recorded. Whereas the preterm infants blinked on only about 33% of the trials, the full-term and postterm infants blinked on 75% of the trials.

Although the preterm infants did respond less frequently than did the two other groups, their behavior may be due to some deleterious effect of prematurity and not simply to their shorter period of gestation. To test whether preterm infants would reach the same level of responding as the other groups given the same time span in which to develop, an additional group of preterm infants were tested at approximately 14 weeks after birth. When tested at 50 weeks of age since conception, the preterm group responded on 72% of the trials, or at about the same level as the full-term and postterm groups.

Since 10 weeks postbirth was apparently too late to detect differences in blink frequency between full-term and postterm infants, we next tested full-term and postterm infants at an earlier point in development, or 6 weeks after birth. Approximately 20 control trials in which the triangle was withdrawn from the infant's eyes were presented in addition to 20 approach trials. Since postterm infants have been reported to have a higher rate of neonatal mortality (Anderson, 1972) and to have scored lower on the Denver developmental scale (Field, Dabiri, Hallock, & Shuman, 1977), one might expect a poorer performance from this group than from the full-term infants. The results were quite different from this expectation. The full-term infants blinked on only 16% of the approach trials, whereas the postterm infants responded on 37% of the trials. Thus, an additional 3 to 4 weeks in utero produced a substantial increase in defensive responses to the approaching object.

These results were confirmed in an independent replication study in which we used an improved method of establishing the gestational age of the infant. In addition, the experimenters did not know whether the infant was part of the full-term or postterm group until after the data had been analyzed. For both groups of infants, there was a very low frequency of blinking on the baseline withdrawal trials. The baseline frequency was so low that although the full-term infants failed to blink on 84% of the approach trials, these infants still blinked more frequently to the approach of the triangle than to its withdrawal. Although there is a striking increase (from 16% to 75%) from the 6th to the 10th week of age in the probability that an approaching object will evoke a blink in full-term infants, even at 6 weeks postbirth, infants show some sensitivity to information for the approach of an object.

The finding that postterm infants blink more frequently at an approaching object than do full-term infants provides a strong argument for a maturational rather than a learning-based account of the development of defensive blinking. However, we cannot rule out classical conditioning entirely. It is possible that if the postterm infants are neurologically more mature than the full-term infants, they may more efficiently learn a conditioned response.

If we accept the hypothesis that it is maturation that accounts for the increase in responsiveness that we have observed, we are left with the question of what is developing. It may be that the perceptual mechanism that detects the optical information for collision is maturing, or it may be some process that connects the blink response to an already effective perceptual process.

There is some evidence that perceptual sensitivity to information for collision is present even in the newborn. Bower et al. (1971) and Ball and Tronick (1971) have suggested that newborns make an integrated avoidant response to an approaching object several weeks prior to blinking to optical information. They report a response consisting of several behaviors, including emotional upset, interposition of the hands between the object and the infant's face, and upward rotation (withdrawal) of the head. Although other experimenters have failed to find emotional upset and interposition of the hands to be reliable responses (Ball & Tronick, 1971; Ball & Vurpillot, 1976; Yonas et al., 1977), backward head movements have been observed consistently when newborn infants are shown looming displays. These head movements may be defensive in character, although an alternate interpretation of these head movements was suggested by Ball (1970), who pointed out that the upward rotation of the infant's head may be due to a tendency of the infants to follow the movement of the upper contour of the display.

Support for Ball's hypothesis was provided by a study in which we measured head rotation of infants presented with three shadow projection conditions (Yonas et al., 1977). A symmetrically expanding contour providing information for collision, an asymmetrically expanding contour specifying an approaching object on a miss path, and a nonexpanding rising contour were presented to twenty-four 3- to 6-week-old infants. Although the collision display evoked more head rotation than the miss display, it was the rising contour that produced the largest amount of head rotation. In his criticism of this study, Bower (1977) argued that the infants may not have been able to withdraw from the display because of the manner in which they were held. Two points should be considered in evaluating this criticism: (1) The method for supporting the infant's head in our study was identical to the procedure used by Ball and Tronick (1971); (2) we replicated Ball and Tronick's findings (i.e., the infants did rotate their heads upward to a greater degree in reaction to the looming display than to the miss display). Although it is possible that this head rotation was an attempt to avoid the looming object, it is also clear that the presence of a rising contour in the visual field evokes strong upward head rotation. Perhaps the two different types of stimulation—one, information for collision; the other, a contour moving upward—evoke the same response but for two different reasons.

Bower (1977) briefly reported a study in which he provided optical information for an object falling on an infant, but that did not include contours rising in the visual field. He used a rear projection screen to present a rectangular silhouette that transformed through a series of trapezoids into a line; there were also several control conditions. Backward head movements were measured by a pressure transducer built into an infant seat. Bower reported that although expansion of the silhouette (which created contours that moved upward in the field) did not produce backward head movement, the downward transformation of the rectangle into a line did.

Bower's use of a sensitive pressure transducer as an objective measure of head movement is clearly an important methodological advance. We have used a similar apparatus in our two most recent studies. In the first of these, twenty 3- to 5-week-old infants were presented a triangle that rapidly approached the eyes, as well as a control condition in which the object was withdrawn. Eighteen of the 20 infants showed more backward head movements to the approaching object than to the receding object. There was slightly more blinking when the object approached than during the control trials, but the difference was not significant. Although this study demonstrated the sensitivity of the head movement measure, it did not rule out the possibility that these young infants were not defending themselves against collision but were instead simply following the upper contour of the triangle.

In a second study, infants 3 to 6 weeks old were shown a rectangle that was rotated 90° so that the top of the rectangle moved downward toward the infant's eyes. In the control condition, the direction of rotation was reversed; the object initially was positioned only 4 or 5 cm from the infant's eyes and was then rotated so that the close edge moved upward, away from the infant. The results of this study were quite clear. The infants produced a large amount of backward head pressure as the rectangle was rotated away from their faces. They appeared frequently to track the upper contour of the rectangle, rotating their heads upward to follow it. In the condition in which the object was lowered and almost collided with the infant, little backward head movement occurred; the infants' eyes generally moved downward. Obviously, further work is needed to clarify the necessary and sufficient conditions that evoke backward head movements.

Adamson and Tronick (1977) reported that newborns became agitated and motorically active when a white cloth was placed in front of their eyes. A transparent piece of plastic did not produce the same effect. They interpreted this behavior as an attempt by the infants to defend themselves. In our own laboratory we have observed that 3-week-old infants will frequently turn their heads and eyes to the side when an object is positioned so that it occludes their field of view. Similarly, Mendelson and Haith (1976) have found that when newborns are presented with a dark homogenous visual field, they make wide lateral eye movements. Unlike Adamson and Tronick, Mendelson and Haith do not interpret these behaviors as defensive. Perhaps depth information indicating that a surface is positioned very close to the face increases the amount of head and eye movements of the newborn. If so, this would indicate an innate responsiveness to depth information. If such responsiveness is present, it may have evolved to protect the newborn from the danger of nasal occlusion and smothering during nursing. It is clear that the newborn does withdraw rapidly from the nipple when his or her nares are blocked, and perhaps some visual information would also evoke this response. Such reasoning adds plausibility to the argument that some depth sensitivity is present in the newborn. However, even if newborns exhibited more head and eye movements when presented with information for a surface very close to the face, the problem of establishing that the newborn possesses something more than a reflex response to an isolated stimulus property remains.

Once again, the transfer paradigm (Yonas & Pick, 1975) provides a methodology that may be helpful in dealing with this problem. If infants who acquire a discrimination based on one type of depth information show transfer of that discrimination to displays providing a second type of information, an account based on a simple reflex process seems unlikely. At this point, such studies have not yet been carried out, and it may well be the case that the rather complex transfer paradigm will simply not be practical with newborns. Because the human newborn possesses so few meaningful responses that could indicate sensitivity to depth information, we may never know with certainty whether this sensitivity develops over the first months of life or whether it is present in some undifferentiated form from birth.

DEVELOPMENT OF SENSITIVITY
TO PICTORIAL DEPTH

Pictorial cues for depth—interposition, linear perspective, relative size, etc.— are perhaps strange things for a student of the Gibsons to investigate. In graduate school I was taught that the Ames (1951) trapezoidal window is a misleading piece of apparatus, phenomenally as well as theoretically. Antirealist philosophers and psychologists have pointed to the illusory experience of depth that occurs when we view a picture to argue that all spatial experience is an illusion, an inference from probabilistic cues projected on a flat retina. Although my background in philosophy is not sophisticated, I have never found this argument convincing. Rather than assuming that frozen monocular perception is fundamental, it seems more likely that we will fully understand the processes that underlie pictorial perception only when we understand perception over time. This point of view has not kept me from exploring the beginnings of pictorial depth perception.

In the last few years, it has been demonstrated in a number of experiments that preschool children are sensitive to several types of pictorial depth information. Yonas and Hagen (1973) found that when 3-year-olds were asked to compare the sizes of two pictured objects, their choice of the larger was reliably influenced by texture gradient information for the distance of the objects. Using a similar size-comparison task, Benson and Yonas (1973) found that 3-year-olds were also quite sensitive to linear perspective information for the distance of objects. Olson and Boswell (1976) have argued that depth sensitivity could be assessed more directly if children were questioned about the distance of pictured objects rather than being asked to choose the larger of two objects that were matched in visual angle. Using this method, they found that 2-year-old children were responsive to pictorial depth as specified by interposition and relative height in the picture plane.

Responsiveness to spatial information carried by cast and attached shadows has also been investigated. Benson and Yonas (1973) found that 3-year-olds could reliably use the orientation of attached shadows to identify convex and concave shapes in photographs. More recently, Yonas, Kuskowski, and Sternfels (1979) explored the frames of reference young children use to establish the direction of illumination within a picture and to interpret attached shadow information. Three frames of reference— egocentric, gravitational, and environmental—were found to be effective in specifying the location of the light source. In a series of studies investigating preschool children's sensitivity to cast shadow information, Yonas, Gold-smith, and Hallstrom (1978) found that 3-year-old children used the location of the shadow cast by an object to judge the object's distance and to decide whether the object was resting on or floating above the earth's surface. Children as young as 33 months reliably used the shape of the shadow cast by an object to judge the object's shape and orientation.

These studies are only a small part of an expanding literature that further establishes that although pictorial sensitivity may increase after the preschool years, 2- and 3-year-olds are far from insensitive to pictorial depth. Although little research on pictorial depth sensitivity with infants has been done, the studies that have been conducted (Bower, 1966; Day & McKenzie, 1973) suggest that responsiveness to this information is absent in young infants. Unfortunately, in both relevant studies, kinetic and binocular information for the flat surface of the picture was present, and this conflicting information may have overriden sensitivity to pictorial depth. In a series of studies on infant sensitivity to pictorial depth completed in our own laboratory (Yonas, Cleaves, & Pettersen, 1978), conflicting information for the surface of the picture was minimized in two ways. First, subjects wore an eye patch over one eye to eliminate binocular depth information. Second, the pictorial surface was minimized. The display was based on an Ames trapezoidal window

(Ames, 1951), created by photographing a rectangular window rotated 45° about the vertical axis. The resulting trapezoidal form and "window spaces" were cut from the photograph so that the infant could see through the internal spaces of the display, thereby minimizing the pictorial surface texture. When viewed monocularly by adults, this display creates a powerful illusion of a rectangular window slanted in such a way that one side appears to be several inches closer than the other. We hypothesized that if infants are sensitive to the depth information in the display, their reaches would be directed to the apparently nearer side.

In our first study we presented twenty 26- to 30-week-old infants with a real rectangular window rotated to bring the left or the right side of the object nearer the infant. We established that 6-month-old infants would direct their reaching with sufficient accuracy to demonstrate sensitivity to the differential distances of the two sides of a slanted object, and that they would do so while wearing an eyepatch. Direction of reaching was scored from a videotape recording. Although no binocular information was available, the infants reached to the closer side of the object on 75% of the trials, indicating sensitivity to accommodation, kinetic, and/or pictorial information.

In our next study, two prints of the trapezoidal window photograph were presented frontally without motion to 6-month-old infants. The larger side of the window was on the left in one print and on the right in the other print. To control for the possibility that infants prefer to reach for the larger side of the display regardless of depth information, a size-control display was created with one side smaller than the other but with no information that the sides were at different distances. A third display, identical in shape to the size-control display, was created to explore the effectiveness of interposition and relative size information. Whereas the size-control display was painted gray and appeared to be a single object, the interposition display was made by combining large and small photographs of the rectangular window (in the frontal plane, not slanted) so that a larger rectangle appeared to occlude a smaller rectangle. A clear contour indicated that two separate objects were in view, and the relative size of these two rectangles could indicate differential distance. Reaching was scored from videotaped recordings according to the location on the display that was first contacted by the infant's hand.

The infants presented with the trapezoidal window reached to the larger side of the display twice as frequently as they reached to the smaller side. The infants presented with the size-control display, in contrast, reached for the two sides with almost equal frequency. There was a significant difference in directionality of reaching between the infants who viewed the trapezoidal window and those who viewed the size-control displays. The group presented with the interposition display showed some tendency to contact the larger rectangle more frequently than they contacted the smaller rectangle, but the difference between this condition and performance in the size-control condition was not significant. Directionality of reaching was sufficiently strong for the infants presented with the interposition window that the difference between that group and the infants tested with the trapezoidal window was not significant. It is likely that if a display containing more effective interposition and relative size information were used, 6-month-old infants might be able to demonstrate depth sensitivity.

Our next study was an attempt to replicate the finding that infants reach to the larger side of the trapezoidal window and to determine whether this is attributable to a preference to reach for some other property, such as acute angles, rather than to the apparently nearer side of the display. Infants were randomly assigned to either binocular or monocular viewing of the trapezoidal window. We reasoned that if depth information were the basis for the tendency to reach for the larger side of the trapezoidal window, we should be able to minimize the effectiveness of pictorial depth by providing binocular depth information for the actual orientation of the object. The results for the group of infants who viewed the trapezoidal display monocularly replicated the results of the previous experiment, showing the infants' preference to reach for the larger and pictorially nearer side. The infants who viewed the display binocularly showed significantly less directionality in their reaching. It is clear, then, that when conflicting binocular information is absent, 6-month-old infants are responsive to pictorial depth information. The study also demonstrates in an indirect way that 6-month-old infants are responsive to binocular depth information.

The final goal of this series of studies was to establish the age at which sensitivity to the pictorial depth information present in the trapezoidal window first appears. We presented the display to a group of 18- to 20-week-old infants but soon found that these infants would not reach for the display with sufficient frequency for us to estimate reliably the proportion of reaches directed at the larger and smaller sides of the display. In the earlier studies the data from a few infants were excluded, because they reached fewer than six times; with 18- to 20-week-old infants, only a small minority contacted the display six or more times. Consequently, the age range was extended to 20- to 22-week-olds. Although 44 of the 96 infants tested did not reach to the display, the remaining infants provided us with enough responses to judge the directionality of their reaching. We were surprised to find that although these infants wore an eye patch that excluded conflicting binocular information, they showed no evidence of sensitivity to the depth information available in the trapezoidal window. They reached almost as frequently to the smaller, pictorially farther side of the display as to the larger, pictorially nearer side. The possibility that these infants were too inaccurate in their reaching behavior to indicate depth sensitivity was refuted when a second group of 20- to 22-week-old infants (also wearing eye patches) consistently directed their reaches toward the near side of a slanted, rectangular window. Accommodation, motion parallax, and pictorial information all provide consistent information for the difference in the distances of the two sides of an actual slanted object. The trapezoidal window makes pictorial information available, but accommodation and motion parallax specify that the window is in the frontal plane. Some pictorial sensitivity may be present in these young infants, but perhaps it is in so fragile a form that conflicting information overrides its effects.

To create a more precise test of pictorial sensitivity, we presented the trapezoidal window with the smaller side slanted 30° toward the subject to infants from 20 to 22 weeks of age. When adults are presented with this display under monocular viewing, they report that the side of the window that is farther from them (the larger side) appears to be nearer than the side that is actually closer. We wondered if the 20- to 22-week-old subjects would also show sensitivity to pictorial information in this situation, either by failing to reach for the closer side of the window or by reaching in the direction of the closer side of the window less consistently. Instead, the 20- to 22-week-olds reached to the actually closer but pictorially farther side of the trapezoidal window with the same high level of consistency as they had to the closer side of the rectangular window. Thus it appears that at 20 to 22 weeks, infants are quite "blind" to the depth information present in the trapezoidal window. Furthermore, although pictorial information seems to be an ineffective indicator of depth, accommodation and/or motion parallax appear to be effective sources of depth information for 20- to 22-week-old infants.

The finding that 6-month-old infants do respond spatially to the trapezoidal window raises questions about the nature of the information that underlies this sensitivity. Ames (1951) suggested that the trapezoidal window illusion is effective because the viewer assumes that the sides of the window are parallel to each other and that the parts of the window join each other at 90° angles. He further argued that these assumptions are learned through exprience in a rectilinear, carpentered environment. But it is possible that an assumption of rectilinearity has little to do with responsiveness to the trapezoidal window. J. J. Gibson (1950) pointed out that since objects tend to be distributed over the ground with an even scatter, the spacing between elements of texture tends to be regular. This fact provides the basis for Gibson's texture gradient theory of slant perception. If the sides and internal spaces of the trapezoidal window are assumed to be equal in actual size, then a gradient of size provides information for the slant of the window. A perceptual process that detects similar elements in a scene and responds to the relative sizes of these elements as depth information may have developed over phylogenetic rather than ontogenetic history. On the other hand, the human infant may have to learn to extract relative size information.

The appearance of pictorial depth sensitivity in 6-month-olds may raise doubts about an experiential account, but it does not rule it out. Two types of studies could help us explore whether experience in a carpentered environment is necessary for the trapezoidal window to be effective. In one type of study, 6-month-old infants could be raised in environments with few parallel surfaces and right angles; the trapezoidal window could then be presented to them and the directionality of reaching assessed. If these infants were sensitive to kinetic and binocular information for depth but did not respond to pictorial information, we would have evidence in support of the empiricist claims of Ames. A second method that could be applied to this question would involve raising primates in special environments. Three possible environments are suggested: One environment could be carpentered and rectilinear; another could be entirely curved with no parallel surfaces; and a third environment would have walls, floor, and ceiling that are trapezoidal in shape. If animals raised in each of the three environments consistently reached to the larger side of the trapezoidal window, this should exclude the hypothesis that experience in a carpentered environment is necessary for the trapezoidal window illusion to be effective.

Another direction for future research involves experimental variation in the display presented to human infants. We have some indications that interposition and relative size may be effective for 6-month-old infants in the absence of linear perspective information, but we really know very little about the kinds of pictorial depth information to which infants are sensitive. By using the direction of the infant's reach, we should be able to investigate sensitivity to interposition, relative size, and linear perspective.

CONCLUSION

The investigation of depth sensitivity in infancy presents difficulties not present in other areas of infant perception. Work on the early development of visual acuity, for example, has progressed rapidly through the use of sophisticated methods that assess whether infants can discriminate displays that vary in spatial frequency. Unfortunately, demonstrating discrimination of displays that differ in depth information does not allow us to conclude that depth perception is present. If infants look longer at a three-dimensional than at a two-dimensional representation of a face, some difference between the displays is obviously detected, but it is not clear what the nature of that difference is.

In studying depth sensitivity in infants, researchers have generally relied on response indicators that seem to have inherent spatial meaning. If an infant avoids the drop-off of a visual cliff or accurately reaches for an object, we are confident that spatial information is detected. Responses such as blinking and movements of the head or eyes may also be indications that the infant is responding to spatial information in an adaptive way, but these responses lack the spatial character of locomotion and reaching. The spatially accurate reach of a 7- or 8-month-old infant is convincing, because it is very unlikely that anything other than spatially information for the location of an object could elicit this specific and complex sequence of behaviors. In contrast, the simple eye and head movements of the newborn and even the blink of the 6-week-old are responses that can be evoked by many nonspatial types of stimulation. Although these responses can be given an adaptive, spatially appropriate interpretation in a particular context (e.g., infants turn their heads to avoid being smothered by a surface that is too close to the face), it is difficult to see how independent evidence of the truth of this interpretation could be provided. Other interpretations are possible (e.g., infants could also be turning their eyes and heads in search of something to fixate).

We are in a period of explosive growth in research on infant perception; new findings and methods are appearing at a rapid rate. It will no doubt take quite a while to sort the reliable from the unreliable findings and to discover the inferences that will successfully withstand the necessary process of challenge by alternate explanations.

REFERENCES

Adamson, L., & Tronick, E. *Infant defensive reactions to visual occlusion.* Paper presented at the meeting of the Society for Research in Child Development, New Orleans, March 1977.

Ames, A. Visual perception and the rotating trapezoidal window. *Psychological Monographs,* 1951, *65*(1, Whole No. 324).

Anderson, G. G. Postmaturity: A review. *Obstetrical and Gynecological Survey,* 1972, *27*(2), 65–72.

Aslin, R. N. The development of binocular fixation in human infants. *Journal of Experimental Child Psychology,* 1977, *23*, 133–150.

Ball, W. A. *Infant responses to looming objects and shadows.* Unpublished honors thesis, Harvard University, 1970.

Ball, W. A., & Tronick, E. Infant responses to impending collisions: Optical and real. *Science,* 1971, *171*, 818–820.

Ball, W., & Vurpillot, E. La perception du mouvement en profondur chez le nourrisson. *L'Annee Psychologique,* 1976, *67*, 393–400.

Benson, K., & Yonas, A. Development of sensitivity to static pictorial depth information. *Perception & Psychophysics,* 1973, *13*, 361–366.

Bower, T. G. R. The visual world of infants. *Scientific American,* 1966, *215*, 80–92.

Bower, T. G. R. The object in the world of the infant. *Scientific American,* 1971, *225*(4), 30–38.

Bower, T. G. R. Comment on Yonas et al., "Development of sensitivity to information for impending collision." *Perception & Psychophysics,* 1977, *21*(3), 281–282.

Bower, T. G. R., Broughton, J. M., & Moore, M. K. The coordination of visual and tactual input in infants. *Perception & Psychophysics,* 1970, *8*, 51–53.

Bower, T. G. R., Broughton, M. M., & Moore, M. K. Infant responses to approaching objects: An indicator of response to distal variables. *Perception & Psychophysics,* 1971, *9*, 193–196.

Carr, H. *An introduction to space perception.* New York: Longmans, Green, 1935.

Day, R. H., & McKenzie, B. E. Perceptual shape constancy in early infancy. *Perception,* 1973, *2,* 315–320.

Dodwell, P. C., Muir, D., & DiFranco, D. Responses of infants to visually presented objects. *Science,* 1976, *194,* 209–211.

Field, J. Relation of young infants' reaching behavior to stimulus distance and solidity. *Developmental Psychology,* 1976, *12*(5), 444–448.

Field, T. M., Dabiri, C., Hallock, N., & Shuman, H. H. Developmental effects of prolonged pregnancy and the postmaturity syndrome. *Journal of Pediatrics,* 1977, *90*(5), 836–839.

Fox, R., Shea, S., Aslin, R., & Dumais, S. *Stereopsis in human infants.* Paper presented at the meeting of the Psychonomics Society, San Antonio, Texas, November, 1978.

Gesell, A., & Thompson, H. *Infant behavior.* New York: McGraw-Hill, 1934.

Gibson, E. J. *Principles of perceptual learning and development,* Englewood Cliffs, N.J.: Prentice-Hall, 1969.

Gibson, J. J. *The perception of the visual world.* Boston: Houghton Mifflin, 1950.

Gordon, F. R., Lamson, G., & Yonas, A. *Reaching to a virtual object.* Unpublished manuscript, University of Minnesota, 1978.

Gordon, F. R., & Yonas, A. Sensitivity to binocular depth information in infants. *Journal of Experimental Child Psychology,* 1976, *22,* 413–422.

Johnson, B., & Beck, L. F. The development of space perception: 1. Stereoscopic vision in preschool children. *Journal of Genetic Psychology,* 1941, *58,* 247–254.

Jones, M. C. The development of early behavior patterns in young children. *The Pedagogical Seminary and Journal of Genetic Psychology,* 1926, *33,* 537–585.

Julesz, B. *Foundations of cyclopean perception.* Chicago: University of Chicago Press, 1971.

Kasahara, M., & Inamatsu, S. Der blinzelreflex im sauglingsalter. *Archive für Kinderheilkunder,* 1931, *92,* 302–304.

Mendelson, M. J., & Haith, M. H. The relation between audition and vision in the human newborn. *Monographs of the Society for Research in Child Development,* 1976, *41*(4, Serial No. 167).

Olson, R. K., & Boswell, S. L. Pictorial depth sensitivity in two-year-old children. *Child Development,* 1976, *47,* 1175–1178.

Peiper, A. M. D. *Cerebral function in infancy and childhood.* New York: Consultants Bureau, 1963.

Pettersen, L., Yonas, A., & Fisch, R. O. *The development of blinking in response to impending collision in preterm, full term, and postterm infants.* Manuscript in preparation, 1979.

Rezba, C. *A study of infant binocular depth perception.* Unpublished undergraduate honors thesis, University of Minnesota, 1977.

Schiff, W. The perception of impending collision: A study of visually directed avoidant behavior. *Psychological Monographs,* 1965, *79*(11, Whole No. 604).

Von Hofsten, C. Binocular convergence as a determinant of reaching behavior in infancy. *Perception,* 1977, *6,* 139–144.

Walk, R. D., & Gibson, E. J. A comparative and analytic study of visual depth perception. *Psychological Monographs,* 1961, *75*(15, Whole No. 519).

White, B. L. *Human infants: Experience and psychological development.* Englewood Cliffs, N.J.: Prentice-Hall, 1971.

White, B. L., Castle, P., & Held, R. Observations on the development of visually directed reaching. *Child Development,* 1964, *35,* 349–364.

Yonas, A., Bechtold, A. G., Frankel, D., Gordon, F. R., McRoberts, G., Norcia, A., & Sternfels, S. Development of sensitivity to information for impending collision. *Perception & Psychophysics,* 1977, *21*(2), 97–104.

Yonas, A., Cleaves, W., & Pettersen, L. Development of sensitivity to pictorial depth. *Science,* 1978, *200*(4337), 77–79.

Yonas, A., Goldsmith, L. T., & Hallstrom, J. L. The development of sensitivity to information from cast shadows in pictures. *Perception,* 1978, *7,* 333–342.

Yonas, A., & Hagen, M. Effects of static and motion parallax information on perception of size in children and adults. *Journal of Experimental Child Psychology,* 1973, *15,* 254–266.

Yonas, A., Kuskowski, M., & Sternfels, S. Role of frames of reference in the development of responsiveness to shading information. *Child Development,* 1979, in press.

Yonas, A., Oberg, C., & Norcia, A. Development of sensitivity to binocular information for the approach of an object. *Developmental Psychology,* 1978, *14*(2), 147–152.

Yonas, A., & Pick, H. L., Jr. An approach to the study of infant space perception. In L. B. Cohen & P. Salapatek (Eds.), *Infant perception: From sensation to cognition* (Vol. 2). New York: Academic Press, 1975.

III PERCEPTION OF PATTERN AND STRUCTURE

5 Letter Discrimination and Identification

W. R. Garner
Yale University

This volume is to honor Eleanor Jack Gibson, a psychologist who has made so many important contributions to developmental and to experimental psychology. Her influence has been especially great in providing us with experimental data and insights into the processes of perceptual development, with her book, *Principles of Perceptual Learning and Development* (1969), quickly becoming a landmark for all other research in the area. And she has been especially interested in the perceptual processes in reading and its development, this interest being best portrayed in her book, *The Psychology of Reading* (1975), written jointly with Harry Levin.

My own interests over many years have been focused on the perception and processing of stimulus structure. My experimental bent has been to use artificial stimulus materials such as patterns of dots, but in very recent years, the research of myself and some of my students has shifted to the study of the perception of the structure of letters and even words. There could be no more fitting way for me to write in honor of Eleanor Gibson than to review some of the concepts and research data that have come from my laboratory, and to relate these to concepts expounded by her. There is, in fact, a quite natural transition from some of her ideas to some of those I write about here.

ASPECTS OF A STIMULUS

In her 1969 book, Gibson presented a chart of "distinctive features" as a means of describing the properties of English uppercase letters. This list contains such features as straight lines (in any of the four primary

111

orientations), curved lines (closed, or open vertically or horizontally), intersection, redundancy (cyclic change, or symmetry), and discontinuity (vertical or horizontal). This is by far the most comprehensive list of features generated for describing any form of written or printed letters, and it has become the comparison list against which other researchers contrast their experimental results. To quote Gibson (1969): "In selecting a list of features, the experimenter's intuition is the principal generator [p. 86]." It is true that the intuition (or plain good common sense) is aided by any available data, including confusion matrices for errors in letter identification as well as latency data for same–different responses to pairs of letters, but the fact is that good intuition was still very important in selecting the final published list of distinctive features.

The question I want to ask is why intuition is so badly needed (and about that, I have no doubt) in this day of massive data collection systems and highly sophisticated multidimensional scaling procedures, and even more sophisticated clustering analyses or even the older factor analyses. Why wasn't it possible, simply to apply one or more of these sophisticated techniques to an analysis of a set of data to tell us empirically and unequivocally what the properties of sets of printed English letters are?

The answer I suggest is that we don't have a clear idea of the basic nature of the properties of any sort of visual figure, thus not for letters of the alphabet either. Furthermore, each of the many techniques for providing lists of properties assumes certain inherent characteristics of the property system itself, and if letters of the alphabet differ from each other in fundamentally different ways, then no single measurement system will be adequate to the analytic task. All the multidimensional techniques, for example, assume that there exists some form of a multidimensional space, that this space is invariant for a given set of stimuli, and that each stimulus in the set can be adequately described by giving it a numerical value on each of the presumed dimensions. But if in fact the space is not properly described by a single n-dimensional system, then an analytic solution that presumes that it is will be inadequate. This inadequacy is generally fairly self-evident for a given set of stimuli, so the experimenter chooses wisely to impose intuition on the description of stimulus properties elicited by the dimensional scaling solution. And, of course, most of what I have just said about multidimensional scaling is equally true for factor-analytic descriptions, such as that provided by Kuennapas and Janson (1969) based on direct similarity judgments of pairs of lowercase Swedish letters.

The various hierarchical clustering analyses in their turn have constraints that seem to limit their usefulness in providing adequate descriptions of letter properties. Probably the most serious constraint is the assumption that the derived clusters form partitions, i.e., mutually exclusive subsets, and this forced outcome will often be at variance with one's intuitions about the proper way to describe the set of stimuli. Possibly the best way to overcome the constraints of the various methods of analyzing the properties of letters is to use some mixed version of the dimensional systems and the clustering systems, as Shepard (1972) has suggested. It is possible, however, that a more conceptual approach to the problem of stimulus properties will lead more rapidly to clarification of some of the problems, and that is the approach I have taken before (Garner, 1978a) and take again here.

Component Properties

Figure 5.1 is a schematic diagram to illustrate what I think are the minimal distinctions we need to make about stimulus properties. We first must distinguish between component and wholistic properties. I prefer using the general term *attribute* for the component properties, but I have found no good single term to use for wholistic properties.

Attributes themselves have to be subdivided into two major types, which I call *features* and *dimensions*. These words are used because they come close to representing average or modal usage, but psychologists (and lexicographers as well) have used many of the terms for these variable properties quite interchangeably, so it is necessary to accept some ambiguity with respect to exact word meaning. We should try to minimize this ambiguity in our actual usage, however. My definitions are:

A **dimension** is a variable property of a set of stimuli such that if it exists in a set of stimuli, it exists at some positive value in each stimulus, and these values are mutually exclusive. To illustrate, if color is a variable in a set of stimuli, then each stimulus has some color. Likewise, if brightness or loudness are variables, then they are dimensions because the possible values are mutually exclusive, and each stimulus must have some value of brightness if it is an appropriate variable or of loudness if it is an appropriate variable.

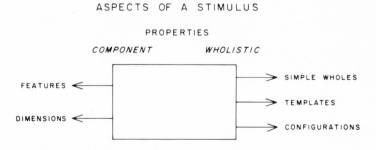

FIG. 5.1. A representation of the dual aspects of stimulus properties: component and wholistic.

A **feature** is an attribute of a stimulus that either exists or does not exist, but if it exists, it has only a single level. Thus the idea of mutually exclusive levels is inappropriate. A feature can be taken away from a stimulus without otherwise affecting the stimulus; thus it might be considered a dissociable element.

The role of zero is quite important in differentiating between dimensions and features. With dimensions, zero may itself be a positive level on a dimension (e.g., zero brightness), especially if the dimension is a quantitative one. With qualitative dimensions such as hue, zero really means the nonexistence of the dimension. But with features, there is a complete confounding between zero as a level on a variable and as an absence of the variable itself. Any component property or attribute is a variable property of a set of stimuli, and a property cannot be a variable unless it exists at two or more levels. Dimensions typically are at least capable of existing at more than two positive levels, but features are always bilevel variables, and one of the levels is zero. But since zero can also mean the nonexistence of the feature, then if for a particular stimulus the value of the variable feature is zero, it is not clear whether the feature could have existed but does not for this particular stimulus, or whether the feature is not an appropriate property for the particular set of stimuli.

A useful way of differentiating between features and dimensions is in terms of the appropriate information-processing interrogations to establish the identity of any particular stimulus in a set. With a dimension, the interrogation is: At what level is the dimension? With a feature, the proper interrogation is: Does the stimulus have this feature? If a set of stimuli is greater than two, then there must always be more than one binary interrogation of features—exactly one for each feature. If the set is greater than two and dimensions define the stimuli, however, the interrogation need not be of a series of binary questions because there may be more than one value per dimension.

I do not want to pursue all the implications of the differences between features and dimensions here, because I have done so elsewhere (Garner, 1978a), but the distinction does affect such things as classification, identification, speed of discrimination, etc. Further, there is an important point about features that I have also made elsewhere (Garner, 1978b) concerning selective attention to stimuli and to their attributes—namely, that when stimuli are generated from features, there are two very special stimuli in the set: the complete stimulus, in which all features are present; and the null stimulus, in which all features are absent. These two special stimuli become important reference stimuli in a set generated by features, but there are no equivalent reference stimuli in a set generated by dimensions.

Gibson's (1969) list of distinctive features is set up primarily in terms appropriate to what I am in fact calling features in that for each letter, she asks whether the particular property does or does not exist. These different properties operate in different ways. Furthermore, there are many mixtures of properties that can and do exist for any given set of letters or other forms. Features may, for example, be nested within levels of dimensions, and dimensions themselves may be nested within levels of other dimensions. To illustrate, I would consider the difference between straight and curved lines to be a dimensional difference. But then within the level called straight, the orientation of the line is a second dimension. Thus of the four categories that Gibson uses—vertical, horizontal, left diagonal, and right diagonal—I would consider dimensional differences within a level of another dimension. On the other hand, within the level called curved, I would consider presence or absence of a gap to be a feature, but if the feature exists (i.e., if there is a gap), then location of the gap becomes a dimensional level.

Thus my suggestion that attributes are of two special types having different properties does not necessarily simplify what is a complicated descriptor system for just the single class of uppercase letters. But then the set of letters is in fact complicated, and with the 12 distinctive features listed by Gibson, 4096 letters are possible (not considering composite letters such as the *H*, which has two separate, vertical straight lines). Nevertheless, it is my hope that these distinctions provide some clarification.

Wholistic Properties

Component properties, or attributes, constitute just one of the two aspects of a stimulus, as indicated in Fig. 5.1. The other aspect consists of the wholistic properties. And I think there are at least three different ideas involved in wholistic properties: simple wholes, templates, and configurations. Of these, the simple whole is the least interesting, because it means that the whole is no more than the sum of the parts or components. This concept is usually defined by default: If we have no evidence that processing or perception is of components, then we conclude that the whole is being perceived or processed. Such a definition is very negative, thus very weak, and I do not consider it a very useful construct. But it is commonly used.

A template is a reasonably useful concept if we use Neisser's (1967) definition of a template as prototype or as canonical form, and if we define template matching as identification by coincidence or congruence with a basic model. And a template as a schema allows the specification of relevant and irrelevant attributes (see also Garner, in press). That is to say, it is quite impossible for a schema to be meaningful in respect to all possible attributes, so some attributes must be considered irrelevant before the template can conceivably be matched. If, to return to our present consideration, we want to argue that a letter is identified by a template match to a form held in memory, then the size of the form must be considered an irrelevant attribute, as must also its particular orientation and even such things as right and left slant. In other words, the idea of a template cannot be considered truly an absolute concept, because it is quite impossible to expect matching in respect to all possible attributes. But if a template is a modal construct, or a schema, then we can have matching in respect to all relevant attributes. I return later to some discussion of templates in letter identification and discrimination.

A configuration is a property of a stimulus that involves interaction between the components, and the property derived from the interaction is the configural property. This is the wholistic construct that has the clearest positive definition; it can be specified without regard to an experimental outcome; and it involves the idea that the whole is at least different from, if not more than, the sum of the parts.

Of Gibson's list of distinctive features, I consider at least three of them to be configural properties. She lists cyclic change (which I would prefer to call repetition) and symmetry as subcategories under redundancy, and both of these are clearly configural properties. In each case, the property involves an interaction between components, and it is this interaction that is of interest. In the case of repetition, the interaction is simply that a component is like another component and is repeated either horizontally (as W) or vertically (as E). With symmetry, the interaction is that a component is like another component and is repeated by reflection either vertically (as E), horizontally (as T), or both (as X and O). It is clear from the examples, of course, that both repetition and symmetry can be further specified as to direction and that they often go together. And I would add intersection as an interactive property, and thus as a configural property, since intersection cannot occur without components that interact.

Dual Aspects

These configural properties are really of a different sort than the component properties, since they require interaction; and I think they operate in letter identification and discrimination in ways different from the ways in which component properties do. I discuss this issue in more detail later, but for now I shall simply note, to illustrate, that if two letters have the property of a closed curved line (such as O and Q), they are alike in a way that is not true of two letters having the property of both vertical and horizontal symmetry (such as X and O). Thus, having a configural property in common does not necessarily make two letters similar, but having a component property in common does make them similar.

But for now, the important point is that component and configural properties are two aspects of the same stimulus and are not capable of being orthogonal to each other. There can be no symmetry, no repetition, and no intersection unless there are components to interact. Thus whenever configural properties exist, these properties coexist with component properties and are therefore redundant to them. It is better to say that the configural properties are redundant to the component properties than the reverse (although technically, either statement is true if the other is), because the component can exist without configuration, but configuration cannot exist without the components to interact. Thus any study of the relative roles of component and configural properties must deal constantly with the problem of the properties being dual aspects of stimuli, not orthogonal properties; and if we want, for instance, to argue that symmetry is the basis of discrimination in a particular situation, we must be able to prove that discrimination did not, or could not, occur on the basis of the differences in the components. It is often very difficult to make the case strongly.

Once these logical distinctions between different properties—both component and wholistic—have been made, do they help us to understand the discrimination and identification of letters? They do indeed, and the rest of this paper is concerned with illustrating the ways in which accuracy and speed of letter discrimination and identification are affected by these stimulus constructs. The illustrations are drawn largely from research by my students and me.

ACCURACY OF LETTER DISCRIMINATION

Accuracy and speed are, of course, the two basic measures of performance used in studies of letter perception. Ordinarily, if speed is measured, errors are few and not very valuable in analysis. So we use speed of performance in tasks that are relatively easy, such as determining whether two letters presented simultaneously or successively are the same or different. When errors are made in sufficient number to be useful in analysis, the task is usually more difficult in two respects: (1) the stimuli are degraded in some manner so as to produce errors; and (2) several stimuli and possible responses are involved in each experimental session. Thus, typically, a single letter is presented, and the subject is asked to state which of the many possible letters it is. Such tasks are more properly called identification than discrimination, but presumably, the same basic perceptual processes are involved in each. I first present data from an identification task in which errors are measured.

Features and Asymmetry of Errors

In first arguing for the necessity of distinguishing features from dimensions (Garner, 1978a), I suggested that under some circumstances, errors of letter identification would be asymmetrical if the pair of letters under consideration differed from each other by features rather than by dimensions. The basic nature of the argument had to do with the difference between a feature that exists or does not exist and a dimension that, if it exists, does so at some positive value. Thus, features are variables for which there is more or less of a component, whereas dimensions are variables that have different values or levels but with basically the same amount of something. If two letters differed as levels on a dimension (e.g., curved vs. straight line), there is no reason for more errors to be made from one letter to the other than in the reverse direction. However, if two letters differ in having or not having a feature, there is reason for errors to be in the direction of the letter not having the feature, since a letter presented could lose something (thus changing from feature present to feature absent), but there was no reason to expect the letter to gain something.

As a first attempt to check this idea, I was able to use some data from Townsend (1971), who had used the complete set of uppercase English letters in a letter identification task. Errors in a task of this sort are, of course, spread over so many possibilities that it is not possible to have enough errors for each pair of letters to do more than a cursory analysis; however, I did examine six letter pairs that seemed to me to differ only in features, and these six pairs are shown in Fig. 5.2. For each letter pair, I simply noted how many total errors were made in which each letter was erroneously identified as the other. These total errors are indicated for each direction of error. Despite the relatively small number of errors made for many of these pairs, the result was clear: For every pair, more errors were made from the letter with the greater number of features than the one with the smaller number of features.

DIRECTION OF ERROR

FIG. 5.2. Number of identification errors for six pairs of letters differing by one or more features. The arrows indicate the direction of errors, and for each pair, the letter with fewer features is on the left. (Data from Townsend, 1971).

There are, of course, many factors that could affect the frequency with which one letter is used erroneously as a response to another letter, and the kind of perceptual factor implied by the definition of features is only one such factor. Certainly there can be response biases that could produce such asymmetries, but there is clear evidence that these particular results were not the effect of simple response bias. Certainly response bias would be related to frequency of occurrence of letters in common usage, but these results do not conform to frequency of occurrence. Of the six pairs, in only the C-G and O-Q pairs is the letter with the fewer features also the letter with the more frequent occurrence in common usage, so in four of the six pairs, errors are made more commonly to the less frequent letter. Thus this result is not an artifact of response bias.

State and Process Limitation

When I first argued for the distinction between dimension and feature (Garner, 1978a) and further argued that there should be an asymmetry of errors of identification when letters differed by features but not when they differed by dimensions, I also pointed out that the asymmetry would occur only with a particular form of stimulus degradation. Errors occur, of course, only if the stimulus is degraded in some way, because adults have no difficulty in identifying letters of the alphabet if they are completely clear and unambiguous.

Earlier, John Morton and I (Garner & Morton, 1969) had distinguished between perceptual interaction as being due to interactive states of the organism or to interactive processes, the distinction having to do with whether different processing channels were functioning inadequately or whether they were interacting directly. Later I extended this distinction between state and process to that of a perceptual limitation (Garner, 1970, 1974) with the same basic distinction in mind. In terms of stimulus control of the limitation, the distinction is primarily between state limitation as energy limitation (i.e., not enough of the stimulus gets into the organism) and process limitation as pattern distortion or as inadequate stimulus differentiation. In interpreted form, with energy limitation, not enough stimulus is generated for the state or action level of the organism to process it. With process limitation, there is some inherent inability to carry out the process as specified by the task; there is, in other words, a limitation of information rather than of energy.

The asymmetry of errors should occur only with state limitation, because only with that type of limitation is there a loss of something in the stimulus that corresponds to the loss of features that define or generate the letters. With process limitation, however, there is no necessary loss of anything, and thus there is no reason to suppose that the errors will be asymmetric. Nor is there any reason to suppose that errors will be asymmetric with any letters that differ only in dimensions with either type of limitation.

Townsend (1971) had used two different experimental conditions to produce stimulus degradation and thus errors of identification. In one condition, the letters were presented at tachistoscopically short durations. This condition is unequivocally what I would consider state limitation. In the other condition, short duration was combined with a poststimulus pattern mask. In this case, it is clear that there was state limitation, but there may also have been some amount of process limitation. The data presented in Fig. 5.2 were from both conditions combined and may therefore be presumed to represent an outcome determined primarily by state limitation. Since the conditions I expected to produce asymmetry of errors with letters differing by features apparently existed for the Townsend data, his data did provide confirmation of my expectations.

In order to pursue this question further, however, Forrest Haun and I (Garner & Haun, 1978) carried out an experiment with much more deliberate experimental manipulation both of letter sets differing by dimensions or features and of the type of stimulus degradation. We used two letter sets with four letters in each set:

1. A feature set consisted of the block letters formed from a vertical straight line as a handle and with two features—top and bottom horizontal lines extending to the right. These four letters are shown in Fig. 5.3, and they can be identified as the uppercase letters *I, T, L,* and block *C,* with only a slight distortion of what an uppercase *T* is.

FIG. 5.3. Proportion of identification errors for six pairs of four letters generated from a feature system of attributes. The arrows indicate the direction of errors, and for each of the five top pairs, the letter with fewer features is on the left. (Data from Garner & Haun, 1978.)

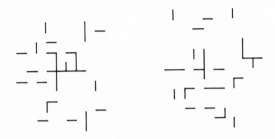

FIG. 5.4. Examples of process-limited stimuli used by Garner and Haun (1978). The letter on the left is *p* and that on the right *L*. Each letter was produced with a noise probability of 0.12.

2. A dimension set of letters consisted of the lowercase letters *p, d, q,* and *b,* formed also as block letters. These four letters are easily described in terms of two dimensions for the location of the loop in relation to the vertical line, up–down, and right–left.

Two forms of stimulus degradation, corresponding to the difference between state and process limitation, were also used. For "state limitation," we used a short duration with tachistoscopic presentation. For "process limitation," we used a type of pattern distortion illustrated in Fig. 5.4. Each letter was considered to be formed from a fixed number of line segments, and then a surround was generated that was twice as great as the width of the basic letters. Each line segment as illustrated in Fig. 5.4 was actually half the length of the shortest line as shown in Fig. 5.3. The pattern distortion was produced by assigning a noise probability for each line segment both within the actual letter and in the surround. If, as in the illustration, the noise probability was 0.12, then each segment in the letter proper had that probability of being missing, and each segment in the surround had that probability of being present. With this technique, variations in amount of distortion can be produced quite readily, variations that systematically influence the error rate. The technique was quite successful, and the primary difficulty wtih it is simply that many different sample patterns have to be produced to avoid sampling artifacts.

Each set of letters was used separately in an identification task, so that for any experimental run, the subject had four possible responses. The critical test, of course, is whether errors are asymmetric when the letters are generated from features and when state limitation is used to produce errors. The results for this condition are given in Fig. 5.3, in which it can be seen that in the five pairs of letters that differ in number of features, more errors were made in the direction of the letter with fewer features. There is also some evidence of response bias, especially with a greater tendency to use the letter *L* as a response compared to the use of the letter *T* (possibly the subjects had some objection to calling that particular letter a *T*). All the other data were in support of the hypothesis that errors were made in the direction of fewer features. Thus the analysis of the Townsend (1971) data in Fig. 5.2 can be accepted as a valid generalizable result.

Since the data are presented in detail in the original Garner and Haun (1978) paper, they are not duplicated here. They can be summarized by stating that this asymmetry in error production occurred only under the unique combination of feature-generated letters and with errors produced by a state limitation. When the *p-d-q-b* set of letters was used, no equivalent asymmetries occurred with either type of stimulus degradation; and when the *I-L-T-C* set of letters was used with pattern distortion, the asymmetry did not occur either.

We can conclude: (1) that the distinction between attributes of letters as features and as dimensions is meaningful; (2) that we cannot understand the nature of identification errors without distinguishing between features and dimensions; and (3) that we must distinguish still further between state and process limitation, or at least define their reasonable equivalents in producing stimulus degradation. All attributes of letters are not equivalent, nor are all forms of stimulus degradation.

SPEED OF LETTER DISCRIMINATION

Now I turn to a discussion of speed of discrimination of letters. In doing so, I refer to a rather large amount of data collected by Peter Podgorny and me (Podgorny & Garner, 1979) as well as data collected by Eleanor Gibson and some of her co-workers at Cornell. The latter data (Gibson, Schapiro, & Yonas, 1968) were used by Gibson to help formulate her list of distinctive features for letters but have not, to my knowledge, been published in the general literature. Nevertheless, because the procedures and conditions used by Podgorny and me are similar to, yet different from, those of Gibson et al. (1968) in certain critical ways, direct comparison of the two sets of data make each set more interpretable than either would be considered individually.

There are two major topics: the nature of letter differences, and the nature of letter identities. This section is concerned with the discrimination of differences. Because differences in experimental procedures are important here, the general procedures used in the collection of each set of data are outlined.

The Gibson data were collected with a fairly straightforward same–different procedure, with pairs of letters presented simultaneously and with the subject being required to make a response of same or different using a manual key response. Pairs of stimuli were presented at a rate of about 3 to 4 sec per trial. Because the exact physical conditions are discussed later, it is important to point out that the letter pairs were presented in adjacent windows 2 in. (5 cm) square and separated by a distance slightly greater than 1 in. (2.5 cm). The subject sat 5 to 6 ft. (1.55 to 1.86 m) away. Thus although the task was a simultaneous same–different one, the stimuli were far enough apart that some spread of attention was probably required, even if there was no eye movement. Gibson obtained data from both adults and children, but I use only the adult data.

Podgorny and I used computer-generated letters viewed on a CRT display. One letter was presented to the subject and was considered the target. The display consisted of one letter at a time being presented at a subject-paced rate of about 2 sec per letter, and the subject pressed one of the console keys if the letter was a target and another key if it was a nontarget. The same letter remained as the target for 50 to 75 displays; then another letter became the target. This procedure is, of course, very much like a sequential same–different task except that the target letter to be held in memory does not change on every trial. Our data were obtained only from adults.

Effect of Context

The first point to be made is that even with these substantial differences in procedure, the results from the two experiments concerning the speed of making the difference response (different in the Gibson procedure, nontarget in the Podgorny–Garner procedure) are in substantial agreement. But an additional procedural difference between the two experiments makes a very particular point, and that concerns the total letter context within which the judgments were made. In the Gibson procedure, two subexperiments, using different subjects, were run. In each subexperiment, only nine different letters were used: *C, E, F, G, M, N, P, R*, and *W* for one group of subjects; and *A, D, H, K, O, Q, S, T*, and *X* for the second group of subjects. The second group of subjects produced somewhat higher reaction times than did the first group, and this fact raises the question of whether the particular context of letters used is an important determinant of the speed of the difference reaction. The Podgorny–Garner data were collected with all 26 letters being used together, and in fact, each run with a particular target held in memory contained all 26 letters. So in this case, the subjects were continually exposed to the entire range of letters, and at a fairly rapid rate. Thus a comparison of the reaction times obtained in the two different experiments can help determine whether the particular context of letters is important or whether the reaction times are determined primarily by the particular pair of letters (two letters displayed in one case, target and nontarget in the second case).

A scatterplot of difference reaction times for the two experiments is shown in Fig. 5.5 (the Gibson data for the *CEFGMNPRW* set are used, and the equivalent measures from the Podgorny–Garner data are included). The correlation between the two sets of data is .54. Considering that the Podgorny–Garner data were extracted from a matrix with 325 difference

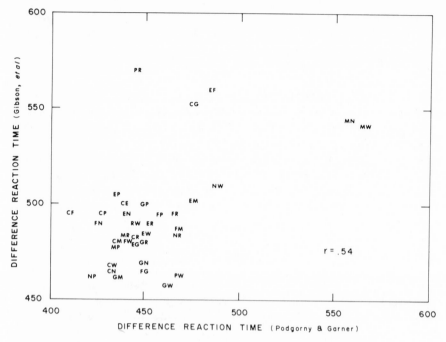

FIG. 5.5.   Reaction times (msec) to letter differences. Each letter pair is indicated. (Data are from Podgorny & Garner, 1979, and Gibson et al., 1968.)

scores (thus each single score is not highly reliable) whereas the Gibson data were obtained from a complete matrix of just 36 difference scores, the high level of agreement suggests that the overall differences in procedure and context are not very important.

This general conclusion is supported even further by the equivalent data displayed in Fig. 5.6 for the *ADHKOQSTX* set of data. In this case, the correlation between the two sets of scores is even higher (.63). Not only are the correlations quite high for the two sets of data, but it is also evident that the general range of reaction times is much the same for the two different procedures. Thus there is overall agreement between the Gibson data and the Podgorny–Garner data and clear evidence that reaction times are determined more by the specific letter differences than by the total context of letters used.

Yet this general conclusion, although valid, needs qualification because there seem to be some local context effects that are also of importance. To illustrate, in Fig. 5.5, there are three pairs of letters (*PR*, *CG*, and *EF*) that have lower correlation between the two sets of data than do any of the other pairs. If these pairs were not considered, there would be a much higher overall correlation. The specific discrepancy is that the reaction times for these letter

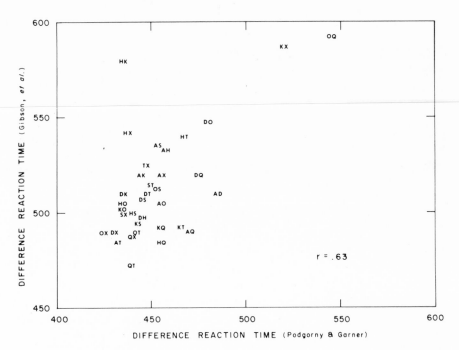

FIG. 5.6. Reaction times (msec) to letter differences. Each letter pair is indicated. (Data are from Podgorny & Garner, 1979, and Gibson et al., 1968.)

pairs are higher for the Gibson data than they are for the Podgorny–Garner data. A similar discrepancy exists for the *HK* pair in Fig. 5.6. In three of these four most discrepant pairs, the Podgorny–Garner data show that for one letter of the pair, there is another letter more confusable with it than the letter paired with the Gibson subsets of letters.

The results of a hierarchical cluster analysis for our data are shown in Fig. 5.7. Although that analysis is discussed in more detail later, for the moment it provides the evidence for arguing that there do appear to be some local context effects. Notice that the discrepant *PR* pair contains the letter *P*, which is more confused with *B* than with *R* in the complete set of data. And the discrepant pair *CG* contains the letter *G*, which is more confused with the letter *A* in the complete set of data. The *HK* pair, also discrepant, contains the letter *H*, which is more confusable with both *M* and *W* in the complete set of data. Only the discrepant *EF* pair is also the most confusable pair in the complete set of data.

There is, of course, always the possibility that these discrepancies are due less to the specific context in which the data were obtained than to the specific letter characteristics. That is to say, the discrepancy in the complete set of data may be due not to the larger context but to the specifics of the geometrical

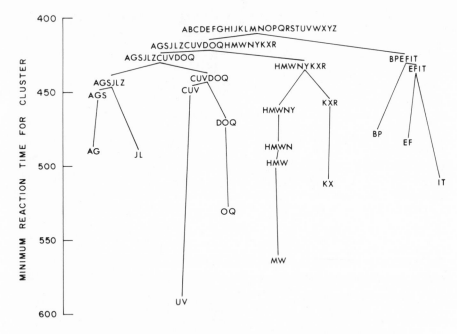

FIG. 5.7. Hierarchical cluster analysis of letters based on reaction measures. The ordinate vaues are the minimum difference reaction times for any pair of letters in the indicated cluster. (Data are from Podgorny & Garner, 1979).

properties of the letters as produced. There is no way to clarify this issue with the present data.

Furthermore, it seems to me that the basic agreement of the two sets of data is far more important than are the few disagreements. Given the large differences in procedures and in the sets of letters used in each particular experiment, it is clear that reaction times to differences in letters do reflect properties of the differences, and that we can expect to understand the nature of these properties by an analysis of the reaction times to the differences.

The Structure of Letter Properties

The high correlations between the Gibson data and the Podgorny–Garner data make clear that any analysis of the properties of letters based on the reaction times to letter differences will be very similar. Podgorny and I have completed several different analyses of the similarities of the reaction time data, including multidimensional scaling of the reaction times, factor analyses, and hierarchical clustering analyses. Since Gibson et al. (1968) presented their analyses in the form of hierarchical cluster analyses, that is the form of analysis that is used to compare the two sets of data.

The cluster analysis for the Podgorny–Garner data based directly on the latency data, rather than on some derived measure, is shown in Fig. 5.7. Of the many methods available for doing this analysis, we chose cluster analysis based on a maximum distance for all items in a cluster, and maximum distance was defined as minimum reaction time. This procedure allowed us to display the data not only in cluster form but also with a maintenance of metric information directly measured in terms of reaction times for letter differences. Thus the ordinate in Fig. 5.7 shows, for each cluster, the minimum reaction time between any pair of letters in the indicated cluster. When the cluster consists of just two items, this minimum time is, of course, the reaction time for that particular pair, and similarities for all pair clusters can thus be compared. To illustrate, the pair *UV* forms one cluster, at a reaction time of 592 msec. The pair *OQ* also forms a cluster, but in this case the reaction time is 534 msec. Thus although each of these pairs forms a cluster, the reaction times (and thus the presumed similarities) are not equivalent. To illustrate the inequality between similarities for pair clusters, note that the letter pair *PB* clusters at a reaction time of 482 msec, more than 100 msec faster than for the clustering pair *UV*. It is for this reason that it is desirable to maintain some metric representation as well as some clustering in the analyses. Neither metric representation nor clustering alone provides as accurate information about the data as does some combination of the two. An alternative way of combining the two representations is to draw the clusters on a two-dimensional representation, as Glushko (1975) did with a similarity representation for dot patterns, following Shepard's (1972) suggestion. And an alternative way of adding metric information to a clustering display has been suggested by Sattath and Tversky (1977).

But these methodological issues are not the main point of the present discussion, which is to demonstrate that the structure of similarities is relatively independent of whether the total letter context has been used experimentally or whether smaller subsets are used, as Gibson et al. did. At this point, I shall simply describe several clustering results from the Gibson data and compare them directly to the clustering analysis shown in Fig. 5.7. For the letter set *CEFGMNPRW*, in the Gibson analysis of reaction times, four pairs of letters formed clusters: *CG*, *EF*, *PR*, and *MN*. Of these, *EF* forms a pair cluster in Fig. 5.7, thus showing complete agreement. *MW* forms a cluster in Fig. 5.7, but within a three cluster of *HMW* and a four cluster of *HMWN*. The letter *H* did not occur in the Gibson set, but a three cluster of *MNW* did occur, so there is complete agreement between the two sets of data at the level of a three cluster. In our data, as already mentioned, the *P* clusters with the *B* rather than with the *R* as it does in the Gibson data; and the *G* in our data clusters with the *A* rather than with the *C*. This indicates that there are some slight effects of context (or possibly orthography) for this set of letters.

There is even less apparent effect of context when we examine the clusters in the Gibson *ADHKOQSTX* set of letters. With the Gibson analysis, *OQ* forms a pair cluster as it also does for our data. Then in both cases, these two letters are joined by *D* to form the three cluster *DOQ*. Also in both sets of data, *KX* forms a pair cluster and then is joined by *R* in the Podgorny–Garner data but by *H* in the Gibson data. Thus the letters *R* and *H*, used in different letter sets for the Gibson data, do show some variation in clustering, yet they come together rather comfortably in the analysis in Fig. 5.7 with the larger cluster *HMWNYKXR*. And last, in the Gibson data *AS* forms a pair cluster, but *A* is first paired with *G* before next becoming part of the three cluster *AGS* in Fig. 5.7.

As I mentioned earlier, each of the methods of describing similarity relations between items has its drawbacks, and hierarchical cluster analysis has them, too—the chief one being the forced partitioning of letters into mutually exclusive sets. But even with this disadvantage, it is clear that there is overall excellent agreement between data obtained by Gibson et al. (1968) with a simultaneous same–different task using sets of nine letters and data obtained by Podgorny and Garner with a target–no-target sequential task using the full set of 26 letters. The agreements between the two studies are much greater than the disagreements, which suggests that similar, if not nearly identical, processes are at work in producing both sets of data.

Configural Properties. I mentioned earlier that configural properties such as repetition and symmetry have a different role in determining letter discriminability or similarity than do component properties such as curved or straight lines. The cluster analysis displayed in Fig. 5.7 helps clarify this point. There are nine pairs of letters that form clusters. Four of these pairs share the property of symmetry: *UV, MW, KX, IT*. (Incidentally, these four pairs also illustrate the point made earlier that configural properties are always confounded with component properties. This is because each of these pairs has very obvious component properties in common in addition to having the property of symmetry in common.) However, five pairs of letters that form pair clusters do not share symmetry: *AG, JL, OQ, BP*, and *EF*. Consequently, even at a first level of analysis, the property of symmetry does not seem to provide a basis for reaction times indicating high similarity.

Still further, note that the two letters that have the greatest symmetry, being symmetrical on four axes (depending on the exact configuration), are highly discriminable from each other. The actual reaction time for the *OX* letter pairs is 427 msec, which is very near the minimum obtained of 411 msec. These two letters do not cluster until 20 letters (all but *BPEFIT*) are contained in a single cluster. And we can pursue this line by noting that the letter pair that gave the fastest reaction time was *CF*, and in this case, one letter was symmetrical and the other was not. This fact might argue that the difference in amount of symmetry was aiding the fast discrimination and that the fact of total curved line in one letter and straight lines in the other was not sufficient. However, consider the letter pair *CI*: Both letters are symmetrical; yet the same difference between curved and straight exists as with the *CF* pair, and the reaction time for this letter pair was 413 msec. It seems clear, then, that two letters that share symmetry are not necessarily similar, and two letters that differ in symmetry are not necessarily dissimilar, at least when similarity and dissimilarity are measured by reaction times to the letter differences.

What role does symmetry play in determining difference reaction times to letter pairs? Its role is to restrict the availability of other letters that are configurally highly similar, but that are rotated or reflected in relation to each other. In my earlier work on pattern perception, I argued that an important factor in the perception of figural goodness (in the gestalt sense) is the number of equivalent patterns that exist by virtue of rotations and reflections. A pattern that is symmetrical on the vertical, horizontal, and both diagonal axes will simply generate itself when it is rotated in 90° steps or reflected on any of its axes of symmetry. If, however, there is only one axis of symmetry, then there exists a subset of four patterns, all of which are identical if rotation and/or reflection are allowed. Further, if there is no axis of symmetry in a pattern, then there are eight patterns that will produce each other with rotation and/or reflection.

Patterns within a subset of equivalent patterns are very similar, and reaction time to pairs of them is high. (For a more complete review, see Garner, 1974.) In the data displayed in Fig. 5.7, two pairs of letters that form clusters exist in the same rotation and reflection subset. These are *M* and *W*— which are mirror images of each other around the horizontal axis—and *J* and *L* which are mirror images of each other around a vertical axis, although lateral displacement must be allowed for *J* and *L* to be reflections of each other.

There is a role of symmetry and other configural properties, but it is a role that limits the number of highly similar letters that can exist within a set. If all letters were symmetrical on four axes, as *X* and *O* are, all letters would be highly discriminable. If there are no configural properties operating, then highly similar letters can and do exist. It is tempting even to argue that configural properties are catalytic properties, making it possible for component properties to operate more effectively. This notion, of course, is inherent in the concept of *redundancy*, which is the term Eleanor Gibson used in describing symmetry and cyclic change. But I think the point is stronger than that term implies. Redundancy simply implies that there is extra, repeated information in the letter properties. Strong joint configural properties require maximum differentiation of component properties and certainly prevent the existence of letters that are simply rotations and reflections of each other. Such letters are perceived as similar because they have the same configuration, but that is quite different from perceiving two letters as similar because they have the same amount of redundancy.

Template Properties.   So far I have considered only component properties and the kind of wholistic properties I have called configural. However, template properties are also wholistic, and I want briefly to consider the possibility that we should not really remove template properties to the back burner in our thinking. As I mentioned in my introductory remarks, templates are difficult to define because there can be no meaningful definition of a template that does not allow for some irrelevant attributes. But if we allow size and location to be irrelevant attributes, then we can define template processing as processing of the configural whole, and speed of processing then is related simply to amount of overlap of two letters, with overlap being maximized by permissible size and location transformations. Notice now the nine letter pairs that form clusters in Fig. 5.7. If we were not used to thinking in terms of attributes, either features or dimensions, the fact that stands out about all these letter pairs is that there is a great overlap between the templates (or configurations, even) in each pair. For many pairs, such as *OQ*, *UV*, *KX*, *BP*, *EF*, and *IT*, the great overlap is simply blatant, with the letters differing by what I would call a single feature, as with the *EF*, *BP*, *OQ*, and *IT* pairs.

Evidence comes from Taylor (1976) of a similar nature. He used a successive same–different task, with reaction time measures, for a set of six letters that were generated from the block numeral 8. Five of these letters are unambiguously identifiable as uppercase *E*, *O*, *F*, *H*, *U*, whereas the sixth could be either the *A* or *R*. The use of these letters allows exact specification and control of amount of overlap in the letters. Taylor found that the difference reaction time was faster, the greater the number of nonoverlapping segments, and he used this result as evidence that analytic processing is used in the difference reaction task. But is it really evidence against template processing? If template processing means that templates can only differ in an all-or-none manner, then of course the fact that a difference in speed of reaction does occur as a function of amount of difference is evidence for attribute (analytic) processing. But it does not seem reasonable to me to put such a rigid requirement on the idea of template processing.

In fact, consider reversing the role of defendant in the consideration of template vs. attribute. We assume a template matching system and that we know nothing whatsoever about such dimensions as straight lines or curved lines, openness, and so forth. We only assume joint occupancy of space for two different letters, and we obtain a measure of overlap for every pair of letters. To simplify and reify my illustration, consider the set of four letters— *O*, *C*, *I*, and *T*—used in overlap measures (so obvious that I do not state them) to generate a multidimensional scale or even a cluster analysis. Is there any question at all that such a procedure would lead to an *OC* cluster pair as well as an *IT* cluster pair, and that a dimensional analysis will show a primary dimension of curved–straight, with a peculiar second dimension that is some mixture of the gap and the top crosspiece? [In my terms, incidentally, I would have described this set of four letters as having a primary dimensional difference, with two levels (curved or straight), and then with a feature nested within each level of the dimension (gap in one case, crossbar in the other).]

I do not pursue this issue much further because I have no data with which to pursue it. As I remarked in the introduction, however, wholistic ideas like simple whole and sometimes template are often defined by default, and the burden of proof is on the template—that it is in fact used. If, however, we can find positive definitions for the wholistic properties, we may discover that the analytic or component processes will not be so readily accepted as primary in perception and information processing.

In summary, based on our evidence, it seems that the discrimination of letters is based on stable processing factors. These are processes that are not easily altered by shifting from a simultaneous same–different task to a sequential task with a single target in memory. Furthermore, the use of smaller subsets of letters does not lead to a drastically different picture of the properties of letters that determine their discriminability. Overall, the picture of a similarity structure based on reaction times is quite consistent from these two circumstances if we consider the similarity structure to be primarily based on component properties. It is clear, however, that configural properties do influence discriminability. And we may also want to keep in mind the possibility that letter discrimination is carried out with a template form of processing, and that the emergence of component properties in our analyses is partly artifactual.

THE PERCEPTION OF LETTER IDENTITY

So far I have discussed the discrimination of letter differences as measured by reaction time for subjects to respond that two letters are different. But in such tasks, there is always an alternative response, which is used when in fact the two letters displayed or the display and the target letter held in memory are identical. It has been known for some time that the reaction time for the same, or identity, response is not the same as it is for the difference response. To illustrate, Bindra, Williams, and Wise (1965) investigated a number of factors such as discriminability and encodability that influence whether identity response is faster or slower than the difference response. With more specific regard to visual patterns, Sekuler and Abrams (1968) showed, with geometric patterns formed from blackened cells in a 4 × 4 matrix of cells, that identity responses were faster than difference responses and furthermore were unaffected by number of cells filled, although the difference response was affected by number of cells. A similar result has been found for letter strings by Bamber (1972) and by Taylor (1976), as well as by others, and this independence of the identity reaction to the number of items processed (filled cells or letters in these cases) has been used to argue that identity perception is wholistic whereas difference perception is analytic.

In emphasizing the relative lack of effect of number of components on the speed of the identity response, these experiments have not investigated the thing that I want to discuss in this section: Although the identity response may be relatively uninfluenced by the number of components, nevertheless, all identity responses in a given experimental context are not in fact the same. There are considerable differences between identity reaction times, and these are what I shall discuss.

Differences Between Letter Identities

To bring this discussion back to letters and to put the issue in perspective, I refer again to the data of Podgorny and Garner (1979). Our identity reaction times ranged from 437 msec to 479 msec. The individual pair-difference reaction times varied over a much greater range, of course, the actual range being 411 msec to 592 msec. However, if we consider the average difference reaction time for each letter used as a target against all possible nontargets, the range is from 431 msec to 468 msec; and if we consider each letter as a nontarget averaged for all target letters, the range is from 441 msec to 464 msec. (These last two numbers are the row and column averages when the matrix of data is arranged with target letters as rows and nontarget display letters as columns.) In this context, it can be seen that there is greater variation in the identity responses from one letter to another than there is for letters used as targets or as nontargets on the average. There is, therefore, a measurable phenomenon worth investigating.

Effect of Context

Gibson et al. (1968), with the simultaneous same–different task, also found differences between letters for the identity condition, and since they used two subsets of letters, a comparison of the data Podgorny and I obtained with the Gibson data provides some evidence of the effect of context on which letters are perceived as identical more quickly than others. The comparative data for the *CEFGMNPRW* data are shown in Fig. 5.8. The correlation between the two sets of data is high at .77. The similarity between the two is also apparent in that the four fastest letters are the same in the two different experiments (i.e., *PCRE*). Still further, the range of values is very much the same. The mean value for the Gibson data is somewhat higher than for the Podgorny–Garner data, but that figure is easily influenced by response sets,

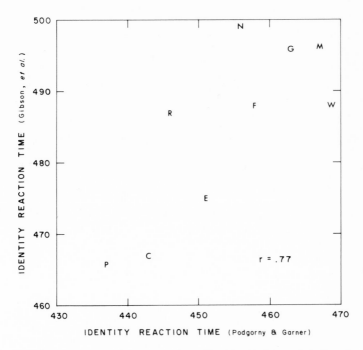

FIG. 5.8.   Reaction times (msec) to letter identities. Each letter is indicated. (Data are from Podgorny & Garner, 1979, and Gibson et al., 1968.)

probability of the identity response occurring, etc., so that the comparison of absolute values is of little import.

The comparison data for the *ADHKOQSTX* data are displayed in Fig. 5.9. Once again the correlation is quite high at .71, and the range of values is slightly higher for the Gibson data. Again, the four fastest letters are the same for both sets of data: *OTSA*. Thus the effect of specific letter context in determining the speed of the identity response is not strong.

Context as Similarity.   If context has little effect in determining the speed of the identity reaction, what does make the differences in speed? One possible answer is that fast responses are to those letters that are isolates in the similarity or confusion space. Lockhead (Lockhead & King, 1977; Monahan & Lockhead, 1977) has argued strongly and convincingly that a single mapping of similarity space can account for most measures of discrimination time as well as speed of the identity response. Let us examine this assumption for the letter data and see to what extent it might account for the differences in speed of the identity response.

There are several ways in which similarity could operate to produce isolation of single letters. One of these is simply for a letter to have no single

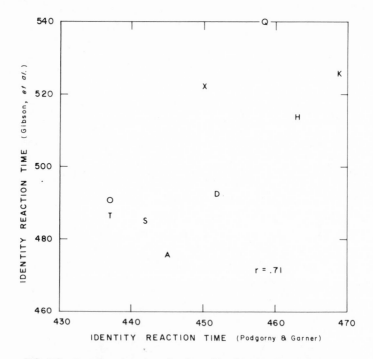

FIG. 5.9.   Reaction times (msec) to letter identities. Each letter is indicated. (Data are from Podgorny & Garner, 1979, and Gibson et al., 1968.)

"near neighbor" in a similarity space. Since similarity is inversely related to the difference reaction time, an examination of the data displayed in Fig. 5.7 will help to answer whether the near neighbor idea has validity. The four fastest letters in terms of the identity response for the Podgorny–Garner data were T, B, P, and O. From Fig. 5.7 it can be seen that B and P together form an initial cluster pair; thus their advantage in being fast identity letters cannot be due to their isolation from any single letter. T and O also form initial pair clusters but with other letters: T clusters with I, which is ranked 8th in identity speed; and O clusters with Q, which is ranked 18th. A similar picture exists if we look at the letters that rank poorly in speed of the identity response. The four slowest letters were M, K, V, and W. M and W formed a pair cluster, and K formed a pair cluster with X, and V with U. Thus the picture concerning near neighbors lends no support to the idea that fast identity responses occur to letters with no near neighbor whereas slow identity responses occur to letters with near neighbors.

Another type of similarity isolation is what might be called "average isolation." By this is meant the extent to which a letter is at the outside of the similarity space and thus is, on the average, further away from the other letters. We can estimate the role of average isolation by using the reaction measures themselves as our measures of similarity; and we can determine the average speed for a letter as a target against all other letters as different displays to provide a single measure of average distance of each letter from all other letters. (This is the row mean of the matrix mentioned just earlier.) The correlation of this measure with the identity reaction times is .78. The correlation of the identity reaction times with the column means is .40. Both these correlations do lend support to the idea that one possible factor in determining speed of the identity response is the average isolation of a given letter from all other letters. (This is further discussed later.)

Another factor that might contribute to the speed of the identity response is frequency of occurrence in printed English (as a measure of familiarity). The correlation between speed of the identity response and frequency of occurrence for different estimates of the frequency was about .50. It is not clear that frequency of occurrence is uncorrelated with various physical properties; and correlation with alphabetic order was .22, which suggests that practice in reciting or using the alphabet in sequence has little influence.

The Unique Stimulus in Memory

It seems to me that the primary factor affecting speed of the identity response involves properties of the individual unique stimulus rather than the contextual properties, and that these properties operate primarily through their role in memory rather than through their role as displayed letters. The fact that a memory component is involved in letter identification tasks is self-evident in the task used by Podgorny and me (1979), because the subject in that study held a single letter in memory and then decided whether a rather long series of displayed letters were or were not the target letter in memory. The Gibson data were, as mentioned, obtained with a simultaneous same–different task, but the high correlations between her data and ours argue not only that context is unimportant in these tasks but also that the same psychological processes were operating in the two tasks, and almost certainly that there is an important role of memory in her task as well as in ours.

Simultaneous Judgments.   All tasks requiring the same–different judgment do not necessarily involve an important memory component, especially when the two letters are presented side by side for a simultaneous comparison and judgment. Several experiments have now been reported using the simultaneous same–different judgment. Clement and Carpenter (1970) showed that the judgment was based on visual rather than on phonological properties of the letters. Fox (1975) argued that symmetry of the letter pair provides a faster identity reaction time, but his results do not correlate well with the earlier Clement and Carpenter data. Still further, Fox's results were not replicated by Egeth, Brownell, and Geoffrion (1976) and were only weakly replicated by Richards (1978). This failure to get equivalent results with these several simultaneous same–different experiments seems to me to imply that specific orthographic properties of the letters are very important in that task, and that display properties specific to the letter pairs may be important, as Fox argued. But the high correlation between our data and those of Gibson suggests that there is a common property or process involved in the identity judgment, and pursuit of its understanding is appropriate.

Pattern Structure.   I want to return to the question of the properties of the unique stimulus and its role in memory, and I want to shift for the moment to a discussion of some data not obtained with letter patterns but with more abstract dot patterns. The experiment most directly relevant was carried out by Marc Sebrechts and me (1979), with the four dot patterns shown in Fig. 5.10. Two of these patterns are good in the gestalt sense, and two are poor. (For a general discussion of this matter of pattern goodness, see Garner, 1974, but for present purposes, I assume it is obvious that the top two patterns have good configuration and the bottom two have poor configuration.) We (Sebrechts & Garner, 1979) conducted the following experiment: All four stimuli were used in each experimental session with a simple sequential same–different task. One of the four stimuli was presented as the memory pattern, and 1 second later, one of the four stimuli was presented as the display pattern. The subject pressed one key if the display pattern was the same as the memory pattern and another key if it was not, and reaction time was measured.

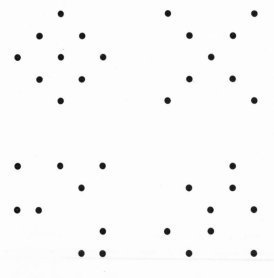

FIG. 5.10.   The two good and two poor stimulus patterns used by Sebrechts and Garner (1979).

TABLE 5.1
Reaction Time (msec) for Difference Responses for Good
and Poor Patterns in Memory and Display[a]

Memory Pattern	Display Pattern		
	Good	Poor	(Mean)
Good	450	463	(457)
Poor	479	476	(478)
(Mean)	(465)	(470)	

[a]Data from Sebrechts & Garner (1979).

The first result of importance is that there was a large difference in the speed of the identity response (398 msec for the good patterns and 446 msec for the poor patterns). Thus here, too, we have evidence that not all identity responses are equal and that the differences are, for this type of task, quite substantial. The identity case involves two stimuli that are the same—one in memory and one in the display—so we cannot disentangle from this result alone whether the difference in reaction time is due to factors involving the display or due to factors involving the memory item. Further analysis will help clarify this.

Table 5.1 shows difference reaction times for four types of difference conditions involving all four combinations of two levels of goodness in the memory and in the display pattern. As can be seen from the row and column means, there is a very slight effect (5 msec) of differences in goodness of the display item, but a much more substantial effect (21 msec) of differences in goodness of the memory item. There is actually an interaction, of course, in which the display stimulus has some effect if the memory stimulus has good configuration, but has no effect if the memory stimulus has poor configuration. These results imply that the differences in reaction time are due primarily to the ability to hold a good item in memory as contrasted to the ability to hold a poor item in memory. By extrapolation, we can argue that the difference in the identity response found in this experiment as well as in the Gibson and in the Podgorny–Garner data is due to the fact that different letters are more or less easily held in memory, even for very brief periods of time.

Another point about these results is noteworthy as well. It might be argued (as Lockhead would) that these results simply indicate that the two good patterns are more isolated in a similarity space than are the two poor items. But Sebrechts and I repeated this experiment with a modification in the procedure: On any single run, of some 100 trials, only two stimulus items were used rather than all four. Thus for a single run, the total context was reduced to just two stimulus patterns, so relative isolation should not have mattered in producing variations in the identity response. But when the data were averaged over all six possible pairs of the four stimuli, the results were essentially identical to those we obtained when all four stimuli were used together in the experimental context. To exmphasize the lack of effect of the general experimental context, I shall note that an identity response for each stimulus is obtained when the stimulus is paired with each of the other three stimuli. The speed of the identity response was not significantly affected by the stimulus with which each stimulus was paired, either for the good patterns or for the poor patterns. Furthermore, note that this result is stating quite unequivocally that if a good and a poor pattern are used in a particular run, the good pattern provides a fast identity response, and the poor pattern provides a slow identity response. Yet there is only a single distance between the two stimuli of a single pair.

It is for these reasons that I am talking about the properties of the unique stimulus as being important in determining the speed of the identity response (as well as the speed of the difference response if one item must be held in memory). It is not the total context that is the major factor in determining speed of the identity response but somehow the properties of the single stimulus. That this type of memory effect occurs has been shown in another experiment of mine (Garner, 1978b). In this experiment, the four stimuli were formed from a pair of parentheses as dimensions, with in and out curvature as the levels on the dimensions: (-(,)-),)-(, and (-). These stimuli are a little more like real letters than are dot patterns and are thus possibly more immediately relevant to the question of speed of letter identity responses. One of the tasks I used required subjects to classify one stimulus against the other three, in what I called a *focusing task*. The result of interest was that the (-) stimulus could be classified against the other three just as fast as it could be discriminated from each of the other three on a one-to-one basis. Presumably, in this task, the subject holds the one item in memory and then performs a go–no-go classification task, simply deciding whether each stimulus is or is not the one held in memory. (In this respect, the task is like the one Podgorny and I used, with one target letter in memory.) The (-) is the configurally best single stimulus, so this result again confirms that good configuration of the memory item will facilitate performance.

What Makes a Good Letter?   I have been arguing that the primary factor that affects the speed of the identity response is the ability to hold the stimulus in memory. But the particular data I have used have also suggested that good configuration is what makes it easy to hold a pattern in memory. What, then, makes one letter easier to hold in memory than another, thus leading to fast identity responses? I have argued that it is not familiarity, not alphabetic order; and only marginally is it location in a similarity space. It is predominantly the physical properties of the letter configuration itself. On these grounds, then, as Fox argues, letters that have symmetry, preferably on many axes, should be good letters for a fast identity response. However, I feel that Fox's data show this to be the case only for a true simultaneous presentation.

Are we then left with the assumption that well-configured letters are easy to hold in memory but with the inability to identify what these well-configured properties are? I think that we can, for letters, identify at least what some of these properties are. As I have mentioned, the four fastest letters for the Podgorny–Garner data were *T, P, B,* and *O. S* and *C* were the next fastest, with *A, I, L,* and *U* following in order. To continue for the full order, *R, X, E, D, J, N, F, Q, Y, Z, H, G, M, K, V,* and *W* were the letters following in speed of the identity response. There is an obvious differentiation between the fast and the slow letters: The fast letters contain single vertical lines or curved lines or a combination of these. The four slowest letters all contain diagonal lines, and *X* is the fastest letter that has clearly diagonal lines (*A* and *V* are somewhat equivocal in this respect with the computer-generated letters). Thus, it appears that symmetry alone, or even amount of symmetry, does not determine letter goodness but that a concept related to simplicity is involved—the simplicity of curvature only, vertical lines only, or curvature plus vertical lines. We have no way of determining whether these constitute general principles for simplicity, and thus for fast identity responses, since there are no letters that, for example, consist only of horizontal lines or horizontal lines plus simple curvature. Also it is still possible that symmetry plays some role; note, for example, the relatively high position for the letter *X* compared to other letters with diagonal lines and compared to its low rank in both alphabetic order and in frequency of usage in English. But within the set of real uppercase letters available to us, simplicity seems to be correlated with vertical lines, simple curvature, and lack of diagonal lines.

CONCLUDING REMARKS

In concluding this discussion about the perception of letter differences and letter identities, I shall simply comment on three important, but as yet unresolved, issues. These issues concern the nature of wholistic properties, the role of configural properties in discrimination and identification, and the problem of ecological validity in studying all the issues involved in letter perception.

Wholistic Properties

Although my introduction to this chapter included my definitions of wholistic properties—including a distinction between simple wholes, templates, and configurations—I do not really feel that these are completely satisfactory definitions. I do feel certain that we must distinguish between wholistic and component properties and that it is important to recognize that these are dual aspects of any stimulus; thus component and wholistic properties are always redundant. But there are difficulties with each of the types of wholistic properties I have mentioned.

Simple wholes have no adequate definition, since it is a construct defined almost entirely by default. For example, in several experiments cited (including Bamber, 1972; Sekuler & Abrams, 1968; Taylor, 1976), the argument that the identity response is based on wholistic properties is an argument by default, since the basic evidence for it is simply that the reaction time does not vary as a function of number of components. However, that experimental evidence does not at all distinguish between complete parallel processing of several independent components and processing of a truly integrated whole. I find that unsatisfactory, partly because I do in fact believe that processing is wholistic. Yet my evidence is inconclusive, since in referring to letter properties that provide fast identity responding, I am forced to describe component properties such as vertical and diagonal straight lines and the like.

The evidence is more conclusive regarding templates, and yet there are two basic unresolved issues mentioned earlier in this chapter. The first is determining which properties are irrelevant in order to discuss a template meaningfully; the second is defining template processing in a way that clearly differentiates it from component processing. As I have discussed, a process model could assume that speed of processing template differences need only be concerned with overlaps of templates without any further definition of component properties. Nevertheless, data from such a model (even data based on physical overlap of letters) can be used to "disclose" the component properties. That we can apply a mathematical analytic model to a set of data in such a way that dimensions (or even clusters) are derived is weak proof that the dimensions or clusters thus generated are psychologically meaningful. This caution is one appropriate not only to measurement models such as factor analysis, multidimensional scaling, and cluster analyses, but equally to data analytic models as commonly used as correlation and analysis of variance. This is not the place to go into a general discourse on how our analytic models have influenced our psychological thinking, but note that our evidence for component processing is weak, because it is often based heavily on unprovem assumptions that the properties of the model are in fact those of the process we are trying to understand.

Last, of course, are configurations, my favorite type of wholistic property. But here, too, we have nothing but weak definitions of a positive form about what constitutes a configural property, and too often it is necessary to use illustrative examples to explain what we mean (see Garner, in press). Most often, symmetry is our exemplar property, sometimes it is repetition, and intersection is a third such property. Can the idea of configural property be that inadequate? Surely we all think that the idea of configural property means more than that, but when we try to extract such properties from a set of data, we end up with component properties. Our mathematical and analytic models are not yet appropriate to the task at hand.

Configural Properties in Letter Perception

I have already noted that configural properties such as symmetry and repetition play a different role in letter (or any other form) discrimination than do component properties. Letters that share component properties— curved lines or diagonal lines—are perceived as similar; and if they do not share these component properties, they are perceived as different. Two letters with equally high symmetry are easily discriminated, as measured by either reaction time or errors. Thus equal symmetry (or repetition, or intersection) does not imply low discriminability. And yet in other contexts, they may be perceived as similar. Certainly, work that I have done on classification of dot patterns (see Garner, 1974, for a review) shows that configurally good patterns (e.g., those that have symmetry) are classed together. More recently, Glushko (1975) has shown that good patterns are perceived as more similar to each other than they are to poor patterns. It may be that discriminability and similarity are not identical constructs and that the configural properties will operate differently in tasks that emphasize similarity than in tasks that emphasize discrimination.

Still further, what role does simplicity play in determining the goodness of patterns, and thus their speed of producing the identity response? Sebrechts and I (1979) showed that patterns having high symmetry produce fast identity responses. However, the letter data from my work with Podgorny show symmetry to be relatively unimportant. In all the work I have done with dot patterns, as well as other fairly abstract patterns, the "amount" of stimulus is the same for all stimuli. Thus in using dot patterns, I have always used patterns of exactly five dots, or nine dots; but I have not mixed the two. The data on letter identification, however, show that letters with single vertical lines, or single curved lines, or combinations of these are identified very rapidly. Perhaps simplicity and goodness have something in common, and we can determine how simplicity affects goodness only by mixing patterns with different numbers of components.

Ecological Validity

The idea of ecological validity is one that constantly crops up when trying to understand perception of any aspect of the world, including the study of letter discrimination. I have myself long felt that ecologically valid experiments (i.e., experiments that reasonably maintain the properties of the real world in which organisms live and develop) have much to offer the psychological study of perception, as contrasted with the experiments that vary physical parameters without regard even to the existence of the parameters in the organism's real world. Emphasis on ecological validity has been made by many, but certainly Brunswik (1955) and James Gibson (e.g., 1966) have been strong proponents in the study of perception. Since this book honors Eleanor Gibson, I quote her (1969) in regard to this issue:

> Ideally, therefore, a laboratory situation which simulates a typical situation in the infant's world should be used. The situation must be controllable so that the information can be analyzed and describable so that it can be replicated, but it should be natural [p. 319].

However, there are problems involved in the ecologically valid approach that are at least as great as those involved in the more traditional laboratory approach with its totally controlled experiments. I discuss briefly some of these issues in the context of material included in this chapter.

The identity reaction times for uppercase letters obtained by Gibson et al. (1968) and those obtained by Podgorny and Garner (1979) were highly correlated, as were these two sets of data for difference reaction times. I argued from these correlations that specific differences in procedure were therefore not important and that changes in the letter context were also not very important. Certainly the data Podgorny and I collected were based on ecologically valid stimuli, since we used the entire set of uppercase English letters with subjects whose native language was English.

Consider some of the questions and how difficult it is to get good answers when we use the letter set as given. Slow letters for the identity response are *M, K, V*, and *W*, all containing diagonal straight lines. Three of them also contain three or more lines, thus confounding diagonality with number of components. Fast identity-response letters include *T, B, P*, and *O;* but these letters confound simplicity with curved lines in three out of four cases. Furthermore, if we want to understand the role of symmetry in discrimination (or its converse, similarity), the only two letters wth symmetry on four axes (depending on exact construction) are the *X* and the *O*, which give very fast difference reaction times. These two letters also differ completely in having nothing but curvilinearity in one letter and nothing but diagonal straight lines in the other. Therefore we really cannot answer the question of whether symmetric letters are perceived as being similar.

Therefore, at times, we must shift back to the totally controlled mode of experimenting, as Haun and I did in generating the letters of Fig. 5.3. But in order to have a set of letters differing unequivocally in just features, we had to use a letter that was more or less like a *T* but not identical. How much this artificiality influenced our results, we have no way of telling.

Which approach is the correct one? The answer has to be that both are necessary, but the two approaches can rarely be combined in a single experiment. With ecologically valid stimuli, we must accept confounding of stimulus factors. But with the controlled experiment approach, we must accept a certain amount of irreality or implausibility. Each approach has its virtues and faults, and I do not think that we can use either approach alone to study letter perception.

And in final conclusion, it would seem that we have more problems left to solve about letter perception than we have so far solved. A not uncommon conclusion, to be sure.

ACKNOWLEDGMENTS

The preparation of this chapter and the research it reports were supported by Grant No. MH 14229 from the National Institute of Mental Health to Yale University. Special thanks are due to the students with whom I have collaborated in this research: Forrest Haun, Peter Podgorny, and Marc Sebrechts.

REFERENCES

Bamber, D. Reaction times and error rates for judging nominal identity of letter strings. *Perception & Psychophysics,* 1972, *12,* 321–326.

Bindra, D., Williams, J., & Wise, S. S. Judgments of sameness and difference: Experiments on reaction time. *Science,* 1965, *150,* 1625–1627.

Brunswik, E. Representative design and probabilistic theory in a functional psychology. *Psychological Review,* 1955, *62,* 193–217.

Clement, D. E., & Carpenter, J. S. Relative discriminability of visually-presented letter pairs using a same–different choice-reaction task. *Psychonomic Science,* 1970, *20,* 363–365.

Egeth, H. E., Brownell, H. H., & Geoffrion, L. D. Testing the role of vertical symmetry in letter matching. *Journal of Experimental Psychology: Human Perception and Performance,* 1976, *2,* 429–434.

Fox, J. the use of structural diagnostics in recognition. *Journal of Experimental Psychology: Human Perception and Performance,* 1975, *1,* 57–67.

Garner, W. R. The stimulus in information processing. *American Psychologist,* 1970, *25,* 350–358.

Garner, W. R. *The processing of information and structure.* Hillsdale, N.J.: Lawrence Erlbaum Associates, 1974.

Garner, W. R. Aspects of a stimulus: Features, dimensions, and configurations. In E. Rosch & B. B. Lloyd (Eds.), *Cognition and categorization.* Hillsdale, N.J.: Lawrence Erlbaum Associates, 1978. (a)

Garner, W. R. Selective attention to attributes and to stimuli. *Journal of Experimental Psychology: General,* 1978, *107,* 287–308. (b)

Garner, W. R. The analysis of unanalyzed perceptions. In M. Kubovy & J. R. Pomerantz (Eds.), *Perceptual organization.* Hillsdale, N.J.: Lawrence Erlbaum Associates, in press.

Garner, W. R., & Haun, F. Letter identification as a function of type of perceptual limitation and type of attribute. *Journal of Experimental Psychology: Human Perception and Performance,* 1978, *4,* 199–209.

Garner, W. R., & Morton, J. Perceptual independence: Definitions, models, and experimental paradigms. *Psychological Bulletin,* 1969, *72,* 233–259.

Gibson, E. J. *Principles of perceptual learning and development.* Englewood Cliffs, N.J.: Prentice-Hall, 1969.

Gibson, E. J., & Levin, H. *The psychology of reading.* Cambridge Mass.: M.I.T. Press, 1975.

Gibson, E. J., Schapiro, F., & Yonas, A. Confusion matrices for graphic patterns obtained with a latency measure. In *The analysis of reading skill: A program of basic and applied research* (Final Report, Project No. 5-1213). Cornell University and U.S. Office of Education, 1968, 76–96.

Gibson, J. J. *The senses considered as perceptual systems.* Boston: Houghton Mifflin, 1966.

Glushko, R. J. Pattern goodness and redundancy revisited: Multidimensional scaling and hierarchical clustering analyses. *Perception & Psychophysics,* 1975, *17,* 158–162.

Kuennapas, T., & Janson, A.-J. Multidimensional similarity of letters. *Perceptual and Motor Skills,* 1969, *2,* 3–12.

Lockhead, G. R., & King, M. C. Classifying integral stimuli. *Journal of Experimental Psychology: Human Perception and Performance,* 1977, *3,* 436–443.

Monahan, J. S., & Lockhead, G. R. Identification of integral stimuli. *Journal of Experimental Psychology: General,* 1977, *106,* 94–110.

Neisser, U. *Cognitive psychology.* Englewood Cliffs, N.J.: Prentice-Hall, 1967.

Podgorny, P., & Garner, W. R. *Reaction time as a measure of inter- and intra-object visual similarity: Letters of the alphabet.* Unpublished manuscript, 1979.

Richards, J. T. Interitem structure and the facilitation of simultaneous comparison. *Journal of Experimental Psychology: Human Perception and Performance,* 1978, *4,* 72–87.

Sattath, S., & Tversky, A. Additive similarity trees. *Psychometrika,* 1977, *42,* 319–345.

Sebrechts, M. M., & Garner, W. R. *Processing consequences of goodness: Context-dependent and context-independent effects.* Unpublished manuscript, 1979.

Sekuler, R. W., & Abrams, M. Visual sameness: A choice time analysis of pattern recognition processes. *Journal of Experimental Psychology,* 1968, *77,* 232–238.

Shepard, R. N. Psychological representation of speech sounds. In E. E. David & P. N. Denes (Eds.), *Human communication: A unified view.* New York: McGraw-Hill, 1972.

Taylor, D. A. Holistic and analytic processes in the comparison of letters. *Perception & Psychophysics,* 1976, *20,* 187–190.

Townsend, J. T. Theoretical analysis of an alphabetic confusion matrix. *Perception & Psychophysics,* 1971, *9,* 40–50.

6 Listening to Melodies: Perceiving Events

Anne D. Pick
University of Minnesota

This chapter is about event perception. But the events discussed are not visible—at least not primarily so. Instead, they are events that we listen to; they are melodies.

What are events? They are things that happen, and we can perceive them happening. They occur over time, and they have a discernible beginning and end. Visible events involve motion, and there is information for perceiving both change and continuity in their motion. They may be long or short in duration, and they may themselves contain embedded events. They have structure; they are organized and constrained, and they behave in lawful ways.

The perception of events and its early development have begun recently to receive the attention of psychologists (Gibson, 1977; Shaw & Pittenger, 1978; Spelke, Chapter 10, this volume). Eleanor Gibson has demonstrated that by analyzing the structure of events and manipulating it in controlled ways, we can discover the particular properties of complex visible events that are perceived even by very young babies (Gibson, 1977). She has also suggested that the perception of some complex events begins with the perception of the shorter embedded events contained in them (Gibson, 1977, p. 4). Thus, she has pointed out how, by appropriately examining the structure of events, we can learn about their perception and about the course of its development.

Although melodies are heard rather than seen, they share many properties with visible events, and the most important of these is change over time (Shaw & Pittenger, 1978). The property of change over time is so obviously fundamental to music in particular, and to auditory perception in general, that we have sometimes mistakenly contrasted visual and auditory perception in terms of the importance of spatial and temporal information. However, Eleanor Gibson (1969) and James Gibson (1966) have taken particular pains to remind us of the importance of change over time for visual perception as well. It is perhaps a more obvious truth for a musical melody than for a visible event that the crucial information for the invariant properties of the event is given *only* over time.

In addition to their essentially temporal quality, the sound sequences that we know as melodies share other properties with visible events. Melodies are highly organized and constrained. The particular patterns of temporal change they can contain are more or less specified, at least if we restrict our analysis to the familiar melodies of our own Western culture. In addition, the limits of these changes, though not bound by physical laws, are more or less bound by convention. Perceiving these changes and their limits may be the basis for how we can distinguish meolodies from other sequences of tones. Thus, the thesis of this chapter is that by analyzing the structure of melodies as events, we will identify the properties by which we can begin to understand their perception. If our analysis is productive, then we may also achieve some insights about general principles of event perception that are valid for events that are seen as well as those that are heard. Much of what can be said now about the perception of melodies is speculative, for the work is just beginning. However, by analyzing melodies as events, and then considering the relevant literature in light of such an analysis, some tentative principles about how melodies are perceived can be derived, and some specific strategies for how the study of their perception should proceed can be made explicit.

PERCEIVING THE STRUCTURE OF MELODIES

Melodies are organized sequences of sound that have structure and constraints. What are the properties of that structure that may be available to the listener? The smallest single elements of the structure of melodies probably are notes, although they themselves have a complex harmonic structure. The notes of a melody vary in frequency and duration. The variations in frequency, perceived primarily as variations in pitch, are an essential property of a melody. It is nearly impossible to conceive of a melody that occurs on only one note—at least in the familiar music of our culture.

The pitch variations of a melody have several characteristics that are relevant for understanding its perception. There is the rising and falling pattern of the pitches that is known as the contour of the melody. There is also a pattern of relative interval sizes between the successive pitches of the melody. In addition, there is a pattern of exact interval sizes between the successive pitches. Melodies also are played in a key, which means that the frequencies of the notes that can make up the melody are those of a particular scale. The key also imposes constraints on the pitch variations that are melodies instead of unsystematic collections of notes. Finally, in addition to variations in pitch, melodies have rhythm, a pattern of note duration and temporal interval duration. In sum, the structure of melodies includes at least the following properties: pitches, variations in pitch that have a contour, relative interval sizes, absolute interval sizes, a key, and finally, a rhythm. What role has each of these properties in the perception of melodies? That is the question that is discussed in the following pages.

The Notes of a Melody

When a melody is transposed (i.e., when it is played in a different key), the frequency ratios among the notes of the melody are preserved. When a familiar melody is transposed in this way, adult listeners ordinarily identify it as being the same melody. This implies that the specific notes of a melody are less important in defining it than are the relations among those notes. However, most adults have heard and sung familiar melodies in a variety of keys. Hence, adults' recognition of transposed familiar melodies might reflect their specific experience with those particular melodies rather than revealing the general basis for how they are perceived. An interesting study by Attneave and Olson (1971) seems to rule out this interpretation. They discovered a familiar melody that had only been heard at three particular pitches: the NBC chimes, which were always played at G below middle C, E above middle C, and middle C. Attneave and Olson asked adults to reproduce that melody on different notes. Even though the listeners had no special training in music, they transposed the melody in a way that preserved quite accurately the frequency *ratios* of its adjacent notes. An important implication of this finding is that it is the relations among the notes that define a melody. In short, although the notes of a melody are its elements, they are not the basic units in terms of which melodies are perceived. Rather, it is relations among the notes that are the essential, irreducible properties of a melody.

Recognizing a Familiar Melody

What specific relations among notes of a familiar melody provide the basis for its recognition? The relevance of exact interval sizes in perceiving familiar melodies is already implied by the way adult listeners reproduce familar melodies. There is other evidence that exact interval sizes are the basis on which familiar melodies are known and recognized. Dowling and Fujitani (1971) asked adult listeners to identify familiar melodies that were distorted in various ways. Recognition accuracy was extremely high when the exact sizes of successive intervals and the contour were preserved. Listeners were somewhat less accurate when the relative sizes of successive intervals and the contour were preserved but the absolute interval sizes were distorted. Accuracy decreased further—but was still well above chance—when only the contour was preserved. Thus, listeners' knowledge of a familiar melody includes knowledge about the exact sizes of the intervals among the notes of the melody as well as less precise information about its relative interval sizes and its contour.

The notes of the musical scale that we are familiar with repeat themselves every octave. Is this cyclical property of the scale revelant for understanding our perception? Adults can identify familiar melodies such as "Happy Birthday" or "Pop Goes the Weasel" when the successive notes of the melody are separated by octaves. This is true so long as the contour and the actual interval sizes (disregarding the octave separation) are preserved (Idson & Massaro, 1976). When either the relative or absolute interval sizes are distorted, recognition is more difficult, and when the contour itself is distorted, recognition is sometimes impossible (Deutsch, 1972b; Dowling & Hollombe, 1977; House, 1977a, 1977b; Idson & Massaro, 1976). Thus when the notes of a familiar melody are transformed across octaves, listeners can still identify it if the crucial property of its structure remains invariant.

In addition to perceiving a melody across octave transformations of its notes, listeners can also perceive familiar melodies in some conditoins when there are notes intervening between successive notes of the melody. Dowling (1973a) asked listeners to recognize melodies when the notes of two melodies were interleaved such that successive tones of one melody occurred between successive tones of the other. Listeners were instructed to say when they knew what the melodies were. When two familiar melodies are interleaved in this way, and when the pitch ranges of the two are initially overlapping and then gradually separated, listeners usually cannot identify the melodies until their pitch ranges are nearly nonoverlapping. However, once a melody is recognized, one can continue to perceive it even when its pitch range again overlaps somewhat the range of the melody with which it is interleaved. Furthermore, if listeners are informed ahead of time what the melody is and are then instructed to say when they can pick it out or identify it, they can do this after some repetitions, even when its pitch range does overlap with that of the melody with which it is interleaved. Thus, knowing what melody to listen for facilitates its recognition—presumably because one knows the specific criterial relations among the notes that must be sought. That one's knowledge of the target melody guides one's search for it is reflected in another finding from the same study. If one is told to listen for one melody but, in fact, a different but equally familiar melody is interleaved with a random sequence of the same pitch range, one does not recognize the melody—even after many repetitions. Thus the effect is not simply hearing something that one has heard before and therefore being able to recognize it.

Knowing what the background melody is does not help listeners to recognize an interleaved target melody—even when the pitch ranges are separated (Dowling, 1973a). However, this finding was obtained with relatively short, five-note sequences, and it might be that knowledge of the background would facilitate recognition of a target melody if both were longer and familiar. The advantage of greater length would be the availability of more structure for the listener to perceive. In any case, if listeners know what the relevant relations are among notes that define a particular melody, they can hear that melody even when it occurs in a highly confusing setting. That the perceiver engages in active seeking after structure is inferred from the fact that without prior knowledge of what the target melody is, the listener cannot identify it until the pitch ranges almost do not overlap at all; but once the melody has been identified, it can be perceived even as the context becomes confusing again.

In sum, what listeners know about familiar melodies includes their contour, pattern of relative interval sizes, and pattern of absolute interval sizes. Listeners do not perceive melodies in terms of the absolute pitches of their notes. Instead, they perceive a melody as being the same when its absolute pitches are all changed and crucial relations among them are maintained. The invariant properties of the melody are perceived over musically relevant transformations such as key changes and even over intervening notes and across octaves.

Perceiving a New Melody

What do we perceive of a melody we are hearing for the first time? Even if a familiar melody is not known by its constituent notes, what about a melody never before heard? Perhaps in this case, the notes of a melody that are its basic elements must be perceived prior to the higher-order properties of its structure.

A study by Dowling and Fujitani (1971) provides some information about what is perceived in an unfamiliar melody, although its generalizability to real melodies may be limited by the fact that the sequences were atonal (i.e., they were not in a particular key on pitches of a musical scale). The study is complicated and has several conditions. In the basic task, listeners heard an unfamiliar five-note melody. Then, after a short delay, they heard a second five-note melody, and they judged whether the second comparison melody was the same as or different from the first one. The specific criteria for their same and different judgments varied in different conditions. In some conditions, the comparison melodies to be judged same were identical in contour and interval sizes to the first melody, and those to be judged different were random collections of notes. In other conditions, the comparison melodies to be judged same were again identical in contour and interval sizes to the first melody, and those to be judged different preserved only the contour but not the interval sizes of the first melody. In still other conditions, the comparison melodies to be judged same preserved the contour of the first melody (but not the intervals), and those to be judged different were random collections of tones.

The design of the study and the task of the listeners were further complicated by the fact that in some conditions, the comparison melodies (both those to be judged same and those to be judged different) began on the same note as the first melodies, but in other conditions they did not. In these latter conditions, listeners were supposed to judge as same the comparison melodies that met the criteria for their particular version of the task, even though the actual pitches of the notes of the melody were all changed from the first to the second melody. Thus, although the form of the task that listeners performed was the same in all the conditions of this study, the particular judgment that they made varied from one condition to another. The extent to which listeners could or could not make the required judgments in the different conditions of this study provides information about what properties of the melodies they perceived and used.

First, what about the notes themselves? Listeners whose comparison melodies always began on the same note as the original melody could distinguish between identical comparison melodies and random collections of notes. They could also distinguish between identical comparison melodies and comparison melodies that preserved only the contour of the original melody. In other words, they correctly judged identical melodies to be the same, and they correctly judged random collections of notes (in the first condition) or melodies that preserved only the contour of the original (in the second condition) to be different than the original. This led the investigators to conclude that when the comparison melodies began on the same notes as the original, listeners' recognition was based on the actual notes themselves, since the notes of the melodies judged different were not those of the original melody, and the notes of the melodies judged same were those of the original. However, it is equally likely that recognition was based on the pattern of interval sizes, since these were also changed in both the random collection of notes and in the melodies that preserved only the contour of the original. In order to conclude that recognition is based on the notes themselves, a condition would be needed in which the comparison melodies to be judged same are identical to the original and in which the melodies to be judged different preserve the contour and relative interval sizes of the original.

From other conditions of the study, it is clear that listeners do use intervals or contour for recognizing melodies. For example, when all comparison melodies began on a different pitch than the original melody, listeners could easily recognize, and judge as same, identical melodies (i.e., melodies whose absolute interval sizes and contour were preserved) and distinguish them from random collections of notes. The relevance of contour for recognition is particularly evident in one final conditon—that in which all the comparison melodies began on different pitches than the original, and the listener's task was to judge as same melodies that preserved the contour and absolute interval sizes of the original and to judge as different melodies that preserved only the contour of the original. Listeners found this task very difficult and were no more accurate in their judgments than would be expected by chance. Since the contours were the same in the original and in both kinds of comparison melodies, we can conclude that the listeners probably perceived at least the contours of the original melodies.

Additional evidence that listeners perceive the contour of unfamilar melodies is found in another recent study by Dowling (1978b). This study also provides some interesting information about the effects of special training on what properties of unfamiliar melodies listeners perceive. The task and conditions were much like those in the study just described except that the melodies were more like ordinary melodies in that they were played on a piano (instead of being computer generated), and they were played in a particular key on the pitches of a musical scale. As before, the listeners heard one melody, and then, immediately after, they heard a second melody. The second, comparison melody always began on a different note than the original. Listeners were supposed to judge as the same comparison melodies that had the same contour and the same relative and exact interval sizes as the original. In other words, they were to recognize the melody when it was transposed to a different key, a task we know is quite easy for familiar melodies. There were three conditions in the study, and they varied in the kinds of comparison melodies that listeners were supposed to judge as different. In one condition, they were melodies that preserved the contour and relative interval sizes of the original but not the absolute interval sizes. In a second condition, they were melodies that preserved the contours but not the intervals—and they were atonal in that they were not played in any key. In the third condtion, they were melodies that preserved neither the contour nor the intervals of the original and were also atonal. Again, in all three conditions, the melodies to be judged same preserved the contour and the relative and absolute interval sizes of the original melody.

The subjects included a musically experienced group with an average of 5 years of formal musical training. This group, as well as a muscially inexperienced group, had great difficulty distinguishing the comparison melodies to be judged same from those that preserved the contour and relative but not absolute interval sizes of the original (the first condition). Both groups performed at about chance level in that condition, being equally likely to judge as same or as different the contour- and relative-interval-preserving melodies. On the other hand, both groups were quite accurate at distinguishing between the comparison melodies to be judged same and the atonal sequences of notes that preserved none of the relevant characteristics of the melodies (the third condition). Thus, both groups perceived at least the contour of the melodies, and probably neither group perceived their absolute interval sizes.

There was an important difference in the performance of the two groups in the conditon in which the comparison melodies to be judged different preserved the contour but not the relative interval sizes of the original melody (the second conditon). The musically inexperienced group performed at little above chance in this condition (Dowling, 1978b, p. 350); they did not consistently distinguish between the melodies that were the same as the original and those that preserved only the contour of the original melody. The musically experienced group, on the other hand, did perform at well above chance in this condition; they correctly identified the comparison melodies that were the same as the original, and they judged as different the comparison melodies that preserved only the contour of the original. Their ability to distinguish between the two kinds of melody suggests that they perceived both the contour and the relative interval sizes of the original melodies, whereas the musically untrained listeners perceived only their contour.

In sum, listeners perceive properties of the structure of short melodies even when those melodies are being heard for the first time. What are perceived are relational properties; ordinary listeners perceive the melodic contour, and listeners with musical training perceive the relative interval sizes as well. The role of the constituent notes themselves in the perception of new melodies is unclear. Whether simple repetition of the melody would enable the ordinary listeners also to perceive the relative interval sizes is an interesting and open question. It has been suggested that recognition can be based on perceiving the pitches themselves, but the evidence is not convincing. Other evidence about perception of single pitches is discussed in a later section.

The fact that the experienced listeners can perceive the more complex level of structure on first hearing a new melody suggests that a hierarchical description of the structure from simpler levels to more complex is indeed relevant for understanding what knowledge the perceiver acquires as a result of repeated listening and learning. Likewise, it would be interesting to know whether the level of structure described by the absolute interval sizes, which is perceived in familiar melodies, is also available in unfamiliar melodies to skilled or experienced listeners after a few repetitions.

Rhythm in Melodies

Thus far, the structure and perception of melodies has been discussed without regard to their rhythm. Yet it is difficult even to imagine or to try to reproduce a melody independent of its rhythm. By the conventions of the music we know, there are many joint constraints on the rhythm and pattern of pitch changes. The contour of a melody has predictable rhythms that are also associated with where in the melody they occur. (For a discussion of the movement of melodies, see Cooper, 1957, pp. 25–31). An obvious example is the slowing tempo at the end of a melody that often accompanies a falling or downward contour.

Rhythm is an important aspect of the structure of melodies, but its role in perception is largely unexplored. It has been suggested (Mainwaring, 1951) and recently demonstrated (Vos, 1977) that at least one aspect of rhythm in music, the measure, is difficult to follow accurately by tapping out the "beat" with an emphasis on the first beat. In one study of the perception of rhythm in melodies, listeners first heard 20 notes that were grouped temporally into 4 sequences of 5 notes each (Dowling, 1973b). Then they heard a 5-note test sequence and were asked to say whether the rhythm of the test sequence was like that of any sequences heard previously. The rhythm of some test sequences was like that of a grouped sequence, and the rhythm of other test sequences was like that across the boundaries of the sequences previously heard. As predicted, the listeners were much more accurate at recognizing the test sequences whose rhythm matched that of the sequences heard previously than they were at recognizing test sequences whose rhythm crossed boundaries of the groups heard previously.

Although these results imply the importance of rhythm in the perception of melodies, it is possible that some of the listeners were using information other than rhythm and another strategy to perform the task. All the initial five-note sequences began on middle C as did all the test sequences that matched the rhythm of the originals. However, the other test sequences began on a different note. Thus, listeners could increase their apparent accuracy for recognizing sequences whose rhythm matched those of the sequences they had heard simply by saying "yes" to all test sequences that began on the same note as those heard previously. Nonetheless, even if this study does not provide a clear demonstration of how rhythm affects perception of a melody, it is certainly reasonable to suppose that it does.

Perceiving Single Notes

We have already seen that there is little evidence that single notes are the basic units in which melodies are perceived, in spite of the fact that the notes of a melody are its obvious basic elements. Nonetheless, adults' perception and recognition of single notes have been studied extensively for the purpose of understanding how pitch is represented mentally. A typical procedure is to present listeners with two successive notes and to ask whether they are the same or different in pitch. Occasionally, the listeners are asked whether the second tone is higher or lower than the first, or they are instructed to adjust a tone to match their memory of the first tone (Olson & Hanson, 1977; for an analysis of the theoretical implications of different types of judgments, see Wickelgren, 1969). Often, other tones are interpolated between the two tones to be judged, and the effects of the interpolated tones on listeners' accuracy are assessed. The degree to which one's immediate memory of a tone shifts toward intervening tones depends on a number of factors, among them the duration and presentation rate of the tones themselves (Elliott, 1970; Olson & Hanson, 1977), the musical training of the listeners (Olson & Hanson, 1977), the specific pitch relations among the interpolated tones (Deutsch, 1972b) and between the interpolated and test tones (Deutsch, 1972a, 1972b), and the time intervening between the first tone and interpolated tones (Deutsch, 1975b). Deutsch concludes that memory for pitch is organized logarithmically and except over the very short term, that it is relations among pitches that are remembered rather than absolute pitches (Deutsch, 1972b, 1975a, 1975b). Thus, her conclusion reached after studying memory for pitches heard in nonmusical contexts is the same as that reached from analyzing how the pitch is perceived in a musical context (i.e., in a melody). It is relations among notes, then, rather than single notes that are the units in which a melody is perceived.

Before leaving the topic of single notes, it should be pointed out that there are situations in which single notes are perceived directly rather than in terms of their relation to other notes. Some people can recognize and label single pitches or notes when played on an instrument such as a piano, a skill known as absolute pitch. What the course of development of this skill is and what individual differences are associated with it are largely unknown. Students in some college music theory classes learn to make such identifications by learning to recognize and identify by name some standard intervals of the familiar music scale (e.g., a third, a fifth, etc.). However, that formal knowledge of the musical scale is not necessasry for the skill to be acquired. There is at least one successful report of training absolute pitch judgments using feedback training with correction and immediate knowledge of results (Lundin, 1963). A small percentage of young children also can demonstrate absolute pitch. A 9-year-old girl of my acquaintance could accurately name all the notes of the piano keyboard except the 15 or so at the very top and bottom of the range. Even on these notes, she made errors of only one or at most two notes (and the piano was not well tuned at the time). When questioned about how she made the judgments, she described the "names" as "just popping into my head." On one occasion she was trying to perform a task in which she was supposed to listen to pairs of intervals played on the piano and compare their relative magnitudes. She had difficulty with the task because she said that the names of the notes came into her head before she could make the comparison, and then, of course, she knew which interval was larger. This child had been taking piano lessons for a few years, and she did have a greater than average interest in music, but she did not have extraordinary talent.

Ward suggests that absolute pitch may be possessed by young children and then lost as a result of hearing melodies in different keys and learning to recognize them over transformations (Ward, 1970, pp. 429–430). This is an intriguing hypothesis, although it is unclear why the individual identity of notes should be lost just because relations among them are the basis for perceiving melodies. Ward (1970) suggests training people with reinforcement techniques to see if they can be "brought (restored?) to a level of proficiency equal to that of a typical 'possessor' of absolute pitch [p. 430]."

It seems, then, that the notes of melodies are not ordinarily perceived directly, but they are not unavailable to listeners either. They are rather easily perceived by experienced listeners and with more difficulty or in special circumstances by ordinary listeners—perhaps when they are especially motivated to do so. It would be interesting to know whether when listeners perceive the notes of a melody directly, they can simultaneously also attend to the relations among notes and perceive the melody itself—or whether the two tasks are simply incompatible.

Summary

The structure of a melody can be described as hierarchical and as including at least the following levels: notes, contour, relative interval sizes, and absolute interval sizes. We have seen that this hierarchical structure is relevant for understanding how listeners perceive melodies. The properties of a melody that are perceived are relational; they are defined by relations among its notes. When listeners hear a short melody for the first time, they perceive its contour, and they recognize it again as being the same melody if it has the same contour. Listeners with musical training hear more of the available information; they also perceive the relative interval sizes of a new melody. The hierarchical structure is also reflected in listeners' perception of a familiar melody wherein they perceive the absolute interval sizes of its notes. These relational properties of melodic structure are properties that are invariant over certain transformations of the notes of a melody. We can hypothesize that experience with these transformations provides the opportunity for identifying the properties that define a melody. The rhythm of a melody is also an aspect of its structure—governing its organization and imposing constraints that may also be reflected in how it is perceived. All properties of melodies are only available to perceivers over time. Thus one task for the future is to identify the particular patterns of change over time that allow perceivers to abstract the properties of a melody that are relevant for identifying it as the same melody when it is heard on different occasions and in different contexts.

NEW DIRECTIONS:
DEVELOPMENT AND LEARNING

Our understanding of melody perception is at a beginning. However, the analysis of the properties of melodies that are relevant for their perception suggests some specific strategies to be used and questions to be answered in order more fully to understand how we perceive these pleasant events. There are several directions that the study of melody perception might take. One that has both theoretical and practical significance is to consider the effects of experience—both controlled and naturally occurring—on how melodies are perceived. In the remaining sections of this chapter, I discuss some of the available information about the kinds of experiences that are relevant for perceiving melodies and suggest some questions to be answered as our study of this kind of perceptual learning proceeds.

The Development of Melody Perception

One strategy for learning more about how we perceive melodies is to study the course of its development. From first grade onward, the acuity of schoolchildren's pitch discriminations increases (Duell & Anderson, 1967; Madsen, Edmonson, & Madsen, 1969). There is also an increase with age in children's accuracy of discriminating between short melodies that vary by one note (Zenatti, 1970). In addition to the developmental trend toward greater accuracy, children also find it easier to discriminate between tonal melodies than between atonal melodies. Thus, by the early school years, children are already sensitive to some of the constraints of the music that is present in their ordinary listening environments. By asking other questions about their discrimination, we should be able to learn about what other specific properties of music children may be sensitive to. For example, are young children—even before they have had formal musical training—more sensitive to changes in a melody that specify a change in its key or that specify a change from a major to a minor key than they are to changes that do not?

A number of investigators have studied children's perception of melodies by asking them to reproduce the sequences—a procedure that has the disadvantage of confounding potential difficulties in production with what is perceived. Petzold (1963) observed a general increase in accuracy through the first six school grades. Burroughs and Morris (1962) tried to teach a group of 13-year-olds to sing a 12-note melody after hearing it played repeatedly on the piano. The children improved very little over several repetitions, but as they had no feedback about the adequacy or accuracy of their performance— except by hearing the melody played again—this is not a strong test of whether accuracy can be increased in such a task. From an early study, it *is* suggested that the singing "ability" of even nursery-school-age children (as well as their interest in musical activities) is improved by training and encouragement (Updegraff, Heiliger, & Learned, 1938). Simple repetition of melodies does affect children's preference judgments (Getz, 1966), and it has also been suggested that young children show preferences for listening to "good" songs (Blyler, 1960), which may refer to songs that adhere to the structure and conventions of Western music.

At how young an age can children distinguish between musical sounds and other sounds? Very young children can distinguish between sounds that are language sounds and those that are not. Do children distinguish musical from nonmusical sounds prior to being able to produce (i.e., sing) a melody? What kinds of sounds or sequences of sound are judged musical by young naive listeners? Answers to these questions will allow us to describe the early phases of melody perception.

What are the conditions in which infants or young children abstract the critical properties of a melody? What, for the immature listener, defines a melody as being "the same" when it is heard again? From what we know about early perception of visible events, we should expect that experience with the relevant transformations is important in providing opportunities for abstracting and learning to hear the properties that remain unchanged and that define the melody. Thus, we would expect that hearing the same melody played on different keys in different pitch ranges and by different instruments would facilitate attention to the properties of the melody in comparison to merely hearing the same melody played on the same notes in the same key and on the same instrument.

Some of the properties of the structure of a melody have been described as a hierarchy, and it has been argued that this hierarchy is relevant for understanding adults' perception of familiar and unfamiliar melodies—both ordinary listeners and those who have musical training. Does the hierarchy that describes the different levels of the structure of a melody also predict the course of development of perception of melodies? Do children rely more exclusively on contour information before they also begin to perceive the pattern of relative and then the exact sizes of successive intervals? Since interval sizes are much more precise information than contour, we should expect such a trend as an instance of the general developmental trend toward increasing precision of perception (Gibson, 1969). Do children perceive familiar melodies in terms of the same properties that adults do? For example, do children perceive the exact interval sizes, or does perceiving those properties of melodies require long experience—of hearing repetitions of melodies played in different keys, in different pitch ranges, on different instruments, and in different voices?

The words in songs that young children learn might serve several alternative functions, and knowing what their role is will help to identify the conditions in which the relevant perceptual learning takes place. The words might help define the structural units in which the melody is most appropriately perceived by directing children's attention to important aspects of the structure of a melody. On the other hand, the words might simply provide an obvious rule for an invariant property of a melody: If the words are the same, then it is the same melody.

Musicians' Perception of Melodies

Another strategy for understanding how we learn to perceive melodies is to study the perception of skilled listeners. There have been cases discussed previously in this chapter in which listeners with musical training demonstrated either finer discrimination or attention to more complex aspects of structure that eluded the hearing of more naive listeners. Another experimental example is the greater accuracy of musically trained listeners at judging whether two simultaneously heard melodies were canons (i.e., "rounds") or different melodies (Dowling, 1978a). In this case, the melodies did not even begin at their beginning! Obviously, there are many nonexperimental examples of musicians' ability to abstract more complex properties of the structure of the melody than nonmusicians can. Musically trained listeners can identify many more properties of the structure of a symphony; to name a few obvious examples— themes, themes under various transformations, themes played by different instruments successively, progressions, and transitions.

However, musicians not only perceive many more properties of the higher-order structure of music; they also perceive more of the structure of the elements of music—the single notes. For example, musicians can make judgments of similarity between notes on the basis of such complex aspects of musical tones as the number and onset times of partials (Miller & Carterette, 1975). What are the relevant experiences or training of musicians that allow them to hear these properties of the notes of music? Perhaps they simply have inborn special abilities. No doubt there are great individual differences in the ease with which people can learn to hear these properties, and some people probably never can. On the other hand, at least some music theorists assume that capacity of human listeners to detect the subtle properties of single notes in music. Consider the following statement from a college textbook (Cooper, 1957) for an introductory humanities course:

> It is quite possible through concentrated listening to detect some of the constituent tones of a musical sound which to the uninitiated ear is simple and

pure. If a low C is sounded vigorously on the piano, the fundamental will at first seem to be the only audible harmonic; but if one concentrates on hearing sounds higher than C, some of the more prominent overtones—the second G above, for example—will emerge so conspicuously as to render incredible the fact that they were previously unnoticed [p. 74].

Skilled listeners recognize the identity of a melody under many more transformations than do ordinary listeners. Ordinary listeners can recognize the identity of a melody transposed to different keys, played by different instruments, and sung in different voices. However, many musically relevant transformations involve vastly more complex changes of the melody. What transformations can a melody undergo that will allow a listener, with sufficient practice, to abstract the critical relations and identify it as the same melody? Conversely, under what transformations is a melody's identity preserved only for a listener such as a musician who has many years of specialized practice and extraordinary knowledge about the structure and rules of construction of music? If we can answer these questions, we will learn a great deal about the conditions and ordinary limits of the perceptual learning that occurs when we learn to perceive the very complex properties of melodies. In order to increase our understanding of how we perceive melodies, we need to know more about what the particular transformations are that leave the basic properties of the melody intact and available for the listener, and we also need to know what the relevant conditions are for the listener to learn to perceive those basic properties.

Rhythm in the Development of Melody Perception

Since rhythm describes the temporal organization of a melody, it may affect directly the units or segments in which it is perceived. Furthermore, since it is a salient aspect of a melody, it may have differential effects on how melodies are perceived over the developmental course of melody perception. At the University of Minnesota, we are beginning to study how young children perceive a melody when they first hear it, and whether the segments or units in which it is perceived correspond to its structure—defined partly by its rhythm. The basic task is a simple one: Children listen to a segment of a song (e.g., 12 to 15 notes). Immediately after, they hear a short, three-note segment, and they judge whether the short segment occurred in the song they heard immediately before. Some of the short segments are taken from between structural boundaries of the song, and others are taken from across structural boundaries. Examples of structural boundaries are the ends of a phrase, a falling contour with a note of long duration at the end. We find that the children are more accurate at recognizing segments from between boundaries of the song than from across its boundaries, which reflects the effect of the structure of the melody on how it is perceived.

In the situation just described, the children listen to songs intact, but in other conditions, we ask children to listen to "songs" played with a constant rhythm or to listen to "songs" with the original rhythm maintained but the melodic line distorted. By artificially separating these two kinds of components of the structure of a song, we want to learn something about the specific effect of the rhythm on how children perceive songs. Our initial findings suggest that the rhythmic organization of a song is an especially powerful property of its structure in affecting how it is perceived—at least for young children. These studies are just beginning, however, and we need to learn much more about how various aspects of the structure interact to affect how a song is perceived. That the melodic line and the rhythm do interact to affect perception is predicted, since these two aspects of the structure are bound up together and jointly constrained. A simple illustration of their joint effect on perception is the fact that musicians' judgments of the time intervals between notes is affected by the frequency ratios among the notes themselves (Divenyi, 1971). We now need to find out whether such interactions occur for children and for ordinary adult listeners as well.

The Contour in the Development of Melody Perception

Previously, the importance of the contour of a melody for ordinary adult perceivers was discussed. Is it an equally important aspect of the structure of melodies for younger, naive perceivers? I have argued that it is probably an aspect of a melody that is perceived directly rather than being perceived only after the separate notes of the melody. If the contour of a melody is perceived directly, then we should expect note changes that affect the contour to be more noticeable than comparable note changes that do not. Another study conducted at the University of Minnesota is relevant for this prediction. Adult listeners heard pairs of three-, four-, or five-note melodies. They first judged whether the second melody was identical to the first, and then if it was not, they judged (on a 4-point scale) how different it sounded. The second melody was either identical to the first or different by one note. The change of the note either did or did not affect the contour, and sometimes the changed note was at the beginning of the melody, and sometimes it was at the middle or the end. It was found that changes that affected the contour were perceived as more different than changes that did not. There was some indication (not significant statistically) that melodies that were different by a note at the beginning were perceived as being more different than those that were different by a note at the end. Such an effect would not be surprising, since the conventions of our music provide more constraints on the ends of melodies than on their beginnings. Since the ends are more predictable and redundant, listeners may simply attend more carefully to the beginnings of melodies than to their ends.

In music, the contour of a melody is sometimes transformed systematically in ways that allow skilled listeners still to recognize it. Dowling (1971, 1972) conducted one study in which he assessed listeners' accuracy at recognizing short melodies under various transformations of their contour. Among the transformations he used are inversions (in which the rising and falling directions of the intervals are reversed), retrogrades (in which the sequence of intervals is reversed, as from beginning to end), and retrograde inversions (in which the pattern of successive intervals is reversed in direction as well as the beginning-to-end sequence). Although these transformations are found frequently in the music of our culture, the listeners found it extremely difficult to recognize many of the melodies under the transformations. However, since the melodies were atonal rather than heard in a familiar scale, and since the interval sizes were smaller than those normally found in our familiar music, the recognition task may have been harder than is ordinarily the case in listening to real music. Clearly, though, melodies are more difficult to recognize under some transformations of their contour than under others. If we can manipulate systematically the conditions in which listeners can learn to recognize melodies under initially difficult transformations, we will learn a good deal more about the course of auditory perceptual learning.

Learning to Read Music Notation

The contour that is so important in what is perceived in a melody is also reflected directly in the music notation system, where differences in height on the staff correspond to differences in relative pitch. The contour is also reflected directly in how music is played, since most musical instruments are constructed so there is a direct spatial relation between the notation that is read and where notes are played. Do these relations affect how we learn to read music? At the University of Minnesota, we are currently studying the role of these relations in the initial phase of learning to read music. Children who do not know how to read music are taught to read and play a simple song on bells corresponding to four or five pitches. The learning conditions are varied in terms of whether the song learned is familiar, whether the spatial relation that is normally present between notation and mode of production is maintained, and whether the relation between notation and the contour of the song is maintained. After the children learn to play a training song, they are asked to play a new song that is composed of the same notes as the training song. This transfer task was selected because it corresponds to what a reader of music can do having learned the separate notes of the pitch notation system and where they are played on a given instrument (i.e., having learned the note–keyboard correspondences). The results of our first study imply that the spatial relation between the notation system and the keyboard may be *more* important in an early phase of learning to read music than the specific auditory feedback provided by the relation of the notation and the contour.

When the spatial relation that is normally present between the notation system and the keyboard is disrupted (by rearranging the spatial order of the bells), learning is tedious and transfer is minimal. On the other hand, when the relation between the notation and the contour is disrupted (by making all the bells have the same pitch), learning occurs as quickly as it does in a normal condition. Furthermore, as in the normal condition, there is immediate transfer to a new song that is also maintained after at least 2 days.

Music notation specifies many things for a reader. For single notes, it specifies what note to play, when to play it, for how long to play it, how to play it (e.g., loudly, softly, accented), and so on. Furthermore, reading and playing single notes accurately as separate items is no closer to skilled reading of music than reading single letters is to skilled reading of text. There are redundancies in music notation, and there is a little information already available about how a skilled reader takes advantage of them. Bean (1938) presented melodies to adults tachistoscopically, at speeds that allowed only one fixation, and assessed how much of the melody could be read and how well it could be played. He found that melodies that were ascending in pitch, descending in pitch, or that followed important harmonic combinations (e.g., a major triad) were much more accurately or easily read than were irregular or less systematic sequences or those that contained a high percentage of sharps or flats.

In reading print, the eye–voice span expands and contracts in coincidence with structural boundaries of the text (Levin, 1979), and the same phenomenon has been demonstrated in music reading. Sloboda (1976) found that the eye–hand span was influenced by phrase boundaries in music notation (i.e., by progressions such as cadences that are constrained to the ends of musical phrases and that are highly predictable within the progression).

There are many questions to be answered about how one learns to read the music notation system. For example, how is the duration and interval notation that specifies rhythm learned by the beginning reader? This notation is more complex than that specifying pitch. It is also less isomorphic to the property of music that it represents. Do these characteristics affect the difficulty with which it is learned as a *system* compared to learning the system of the pitch notation that may be apparent to the naive reader from the start because of its straightforward relation to the contour of music?

As one begins to acquire some skill in reading music, how is the notational information organized or "chunked"? How large are the units in which the notation is read, and what information do they contain? How do the size and organization of the units change with increasing reading skill? What is the role of motor patterns in defining the units in which the material is read—for example, whether one is learning to read and play a piano, or a clarinet, or a violin? One aspect of music notation that is different from alphabetic text and also that is especially interesting is that it has a vertical organization—

specifying notes to be played simultaneously (for some instruments)—as well as a horizontal organization. By systematically varying what information is available in notation (e.g., by deleting some information and assessing its effect on reading and playing), we may be able to begin to describe how skilled readers use redundancy in music notation and what information they use to guide their playing.

SUMMARY AND A FINAL COMMENT

We perceive melodies not as a particular set of notes but as notes that stand in a particular relation to each other. Recognizing a melody over transformations of its notes is evidence that a perceiver has identified the invariant relations that specify that melody and not another. Furthermore, considering some structural properties of a melody as hierarchically organized is relevant for understanding how we perceive that melody and how we come to know it. As we become more skilled perceivers of music, we are able to identify more properties that remain invariant in exceedingly complex and interesting transformations. Skilled listeners can recognize a melody as being the same melody when it is transformed in ways that make ordinary listeners unable to recognize it as the same melody.

Although our knowledge of melody perception is still very limited, some things are clear about how the study of it might proceed. Seeking knowledge about how we perceive music requires careful analysis of the properties of music that may be relevant for its perception. We need to use musical material and to ask about its perception in situations and under transformations that are musically relevant. This caveat may be so self-evident as to be trivial, but in the procedure of many studies reviewed of how listeners perceive sequences of notes, the material to be listened to lacked the harmonics of the notes of music, and the sequences were atonal and not organized according to the constraints of real music. How listeners perceive such sequences may have limited generality for how we perceive the rich structure of melodies.

The property that this analysis began with is change—the fundamental property of all events—for it is changes that contain the information upon which our perception of music is based. Studies of perceptual development, observations of skilled musicians, and studies of the perception of different kinds of melodies will help us understand how we learn to perceive music. What are the conditions in which we learn the conventions of our music that determine how we perceive it? We will probably never be able to describe the requisite knowledge and aesthetic experience of listing to a great symphony nor all the processes required for an expert rendering of a performance of that symphony. However, our understanding of human perception can be advanced to the extent that we can learn how listeners perceive just some aspects of that symphony.

ACKNOWLEDGMENTS

Preparation of this chapter was supported by a grant from the National Institute of Child Health and Human Development to the University of Minnesota, Institute of Child Development (No. HD 05027). An early version of the chapter was written while the author was Visiting Professor at the University of Nijmegen in The Netherlands. The hospitality and interest of colleagues there is very much appreciated. The assistance of Steven Metz and Marsha Unze is also acknowledged with thanks. In addition, Margaret Hagen and Herbert Pick, Jr., have both made comprehensive and valuable comments for which the author is grateful.

REFERENCES

Attneave, F., & Olson, R. K. Pitch as a medium: A new approach to psychophysical scaling. *American Journal of Psychology,* 1971, *84,* 147–166.

Bean, K. L. An experimental approach to the reading of music. *Psychological Monographs,* 1938, *50*(6, Whole No. 226).

Blyler, D. The song choices of children in the elementary grades. *Journal of Research in Music Education,* 1960, *8,* 9–15.

Burroughs, G. E. R., & Morris, J. N. Factors involved in learning a simple musical theme. *British Journal of Educational Psychology,* 1962, *32,* 18–28.

Cooper, G. *Learning to listen.* Chicago: The University of Chicago Press, 1957.

Deutsch, D. Mapping of interactions in the pitch memory store. *Science,* March 3, 1972, pp. 1020–1022. (a)

Deutsch, D. Octave generalization and tune recognition. *Perception & Psychophysics,* 1972, *11,* 411–412. (b)

Deutsch, D. Musical illusions. *Scientific American,* 1975, *233*(4), 92–104. (a)

Deutsch, D. The organization of short-term memory for a single acoustic attribute. In D. Deutsch & J. A. Deutsch (Eds.), *Short-term memory.* New York: Academic Press, 1975. (b)

Divenyi, P. L. The rhythmic perception of micro-melodies: Detectability by human observers of a time increment between sinusoidal pulses of two different successive frequencies. *Research in the Psychology of Music,* 1971, *7,* 41–130.

Dowling, W. J. Recognition of inversions of melodies and melodic contours. *Perception & Psychophysics,* 1971, *9,* 348–349.

Dowling, W. J. Recognition of melodic transformations: Inversion, retrograde, and retrograde inversion. *Perception & Psychophysics,* 1972, *12*(5), 417–421.

Dowling, W. J. The perception of interleaved melodies. *Cognitive Psychology,* 1973, *5,* 322–337. (a)

Dowling, W. J. Rhythmic groups and subjective chunks in memory for melodies. *Perception & Psychophysics,* 1973, *14*(1), 37–40. (b)

Dowling, W. J. Dichotic recognition of musical canons: Effects of leading ear and time lag between ears. *Perception & Psychophysics,* 1978, *23,*(4) 321–325. (a)

Dowling, W. J. Scale and contour: Two components of a theory of memory for melodies. *Psychological Review,* 1978, *85,* 341–354. (b)

Dowling, W. J., & Fujitani, D. S. Contour, interval,and pitch recognition in memory for melodies. *The Journal of the Acoustical Society of America,* 1971, *49*(No. 2, Part 2), 524–531.

Dowling, W. J., & Hollombe, A. W. The perception of melodies distorted by splitting into several octaves: Effects of increasing proximity and melodic contour. *Perception & Psychophysics,* 1977, *21,* 60–64.

Duell, O. K., & Anderson, R. C. Pitch discrimination among primary school children. *Journal of Educational Psychology,* 1967, *58,* 315–318.

Elliott, L. L. Pitch memory for short tones. *Perception & Psychophysics,* 1970, *8,* 379–384.

Getz, R. P. The effects of repetition on listening response. *Journal of Research in Music Education,* 1966, *14,* 178–192.

Gibson, E. J. *Principles of perceptual learning and development.* Englewood Cliffs, N.J.: Prentice-Hall, 1969.

Gibson, E. J. *The ecological optics of infancy: The differentiation of invariants given by optical motion.* Presidential Address presented at the meeting of Division 3 of the American Psychological Association, San Francisco, August 1977.

Gibson, J. J. *The senses considered as perceptual systems.* Boston: Houghton Mifflin, 1966.

House, W. J. Addenda: Octave generalization and the identification of distorted melodies. *Perception & Psychophysics,* 1977, *22,* 601. (a)

House, W. J. Octave generalization and the identification of distorted melodies. *Perception & Psychophysics,* 1977, *21,* 586–589. (b)

Idson, W. L., & Massaro, D. W. *Octave convergence in melodic perception.* Paper presented at the meeting of the Acoustical Society of America, San Diego, November 1976.

Levin, H. *The eye-voice span.* Cambridge, Mass.: MIT Press, 1979.

Lundin, R. W. Can perfect pitch be learned? *Music Educators Journal,* 1963, *49,* 49–51.

Madsen, C. K., Edmonson, F. A., III, & Madsen, C. H., Jr. Modulated frequency discrimination in relationship to age and musical training. *Journal of the Acoustical Society of America.* 1969, *46,* 1468–1472.

Mainwaring, J. Psychological factors in the teaching of music. *British Journal of Educational Psychology,* 1951, *21,* 105–121; 199–213.

Miller, J. R., & Carterette, E. C. Perceptual space for musical structures. *Journal of the Acoustical Society of America,* 1975, *58,* 711–720.

Olson, R. K., & Hansen, V. Interference effects in tone memory. *Memory & Cognition,* 1977, *5,* 32–40.

Petzold, R. G. The development of auditory perception in musical sounds by children in the first six grades. *Journal of Research in Music Education,* 1963, *11,* 21–43.

Shaw, R., & Pittenger, J. Perceiving change. In H. L. Pick, Jr., & E. Saltzman (Eds.), *Modes of perceiving and processing information.* Hillsdale, N. J.: Lawrence Erlbaum Associates, 1978.

Sloboda, J. A. Visual perception of musical notation: Registering pitch symbols in memory. *Quarterly Journal of Experimental Psychology,* 1976, *28,* 1–16.

Updegraff, R., Heiliger, L., & Learned, J. The effect of training upon the singing ability and musical interest of three-, four-, and five-year-old children. *Iowa Studies in Child Welfare,* 1938, *14, Studies in Preschool Education,* pp. 85–131.

Vos, P. G. *Identification of metre in music.* Unpublished manuscript, 1977.

Ward, W. D. Musical perception. In J. V. Tobias (Ed.), *Foundations of modern auditory theory* (Vol. I). New York: Academic Press, 1970.

Wickelgren, W. A. Associative strength theory of recognition memory for pitch. *Journal of Mathematical Psychology,* 1969, *6*(1), 13–61.

Zenatti, A. Perception mélodique et acculturation tonale. Étude expérimentale de l'influence du sexe sur les performances d'enfants agés de 5 à 10 ans. *Scientific Aesthetics,* 1970, *7*(Nos. 1 & 2), *Special Section: Child and Adolescent Psychology,* 71–76.

IV PERCEPTION OF MEANING

7

Reading Silently and Aloud

Harry Levin
Cornell University

Reading is a private process. The consequences of reading such as memory for or comprehension of the text are readily available, but information about the ongoing process of reading is difficult to come by. The measurement of eye movements is the most obvious and the most thoroughly studied component of the reading process. Electromyography of the speech musculature during silent reading has been carried out, but the relations between implicit vocalizations and reading are obscure.

Oral reading—reading aloud—is easily arranged and observed, but researchers and practitioners are rarely interested in oral reading for its own sake but most often as observable behavior that may provide information about the process of silent reading. The essential question, then, is the nature of the relations between oral and silent reading. If these relations are obscure or complex or nonexistent, the interest in oral reading pales. If the two modes of reading are similar and their similarities and differences are understandable, our interest in oral reading is justified. The intention of this chapter is to review and evaluate the research in which oral and silent reading have been compared. The two modes of reading are compared on the following features: (1) nature of the text, (2) characteristics of the readers, (3) eye movements, (4) reading speed, and (5) comprehension and memory.

We can anticipate the principal points of view and the major cast of characters in this way. This summary paraphrases Anderson and Dearborn (1952). On one side are investigators such as Judd, Buswell, and Cole, who see the two modes as involving different processes. They emphasize differences in eye movements and reading speeds. Other investigators (e.g., Anderson & Dearborn; Rogers, & Swanson) believe that the processes are similar and, though accepting the eye-movement findings, dwell on the similarities of silent and oral reading. Those who read well in one mode do so in the other. Comprehension is similar as is the course of the development of the skills. Anderson and Dearborn conclude that silent and oral reading may be implicit and overt expressions, respectively, of the same underlying processes. This chapter is devoted, among other purposes to understanding that assertion.

THE NATURE OF THE TEXT

Judd's (1918) study was the only one that compared oral and silent reading as they were affected by typographic variations: the size of type. Three adult readers, two skilled and one a poor reader, read text printed in three sizes— standard type, twice as large, and half as large as standard. There were negligible differences in eye movements during silent and oral reading that were attributable to the physiognomic variations of the text. The results reinforced Judd's belief that reading in the two modes is similar and that the distance the eyes span depends more on the person's "central processing" than on the physical characteristics of the visual display.

There has been much conjecture and some research on the ways that the grammatical and meaning structure of the text influence oral and silent reading. Or it may be more to the point to say that the earlier interest was devoted to how the two modes created different conditions for taking advantage of the structures that did exist in the text. Accordingly, Clark (1915) and Bond and Tinker (1973) believed that in both modes, reading must occur in "thought units" that allow the organization of material in logical phrases, thus facilitating comprehension.

Judd (1918), Gray (1925), and Tinker (1965), in an earlier report, distinguish the two reading modes precisely by the nature of the units that the mode induces. In oral reading, because some attention must be given to making the sounds (to the articulatory mechanisms), the units may be speech units—that is, words. In silent reading, attention does not have to be divided between the eye and the voice, so there can be undivided attention to meaning, and the units can be larger and more meaningful—that is, phrase units: "Readers who move the lips in silent reading lose the advantage of rapid fusion of words into ideas which is made possible by focussing the attention entirely on the substance of the material being read without any obligation to pronounce the words either orally or to one's self" (Buswell, 1937, p. 87).

Notice that the implication in Buswell's writing is that units are built or fused rather than extracted or reorganized, two points of view that are extensively discussed by Gibson and Levin (1975).

Wanat (1971) reported a detailed analysis of eye movements of persons reading several types of grammatical constructions silently and aloud. The reading of right- and left-embedded sentences was compared (e.g., *The sculptor carved the chapel which was extraordinarily detailed* vs. *The sculptor who was very skilled carved the chapel*). Taken over all types of sentences, oral reading required greater amounts of visual attention than did silent reading. Oral reading took more time and required a larger number of fixations than did reading silently. The two modes of reading did not differ on various kinds of visual regressions.

Wanat (1971) also compared the silent and oral reading of active (*The boy hit the ball*) and passive (*The ball was hit by the boy*) sentences. Reading aloud required more visual attention as indexed by the amount of time spent on each sentence and the number of forward fixations, but the differences between oral and silent reading as already described tended to be similar for all sentences types. Regressive eye movements were different, however, for active and passive sentences. The regressions were most marked in the agent-deleted passives (*The ball was hit by the park*). There were more regressions for this type of passive sentence, but the differences occurred only in oral reading. In summary, when reading silently, the eye movements on all sentence types were similar, but regressions were more marked in the oral mode for certain kinds of passive sentences. There is no simple or obvious explanation for these findings.

The two reading modes have been compared for various languages. In Chinese, Ai (1950) reports that by the fifth and sixth grades, silent reading was superior by about one word per second. Gray (1958) summarizes findings from studies of various languages carried out by others as well as his own comparisons of 14 languages. Results from France and Germany showed silent reading to be faster than oral, beginning in about the fourth grade.

In Chinese (Hu, 1928), fiction was read aloud at the rate of about 3.7 words per second and silently at 5 words per second; nonfictional prose was read aloud at 3.7 and silently at 4.2 words per second; and for poetry, the rates were 2.9 (aloud) and 3.4 (silently) words per second. Similar results are true for Japanese. The results from writing systems that contain ideographic elements must be compared cautiously if at all to alphabetic systems (Gibson & Levin, 1975). More detailed comparisons of poetry would be interesting, since certain types of poetry are designed to be read aloud, making use of stress, rhythm, and rhyme, which should facilitate oral reading. The small amount of information we have suggests that poetry is read more slowly than prose in both modes.

As may be expected, there were language-to-language variations among Gray's 14 languages, though some consistencies are notable. Comprehension scores after oral and silent reading were found to be about equal in all cases. The durations of visual fixations were longer during oral reading than during silent reading in all languages, but the average number of words recognized per fixation varied among the languages. For English and French, the span of recognition (fixation to fixation) was larger in silent reading; in Korean, the oral mode was longer; for the others, the two spans were similar. There were more regressions during oral reading for all languages but Korean and Burmese. We note again that the foregoing findings are difficult to explain without reflection on the nature of the writing systems. Gray asserts that the number of regressions was not affected by the language's orthography, by topographical variations such as printing text without spaces between words, or by the numbers of words needed to express the same idea in the various languages. He cites the following reasons for regressions in oral reading (in addition to the reasons that also exist in silent reading): (1) to check pronunciation and the order of words, (2) to determine the correct inflections, and (3) to allow the voice to catch up to the eye.

Gray concludes that surface characteristics of the text have little influence on oral vs. silent reading. Rather, the differences are due to ways in which reading has been learned (e.g., the Hebrew and Arabic readers reported that they had been taught to pay detailed attention to the text) and to the "syntactic–semantic" characteristics of the text. In summary, one can say that although the relations differ somewhat from one language to the next, except for comprehension, silent reading is the more efficient of the two modes.

CHARACTERISTICS OF THE READERS

Ages

In this section, we review the developmental courses of oral and silent reading. Pintner and Gilliland (1916) devised a score—the reading value—to compare the two modes of reading by groups of various ages. The reading value is the number of correct ideas recalled after reading a passage, divided by the number of seconds needed to read the selection—a sort of piece of idea per second. Taking apart the components of the ratio, the high school and college students read silently faster than orally. The other grades show no differences. "This would seem to suggest that increase in rapidity of reading comes relatively late and that with children silent reading differs from oral reading merely in the fact that the words are not pronounced aloud and there may be in this silent reading almost as much articualtion as in oral reading" (Pintner & Gilliland, 1916, p. 204).

The number of ideas reproduced was about equal for both types of reading in all groups. Silent reading led to substantially higher "reading values" for college students and high schoolers. Among the younger students, the silent–oral differences were trivial or nonexistent.

Most researchers report that in the early grades, the rates of reading silently and aloud are similar or that oral is faster (Ai, 1950; Cole, 1938; Gray, 1925;

Oberholtzer, 1915; Stone, 1922). Oberholtzer believes that oral superiority is due to young children's dependence on sound for comprehension. Given the variations in materials and methods, it is not surprising that there is little agreement about the ages at which the rate of silent reading surpasses oral. Judd (1918) thought that a child's silent reading resembles the adult's reading aloud. The implication is reasonable in that oral reading requires the adult to attend to smaller units of text, which is characteristic of a child's reading regardless of the mode.

Besides the generalization that reading rate is similar in both modes for young children, there is considerable variation as to when children read silently more quickly than aloud: at the end of the first or the beginning of the second grade (Cole, 1938); in the third grade (Stone, 1922); in the fourth grade (Ai, 1950); or in the second to the fourth grade (Gray, 1925). At some deviance from these findings, Pintner and Gilliland (1916) report that the differences in rate did not occur until high school.

The developmental curves of reading rate add to the findings of the crossover points of the two modes. Eye-movement records provide the basic data. Researchers report similar courses of development of the recognition span (saccade length) for oral and for silent reading. There is rapid growth in length of "span" until the fourth grade, followed by a plateau until the middle of high school when a smaller increase in saccade length occurs (Buswell, 1920; Gray, 1925; Stone, 1922). The curves for both reading modes are similar, with oral reading below silent reading. Buswell (1922) explained:

> The principal significance of a comparison of the oral and silent curves lies in the fact that throughout the grades, at least above the first, the silent-reading process makes possible or stimulates broader recognition units, while in oral reading the use of these wide fixations is inhibited.... In oral reading some attention must be given to each word as it is pronounced [p. 39].

The growth in regularity of eye movements, as measured by the number of regressions per line, is similar for oral and for silent reading (Gray, 1925; Stone, 1922). There was a rapid increase in regularity through the fourth grade. The regularity was greater for silent reading, and the differences between the two modes increased wtih age.

To understand the pedagogical implications that were drawn from the studies of eye movements while reading aloud or silently, one must be informed about the importance attached to eye movements in the twenties. Skilled readers exhibited smooth eye movements, so that training in moving one's eyes while reading was thought to be critical in learning to read. Hence, if oral reading showed some benign forms of eye movements, reading aloud was applauded as a necessary skill for mature reading. The following statement is more or less typical: "Consequently, until the child has reached a certain stage of maturity in reading habits, the development of fluency in oral reading is an aid in establishing good eye-movements" (Stone, 1922, p. 16). However, McDade (1941) argued that oral reading, which is usually taught first in school, hinders silent reading—the more efficient mode.

Reading Skill and Oral/Silent Reading

Do people who read well out loud also read well silently? Most investigators report that those who do well in one mode of reading also do well in the other. Gray's (1916) statement is characteristic: "A careful study of individual records shows clearly that those pupils who are able to move forward quickly in oral reading are the pupils who read most rapidly silently [p. 184]." Swanson's (1937) is the most thorough study of this question. His subjects were 70 poor silent readers and 10 good silent readers selected according to their scores on the Iowa Silent Reading Test. There was some correlation in the comprehension scores of oral reading with the silent comprehension by which the groups were selected, indicating again that readers remember equally well from both modes. There was little difference in the rate of oral reading between good and poor silent readers. Poor silent readers made more oral reading errors than the more skilled group.

The foregoing study was elaborated by Anderson and Swanson (1937). The eye movements during oral and silent reading were compared for poor, unselected, and good readers. The patterns of eye movements were most similar for the poor readers, less so for the unselected group, and most dissimilar for good readers. The authors conclude: "It follows that the central processes occurring in the two types of reading are more intimately related in poor readers than in average or good readers [p. 63]." If by "central processes" the authors mean general ability, it is not surprising that poor silent readers do poorly in many intellectual tasks. Also, the differences between good and poor readers was greatest for silent reading, because the demands of oral reading, such as articulation rate, put a ceiling on performance for both groups. Further, poor readers may still be using oral reading habits in their silent reading, thus exaggerating the similarity in the performance in the two modes.

Jones and Lockhart (1919) inadvertently demonstrated a substantial correlation between oral and silent reading. They drew four groups—a *small* group that performed well orally but poorly on the silent test; a *large* group that did well on both; a *large* group that performed poorly on both; and a *small* group that did well on the silent test but poorly on the oral one. This pattern of frequencies demonstrates a relation between the two reading modes. The study, though, may be faulted on the tests used, which seemed to compare silent reading comprehension with oral reading pronunciation.

Early researchers characterized good and poor readers in terms of their "perception accuracy," but it is difficult to know what they meant by this archaic concept. Presumably, they were saying that good readers are less bound by the text, whereas poor readers attend to small units (words?). The ability to use larger-than-word units implies attention to meaning as a direct act of reading, the use of so-called central processes. Good readers, compared to their less able fellows, evidenced higher degrees of perception accuracy in both silent and oral reading.

EYE MOVEMENTS DURING
ORAL AND SILENT READING

Almost from the beginning of the research concern with oral and silent reading, recording and interpreting of eye movements represented the most "scientific" study of the reading process. It is not surprising, therefore, that a number of scientists recorded eye movements during the two modes of reading. The results are fairly consistent. There are more fixations in oral than in silent reading (Judd, 1918; O'Brien, 1926; Schmidt, 1917). Buswell's (1937) explanation is reasonable: "Oral reading necessarily requires attention on each individual word since every word must be pronounced, whereas in silent reading certain words play a small part in the total composite meaning and may be passed over with only a small amount of attention [p. 86]."

Wanat's (1971) study of oral and silent reading of sentences of varing gramatical structure has already been mentioned. Briefly, in reading right- and left-embedded sentences, oral reading required more fixations per line (2.8) than did silent reading (2.6). Active and passive sentences also required more fixations in the oral than in the silent mode (2.4 vs. 2.1 respectively).

Almost as consistent as the fixation results are those about regressions during oral reading (Gray, 1925; Schmidt, 1917; Stone, 1922). Oral reading is slower than silent reading, possibly because it may require more regressions in order to remember the earlier text. Regressions also provide information about appropriate sentence intonation, and they allow the voice to catch up with the eyes.

Wanat (1971) separated the regressions in terms of the types of sentences, and he also made a more detailed analysis of the regressive eye movements themselves. He reported no differences in regressions for silent and oral reading of left- and right-embedded sentences. Oral reading of active and passive sentences did not require more refixations and regressions, but more time was spent on regressions. This finding is particularly marked in agent-deleted passives (e.g., *The ball was hit by the park*). The reading regression times on such sentences were twice that of oral reading on all other sentences and several times the amount required for silent reading. Agent-deleted passives also required more regressions.

Wanat offered several explanations, none of them entirely satisfactory, for the longer regression times in oral reading. The less constrained locative form (*by the park*) must be given an intonation pattern different from the one appropriate for an agentive "by" phrase. This sequence, however, would require more processing time, not more regressive eye movements. A second solution is that the auditory form gives the reader further information that the word after *by* was not the expected word. This explanation implies that when there were no regressions, the conflict was not detected, and the word was incorrectly identified and misread. There is the further implication that there were many misreadings in silent reading, a conjecture that is not borne out by tests of comprehension. Wanat concludes that all we know is that different modes of reading different forms require different allocations of visual attention. The conclusion is certainly as true as it is unsatisfying.

Buswell (1920), in his classic research on the eye–voice span, varied the text in ways that provide data analogous to Wanat's. He studied eye movements during oral and silent reading of paragraphs containing words that may be pronounced in several ways depending on the context. An example of such a sentence is: "She had tears in her dress and also tears in her eyes [p. 87]." There were characteristic eye movements that accompanied any difficulties, and these "confused" eye movements were the same in oral and silent reading. "This shows that the eye-movements in both oral and silent reading are largely controlled by the recognition of meaning" (Buswell, 1920, p. 99).

One final comment about eye movements. Anderson and Swanson (1937) report that the differences in eye movements between the two modes of reading increase with reading ability. They also increase, at least slightly, with age and school grade.

The findings for "attention spans" or "spans of recognition" in oral and silent reading are analogous to the eye movement results, since they are derived from the number and pattern of fixations. Stated simply, that there are fewer fixations per unit of text is interpreted as the existence of longer spans. All authors report narrower spans in oral reading. Judd (1918) wrote: "In oral reading the eye moves from word to word, directing in this way the vocal apparatus as it utters each unit. . . . If the mind can grasp a phrase, that becomes the unit governing fixation [p. 21]." Cole (1938), on the other hand, assumes that the eye is always with the voice in oral reading and that the units of fixation are syllables. Cole's findings, since they fly in the face of much that we know about the eye–voice span, seem unlikely.

Smith (1971) using at least more modern terminology, believes that the limit in oral reading is four or five words, this being the amount that will fill short-term memory. This same limit does not apply to silent reading, because the reader does not have to identify every word. The stimuli can be organized into a more permanent form and stored in this form. In silent reading, then, short-term memory is not filled with individual letters or words but with meanings." If he [the reader] were able to fill his memory with meanings, he might well be responsive to dependencies extending over a dozen words or more [p. 198]." Chunking allows the reader to grasp meaningful segments and to store only their total meaning in short-term memory. This is not possible in oral reading where the reader must recall all the words seen.

As with eye movements, spans are wider in silent than in oral reading (Gray, 1925); good readers have larger spans in both reading modes (Tinker, 1965); in both modes, the spans are narrowed when the reader encounters difficulties (Buswell, 1920).

These findings are substantially confirmed even when other measurement methods for sizes of spans are used (Bouma & deVoogd, 1974):

> The higher span for silent reading found in the experiments probably indicates that silent reading proceeds less carefully in the sense that a lower proportion of words has to be identified as such.... correct oral reading of text seems to require nearly perfect recognition of each individual word (reading for reproduction), whereas silent reading proceeds somewhat more loosely (reading for meaning) [p. 26].

Bouma and deVoogd believe that the spans are similar in both modes—that is, the number of words simultaneously available for processing—but that the silent span is not directly available for measurment.

The main findings emerging from the studies of eye movements during silent and oral reading are these: There are more fixations when reading aloud; the distances between fixations are longer when reading silently; and regressions during reading depend on the complexity of the text in both modes, though there tend to be more regressions during oral reading.

Rate of Reading

The literature comparing the rate of reading aloud with the rate of reading silently is voluminous. All investigators report that silent reading is faster than oral reading (e.g., Buswell, 1937; Gray, 1925, 1958; Huey, 1968; Quantz, 1897; Schmidt, 1917; Wanat, 1971). Buswell suggests that it is not possible to read aloud at a rate faster than 250 words per minute, although silent reading may be as high as 600 words per minute. The differences in rate are universally explained by one or another physiological factor. Huey (1968), for example, pointed out that oral reading and speaking can occur only on the expiration of breath, wheras silent reading, which they thought involved inner speech, can occur during expiration and inspiration. Judd (1916) wrote that oral reading is limited by the speech musculature.

The rate ceiling imposed by the limits of the speech musculature occasionally reduce the difference in the speed of reading from one mode to another. Quantz (1897) found that if a reader moved his or her lips, the rate of silent reading would be low. The 10 slowest readers had almost double the amount of lip movements as the 10 fastest readers. Since the limits imposed by the vocal musculature are similar for all readers, the range of possible rates is much narrower for oral than for silent reading. Schmidt's (1917) summary is apropos:

> The very marked differences which are in evidence in the case of some individuals indicate very clearly that it is possible to make much greater distinctions between the two types of reading than are ordinarily made. The rate of oral reading, although subject to considerable variation is confined within relatively narrow limits because of its dependence upon the physiological mechanism involved in vocalization. Silent reading, on the other hand, is much more independent of physiological factors, though by no means entirely so, since the great majority of readers are dependent upon the so-called inner speech of reading [p. 82].

MEMORY AND COMPREHENSION
AFTER ORAL AND SILENT READING

Memory is usually measured as the readers' accuracy in reproducing the materials read; comprehension is measured by the ability to answer questions about the text. Memory is certainly implicated in comprehension, although it is possible to reproduce by rote with little or no real understanding.

In four of the five studies of memory, the same methods were used: Passages were analyzed into the number of "points" or "thoughts" or "ideas" each contained. Equal numbers of passages were read silently and aloud. Pintner (1913) reported that the average number of points reproduced after oral reading was 15 vs. 18 after silent reading. Pintner theorized that the differences would have been larger if the children had received some training in reading silently. Two additional studies yielded the same results (Mead, 1915, 1917). Pintner and Gilliland (1916) found no differences between the two modes in number of ideas remembered.

Memorizing poetry is a special kind of task. The results depend on whether the verse is to be recalled orally or in writing. Poetry provides the opportunity for the memorizer to use rhythm to chunk the text and to use rhyme as a mnemonic device. Woody (1922) reported that memorization of poetry as well as speed of reading (contrary to results previously reported) was superior for oral reading. However, the mode of testing used in the study has been questioned, and the fact that those who performed well in one mode did so in the other also suggests high overall subject ability, which may have affected results.

Controversies over whether one understands text better during oral reading compared to silent reading have appeared in the literature for many years. Some conjectures about the superiority of oral reading include the belief that the added auditory stimulation aids comprehension. An obvious contrary hypothesis holds that the requirement of making sounds—attention to vocalizing—detracts from comprehension. The possibility of no differences is based on the assumption that comprehension depends on central rather than peripheral factors. Another hypothesis is that skilled readers better understand materials read silently, whereas poor readers profit from reading aloud, presumably because of the contribution of the second modality as well as the focused attention required by oral reading.

Consensus was that attention paid to vocalizing detracted from the attention to understanding what was read. Jones and Lockhart's (1919) conclusion was typical: "The necessary innervations to the vocal organs tend to inhibit the nerve currents stimulating thought processes.... The visual impression of the printed word sets off the speech reaction, but in doing so inhibits thought reactions [p. 590]." This point of view was generally shared (Buswell, 1937; Cole, 1938; Gray, 1925; Judd & Buswell, 1922; O'Brien, 1926; Stone, 1922).

Attention to articulation is likely to occur in a test situation where a subject tries to enunciate clearly and pronounce correctly. Buswell (1927) found a situation that most of us would agree requires extraordinary attention to articulation probably to the detriment of understanding. The subjects were instructed to read aloud and to understand a passage in a foreign language that they were studying. The subjects said they paid attention to the pronunciation rather than to the meaning of the text.

More recent research (e.g., Anderson & Swanson, 1937; Gray, 1958; Swanson, 1937) show consistently that there is little difference in the comprehension of materials read orally and silently. Rogers (1937) reported no differences in comprehension after three experimental variations. In the first, subjects read for a fixed length of time; in the second, they read a fixed amount of material; and in the third, they had various amounts of time during which to read. The slight advantage of silent reading was lost as the readers had more time, but there was no progressive improvement with increases in time. "The notion that good but not poor readers are handicapped by oral reading because the latter have never relinquished their early habits is not supported by this research [p. 397]."

Poulton and Brown (1967) found no clear differences in comprehension. They questioned the idea that attention to vocalizing reduces comprehension. "But since reading aloud is a highly overlearnt skill, after approximately 150 words she was able to programme her [the reader's] vocal output satisfactorily. It could then continue to run with the minimum of attention, leaving her more free to concentrate upon storing the information in the passage [p. 221]."

Questioning the other supposed advantage of reading aloud—the bimodality practice through sound and vision—Smith (1971) emphasized that the reader still must extract the meaning from the words: "The meaning of a language is no more given directly in its sound than it is available in the surface structure of writing [p. 200]." Later in the study he states, "There is another widespread misconception that spoken words have a kind of magical character; that their meaning is apparent the moment they are uttered [p. 207]."

The research on memory and comprehension, much of it carried out many years ago, does not give an unequivocal picture of findings, though it is clearer than the picture for many other topics of this chapter. In testing memory for materials read, silent reading in most cases was superior to oral reading. One wonders, though, whether the results would have been different if oral memory tests followed oral reading. Early findings on comprehension favored silent reading, and these findings were usually explained by the supposition that attention given to vocalization detracted from understanding the text. In more recent research, with more sophisticated methods, differences have not been found between the two modes in comprehension, and it has been concluded that the central processes underlying comprehension are similar in both types of reading.

The intention of this chapter was to summarize the similarities and differences between silent and oral reading in order to assess whether oral reading, which is more available to observation, can be used as a guide to the processes of silent reading. The similarities warrant attention to oral reading, although the two modes are sufficiently different to require caution in extrapolating from one to the other. Anderson and Dearborn's (1952) conclusion, although encouraging, is probably too optimistic: "The evidence suggests rather that silent and oral reading are significantly related and have many elements in common. An alternative hypothesis, therefore, is that oral and silent reading may be the overt and implicit expressions, respectively, of the same fundamental process [p. 160]."

What are the similarities? First, all the curves plotting the development of reading skills show parallel curves for the two modes, though skill in silent reading develops more rapidly. Second, those readers who perform well in one mode also do well in the other. Third, memory for text is superior after silent reading, though text is understood equally well in both modes. Fourth, perception of text as indexed by eye movements is similar for both modes. More skilled readers use more efficient eye movements when reading both silently and aloud. Fifth, difficulties in reading material lead to characteristic regressions, and sometimes to what Buswell (1920) called confused eye movements, during both types of reading. Sixth, as was shown by the eye-voice-span studies, skilled readers process the text in systematic or meaning units. Most investigators infer that the "idea" or "meaning unit" is operative in silent reading. Therefore, reading in either mode involves extracting the meaning from the text, and beyond the superficialities of vocalizing, many of the findings hang together if we assume that higher-order processes are simialr for silent and for oral reading.

ACKNOWLEDGMENTS

I wish to thank Anne Buckler Addis for her help with this paper, which is adapted from *The Eye-Voice Span* (Cambridge, Mass.: M.I.T. Press, 1979).

REFERENCES

Ai, J. W. A report on psychological studies of the Chinese language in the past three decades. *The Journal of Genetic Psychology*, 1950, *76*, 207–220.

Anderson, I. H., & Dearborn, W. F. *The psychology of teaching reading*. New York: Ronald Press, 1952.

Anderson, I. H., & Swanson, D. E. Common factors in eye-movements in silent and oral reading. *Psychological Monographs*, 1937, *48*(3), 61–69.

Bond, G. L., & Tinker, M. A. *Reading difficulties—their diagnosis and correction* (3rd ed.). Englewood Cliffs, N.J.: Prentice-Hall, 1973.

Bouma, H., & deVoogd, A. H. On the control of eye saccades in reading. *Vision Research*, 1974, *14*, 273–284.

Buswell, G. T. A study of the eye–voice span in reading. *Supplementary Educational Monographs*, 1920, *17*.

Buswell, G. T. Fundamental reading habits: A study of their development. *Supplementary Educational Monographs*, 1922, *21*.

Buswell, G. T. A laboratory study of the reading of modern foreign languages. *Publications of the American and Canadian Committees on Modern Languages* (Vol. 2). New York: MacMillan, 1927.

Buswell, G. T. How adults read. *Supplementary Educational Monographs*, 1937, *45*.

Clark, S. H. *Interpretation of the printed page*. Chicago: Row, Peterson, 1915.

Cole, L. *The improvement of reading*. New York: Farrar & Rinehart, 1938.

Gibson, E. J., & Levin, H. *The psychology of reading*. Cambridge, Mass.: M I T Press, 1975

Gray, W. S. A study of the emphasis on various phases of reading instruction in two cities. *The Elementary School Journal*, 1916, *17*(3), 178–186.

Gray, W. S. Summary of investigations relating to reading. *Supplementary Educational Monographs*, 1925, *28*..

Gray, W. S. *The teaching of reading and writing*. Chicago: UNESCO, Scott, Foresman, 1958.

Hu, I. *An experimental study of the reading habits of adult Chinese*. Unpublished doctoral dissertation, University of Chicago, 1928.

Huey, E. B. *The psychology of reading*. Cambridge, Mass.: M.I.T. Press, 1968.

Jones, E. E., & Lockhart, A. V. A study of oral and silent reading in the elementary schools of Evanston. *School and Society,* 1919, *10*(225), 587–590.

Judd, C. H. Measuring the work of the public schools. *Cleveland Education Survey* (No. 10). Cleveland, Ohio: Survey Committee of the Cleveland Foundation, 1916.

Judd, C. H. Reading: Its nature and development. *Supplementary Educational Monographs,* 1918, *10.*

Judd, C. H., & Buswell, G. T. Silent reading: A study of the various types. *Supplementary Educational Monographs,* 1922, *23.*

McDade, J. E. *Essentials of non-oral beginning reading.* Chicago: Plymouth Press, 1941.

Mead, C. D. Silent versus oral reading with one hundred sixth-grade children. *The Journal of Educational Psychology,* 1915, *6*(6), 345–348.

Mead, C. D. Results in silent versus oral reading. *Journal of Educational Psychology,* 1917, *8*(6), 367–368.

Oberholtzer, E. E. Testing the efficiency in reading in the grades. *The Elementary School Journal,* 1915, *15*(6), 313–322.

O'Brien, J. A. *Reading; its psychology and pedagogy.* New York: Century Co., 1926.

Pintner, R. Oral and silent reading of fourth grade pupils. *Journal of Educational Psychology,* 1913, *4*(6), 333–337.

Pintner, R., & Gilliland, A. R. Oral and silent reading. *Journal of Educational Psychology,* 1916, *7,* 201–212.

Poulton, E. C., & Brown, C. H. Memory after reading aloud and reading silently. *British Journal of Psychology,* 1967, *58,* 219–222.

Quantz, J. O. Problems in the psychology of reading. *Psychological Monographs,* 1897, *2.*

Rogers, M. V. Comprehension in oral and silent reading. *Journal of General Psychology,* 1937, *17,* 394–397.

Schmidt, W. A. An experimental study in the psychology of reading. *Supplementary Educational Monographs,* 1917, *2.*

Smith, F. *Understanding reading.* New York: Holt, Rinehart & Winston, 1971.

Stone, C. R. *Silent and oral reading.* Boston: Houghton Mifflin, 1922.

Swanson, D. E. Common elements in silent and oral reading. *Psychological Monographs,* 1937, *48*(3), 36–60.

Tinker, M. A. *Bases for effective reading.* Minneapolis: University of Minnesota Press, 1965.

Wanat, S. F. *Linguistic structure and visual attention in reading.* Newark, Del. The International Reading Association Research Reports, 1971.

Woody, C. The effectiveness of oral versus silent reading in the initial memorization of poems. *Journal of Educational Psychology,* 1922, *13,*(8), 477–483.

8 The Origins of Meaning in Perceptual Development

T. G. R. Bower
University of Edinburgh

One could argue that modern experimental psychology began with the problem of meaning. Certainly the question of how one particular item of sensory information can stand for—signify or represent—some other currently absent item of information preoccupied the early philosophers who laid the ground plan for much of our present-day field. Their answer to the problem was expressed in terms of the doctrine of association. We see that something is hard, without touching it, because in the past we have experienced the hardness of the thing while simultaneously experiencing its visual qualities. The doctrine of association has been applied in many areas of psychology, in particular to the acquisition of word meaning. The meaning of a word is supposedly acquired by association with the sensory qualities that that word represents. *Fire* evokes the sound of crackling, the sight of flames, and the feeling of heat.

Associationist accounts of word meaning have been severely criticized by philosophers and linguists (e.g., Fodor, Bever, & Garrett, 1974). These critiques, by and large, have not considered associationist accounts of the acquisition of perceptual meaning. This omission, in my view, leaves their alternative accounts of word meaning dangerously exposed. I return to this problem later.

Meantime, let us look at the associationist account. It appears to me to make a variety of assumptions about perceptual experience and the nature of representation that are by no means obviously true. The first assumption is that there are qualities of experience that are directly given. I find it difficult to expand "directly given" into anything more comprehensible. The assumption seems to be that some sensory qualities are directly experienced. They do not

183

require translation or mediation. Given the appropriate physical input, the structure of the human sensory apparatus, in a human of any age, will ensure registration of the appropriate sensory experience. There is no developmental change in the registration of these direct givens, nor should there be any cultural diversity whatsoever. Although one could use these criteria to isolate the directly given, no one has done so, as far as I know. Instead, "directly given" is equated with "psychologically simple," which has been understood as "chemically simple" and equated with "physically simple." Thus the constructs of physics came to dominate the construction of psychology.

It was this process of psychological analysis that led to the problem of meaning in the first place. The separation of the senses created the problem of intersensory meaning already described. Indeed the ongoing analysis produced for the first time an appreciation of the problem of word meaning. Prior to that, words, and names in particular, were considered essential properties of objects or events—like their color, size or loudness—and were presumed to be perceived in the same direct way.

Needless to say, the associationists did have a complex theory of meaning and its development. The core of the theory of meaning was a theory of representation. Representation in an associationist context must be understood in a very literal way, as re-presentation. An internal representation functions as a surrogate for an absent percept. Indeed in most associationist writing, the word reperception could be substituted for the word representation. Alternatively, as Ward (1918) proposed, we could substitute presentation for perception and then discuss presentation and representation. In this model, meaning grew very much as representation grew. Direct givens are represented by literal copies, stored in memory. Real objects and real events are represented by agglomerations of representations of direct givens. Word meaning is initially given by the association of a word with such agglomerations. Some words, however, come to represent abstract properties of classes of real objects or events. The details of how these higher-order words acquire meanings varies from theory to theory. The assumption that such higher-order meanings are acquired after first-order meanings is common to all theories.

Lest it be thought that I am merely setting up straw men, I should point out that the two major components of classical associationism are still with us, even if they are no longer as precisely associated as they once were. For example, the findings reported by Dodwell, Muir, and DiFranco (1976), Field (1977), Gordon and Yonas (1976), and McGurk, Turnure, and Creighton (1977) are seen by them as being consistent with the doctrine of separate senses, corresponding to the psychological or physical simples of associationism, in early life. Bruner (1966) has proposed yet again the hierarchy of meaning at the core of associationism; his argument is that in development, representation goes from literal copies, enactive or iconic representation, to more abstract symbolic representation. Bruner's is the most explicit version of this theory of the growth of meaning; I know of no one else who has proposed an alternative, psychologically coherent view.

The two essential components of an associationist theory of meaning are thus still alive and well and generating research. The two components are the theory of direct givens and the theory of a developmental hierarchy of representational systems. Indeed I think it significant that challenges to strict associationism have taken place within an associationist framework. Thus J. J. Gibson (1950) expanded the idea of what could be directly given—a line followed by many subsequent investigators, both psychologists and philosophers. An expansion of the range of information that can be directly given does not affect the assumption that there are direct givens. As long as that assumption remains, a theory of how behavior can be controlled by that which is not direct will be necessary. That theory will almost inevitably become something like an associationist theory, with one or another apparatus for the extraction of those higher-order features that are not directly given (see, e.g., Anglin, 1977). In this paper I propose that the whole enterprise is misconceived: Nothing is directly given; from the very beginning, perception is a process of representation; representation does not go from literal to abstract; rather, it goes from abstract to literal. In other words, I propose a theory of meaning as opposed to that of classical associationism as I can conceive.

In the account that follows, it is assumed that the meaning that an event has for an organism can be inferred from the behavior of the organism. It is further assumed that our inference about the meaning can be made more precise by comparing events across time. Thus, habituation experiments and transfer experiments are important tools in the analysis of meaning.

The key assumption in the theory I am criticizing is the assumption of the directly given. At this point, I should like to examine that assumption. As I said earlier, the major controversy in recent years has been over how much is directly given. Nativists typically assume that a great deal is directly given; empiricists, that rather little is directly given. The essential idea in both theories, however, is that there are some percepts that do not vary with experience or culture. These percepts are the building blocks from which the rest of perception or cognition is constructed. This remainder will show interpersonal variation depending on experience or culture. The notional core percepts vary between theories. All theories admit that the core percepts depend jointly on events in the world and the structure of the perceptual system of the experiencing organism. Nativists tend to assume that the core structure of the human perceptual system is that of the normal adult (the perceptual world of the newborn is thus very much like that of the adult); empiricists tend to maintain that the core structure is rather like the theoretical structures of a physicist (the world of the newborn is thus very different from that of the adult). For many present-day psychologists, these two positions seem to exhaust the theoretical possibilities (see, e.g., Gordon & Yonas, 1976; McGurk et al., 1977). They do not discuss the venerable[1] opponent of both of these positions, an opponent I shall refer to as differentiation theory, whose most distinguished modern proponent is E. J. Gibson. Differentiation theory is different in kind from nativism/empiricism, not least in its assumption that there is no variety of perceptual experience that is not subject to developmental variation. The differentiation theory thus strikes at the very root of nativism/empiricism, the idea of the directly given.

The development of intersensory coordination is a convenient paradigm to analyze the differences between these theories. Suppose, for example, we have a newborn baby in the light. Suppose we then present him with a sound that is off his midline to his right. What account will an empiricist give of the baby's experience? More important, what behavior would an empiricist expect of a newborn baby in such a situation? Straightforward modern empiricists such as McGurk et al. (1977) assume that the baby's response to such a presentation is, "There is a sound." Since they assume no intersenory coordination, they would expect no eye or hand movements—no behavior at all, in fact, save whatever autonomic correlates of auditory attention there are. What account would a nativist give of such an event? Since the newborn is supposed to be basically like the adult, the baby would presumably register the presentation as: "I hear a sound on my right." This, in turn, would produce: "Since sounds have sources that can be seen, I will look to the right to see what is making the noise." Nativism thus predicts that eye movements will be elicited by presentation of sounds in light.

What has a differentiation theory to say about such a simple event? An adult response in this theory is considered the end point of a differentiation process. It follows that the response of the newborn will be less differentiated than that of an adult. The major problem is to define "less differentiated." Recently, following Bateson (1972), I have found it convenient to do so in terms of the Theory of Types. Let us begin with an adult percept of our simple situation:

Level I: "I hear a sound coming from 60° to my right."
That statement is as differentiated or as complete a description of the event as one could wish. A less differentiated version of that might be:
Level II: "There is something happening 60° to my right."
This level of description is ambiguous about precisely what is happening on

---

[1]As far as I have been able to determine, the first differentiation theory of psychological development was offered by Duns Scotus (alternatively known as John the Scot) in the 14th century.

the right; it could be an auditory event or a visible event or both or neither. Less differentiated yet is:

Level III: "There is something happening to my right."

This level of description is ambiguous about both precisely what is happening and precisely where it is happening. The least differentiated level of description we shall consider is:

Level IV: "Something is happening."

These four statements are each of a different logical type. Specifically, where $\rightarrow$ = "implies," and $\sim$ = "not":

$$I \rightarrow II; \, II \rightarrow III; \, III \rightarrow IV.$$
$$\sim IV \rightarrow \sim III; \, \sim III; \, \rightarrow \sim II; \, \sim II; \, \rightarrow \sim I.$$

and IV $\rightarrow$ III or $\sim$III; III $\rightarrow$ II or $\sim$ II; II $\rightarrow$ I or $\sim$I.

A differentiation theory contends that the perceptual world of the young infant is less differentiated than that of the adult. In other words, the Level I description is not appropriate. What behaviors could we expect to correspond to Levels II, III, and IV? Level II should produce precise multimodal inspection of a location. There should be both eye movements and hand movements to the location, if these are in the child's repertoire. The same sort of behaviors should occur with Level III except that the exploration should be lateralized but imprecise; with Level IV, the movements should have no determinate direction.

Suppose now that we present an infant with a sound in the same way as before but this time in darkness. What will the three theories say about this? There is no change in the empiricist account; no nonauditory behavior should occur. What of the nativist account? In darkness, it should predict no eye movements, since the system should know that there is no possibility of vision in darkness. Differentiation theory, because it does not assume modality differentiation at this stage in development, by contrast predicts that behavior in darkness should be the same as behavior in light.

What accounts do the three theories give of developmental change? Nativism predicts no change. Empiricism predicts that eye and hand movements elicited by sounds, in light or dark, will become more and more likely as the baby grows older. Differentiation theory predicts that such movements will become less and less likely, particularly in darkness.

What are the data? First of all, it is clear that newborn infants do turn their eyes toward the source of a sound in light (Alegria & Noirot, 1979; Turkewitz, Birch, Moreau, Levy, & Cornwell, 1966; Wertheimer, 1961) and in darkness (Mendelson & Haith, 1976). Differentiation theory is the only theory that gives an account of this. Which level is an appropriate description? The movements are correctly lateralized (Level III) and indeed take some account of the amount of movement required in that presentations that demand very large eye movements are less likely to elicit eye movements at all (Alegria & Noirot, 1979; Macfarlane, 1977; McGurk et al., 1977). However, the precision does not approach that demanded by Level II (Bechtold & Salapatek, 1976–1977). Level III thus seems the most likely description of the way infants respond to sound presentations.

What of developmental changes? Reaching for noise-making objects in darkness declines with age (Wishart, Bower, & Dunkeld, 1978). Looking at sound sources in darkness likewise appears to decrease if we compare the results of Mendelson and Haith (1978) with those of Wishart et al. (1976). What happens in light is less clear.

The data on auditory–visual and auditory–manual coordination thus support a differentiation theory as do the data on visual–manual co-ordination. In a differentiation theory, a seen object does not exist as such in the perceptual world of the young infant. A visible object is simply an event in a place, to be explored multimodally or amodally. Thus, visually presented objects should elicit compulsive manual exploration in young infants but not in older ones. This does seem to be the case (Bower, Broughton, & Moore, 1970; Schaffer & Parry, 1969, 1970). Field (1977) and Dodwell, Muir, and DiFranco (1976) have argued for the opposite position. However, Dodwell's study is seriously flawed (Bower, Dunkeld, & Wishart, 1979), and Field's data do not support his conclusions. In particular he found that old infants are less likely to try to grasp seen objects than are younger infants (Table 8.1), a result in accord with differentiation theory.

The study of reaching, too, supports a differentiation theory. Reaching in adults is an example of visual–motor coordination. In infants it is not, presumably because the visual sense and the proprioceptive sense are not yet differentiated. Thus the reaching behavior of young infants is not disturbed if

TABLE 8.1
Number of Subjects Showing Each of
Three Categories of Hand Shaping When Reaching

Age Group	N^a	Fisted[b]	Convergent	Divergent
3 months	6	5	5	0
5 months	6	3	4	6
7 months	8	1	6	8

[a]Number of subjects who made at least one oriented hand extension (from Field, 1977).
[b]A fisted response means that the hand has closed before reaching the object; a convergent hand movement means that the hand is closing before it gets to the object; divergent means that the hand stays wide open (fully flexed) until it reaches the object. A divergent hand posture thus corresponds to a tactually elicited grasp, whereas fisted and convergent correspond to visually elicited grasping.

they cannot see their hand, whereas that of older infants is (Wishart et al., 1978; Yonas & Pick, 1975).

Some of the best evidence in favor of a differentiation theory comes from studies of the blind child. What could an empiricist make of data indicating that a blind baby will "look" at sound sources, "look" at his or her hand, reach for noise-making objects, and then suddenly stop all these behaviors (Bower, 1974; Freedman, 1964; Urwin, 1973)?

What has all of this to do with the development of meaning? It seems that the young baby perceives the world in a less differentiated way than the adult does. Reference to the Theory of Types will be convincing evidence, I hope, that "less differentiated" as I have used it means "more abstract" or "less literal." These percepts are not direct copies of the world; they are *representations* of the world.

The point may be reinforced if we look at experiments in which representation in a conventional sense is demanded. Consider one experiment on habituation to presentations of a cube (Day & McKenzie, 1973). One group of babies was given ten 20-second presentations of a constant cube in a constant orientation. They duly habituated. A second group was shown a series of life-size photographs of the cube, each presentation showing the cube in a different orientation. They did not habituate. A third group was shown the real cube in a different orientation in each presentation. They habituated; indeed their rate of habituation was indistinguishable from that of the first group, who saw the real cube in a constant orientation. This is an important experiment in many respects. For our present purpose, let us focus on the nature of the representation that mediated habituation in the third group. It cannot in any sense have been a literal icon of the presentation, for if it had, the difference between presentations would have militated against habituation. The representation must have been something quite abstract, as abstract as a word.

Caron, Caron, and Carlson (1977) completed a similar experiment producing similar results. In their study, a constant form was presented in a constant orientation to produce habituation. The shape, or the orientation, or both were then changed. This last change was arranged so as to minimize the iconic difference between habituation and test presentation. Indeed in terms of retinal image, there was no difference at all between the two. Despite this, it was the dual change that produced the greatest recovery of attention.

Similar conclusions, albeit for older infants, can be drawn from an experiment of Bryant (Bryant, Jones, Claxton, & Perkins, 1972). A pair of objects were used—one an ellipsoid and the other an incomplete ellipsoid of the same dimensions as the first but with a deep ridge cut into the top of it. Each contained a bleeper that would emit a sound when the object was tilted. On the first presentation, the infant saw both objects, but neither bleeper was activated and the infant was not allowed to touch either of the objects. One of the objects was then presented to the infant in such a way that he or she could feel but could not see it, and the experimenter caused the object to produce a noise. The final presentation consisted of a vision-only presentation of both objects again, but this time the infant was allowed to choose one of the toys. The infants showed themselves able to distinguish visually between the objects on the basis of the tactual information given in the previous presentation, preferring to choose the toy that they now knew to be capable of producing a noise. The babies must have recognized the rattle as "rounded with a piece cut out," a rather abstract description that can be based on visual or tactual input equally well.

I propose that there is a similar kind of representational process underlying cognitive development: As infants grow older, they progressively elaborate their internal descriptions of events to make them more specific. Such a change in favor of more specific description acts to decrease the likelihood of a smooth transfer from one skill to another, thereby increasing the likelihood of a seeming repetition. Consider the problem presented to an infant by the sight of an object entering one end of a tunnel and emerging from the other end. Initially, the infant may refuse to look at this kind of display. Once recognizing that the object he or she sees at either end of the tunnel is the same object (which is no easy feat) the infant must then figure out what is happening to the object when it is out of sight.

I propose that the infant's first discovery is that one object can go inside another and still exist. That is a relatively abstract hypothesis about the world; it will not particularly improve the infant's skill at tracking the object through the tunnel. What the hypothesis will do is allow the infant to shift that understanding from the tracking situation to other situations. Suppose an infant who understands this hypothesis now sees a toy placed in one of two cups. The infant should now know that the toy is inside a specific cup and therefore be able to retrieve it. If the toy is then placed in the other cup, he should also be able to retrieve it from inside that cup. That is exactly what happens if the infant is given this transfer task (Wishart & Bower, 1978).

If the infant is then given more practice with the tunnel-tracking task, however, something quite different happens. After a while, he readily works out specific sensorimotor rules enabling him to track the object quite efficiently. He shows by his behavior that he knows that in order to see the object that has vanished at the left end of the tunnel, he must look for it at the right end of the tunnel after x seconds. His knowledge of the spatial and temporal nature of the tracking task becomes very detailed indeed. Infants who have had weeks of experience with tracking tasks do not spend much time looking at the display, but they can move their eyes unerringly to catch the object at any point in space.

If such infants are again given the toy-in-the-cup transfer task, they do better than infants with no experience in the tracking task. The experienced infants do not do as well, however, as other infants who are given the transfer task after having had briefer tracking practice. Specifically, if the infant watches the toy being placed inside the second cup after a few trials of seeing it placed inside the first cup, he or she will still tend to look for it in the first cup. Thus the infant seems to repeat a phase in development, failing to understand for a second time the relation between two objects when one is inside the other. What causes such a repetition, I suggest, is that with so much practice at tracking an object going through the tunnel, the infant has evolved such specific rules in dealing with the tracking task that he is actually hampered by them when he is faced with a similar but not identical situation. An infant who has had less practice with tracking has the initial conceptual discovery (one object can go inside another and continue to exist) still at the forefront of his mind to help him perform the transfer task.

This kind of model of cognitive development can explain puzzling instances of repetitive processes in which young children give correct verbal responses to a problem in situations where older children give incorrect responses (Maratsos, 1973; Mehler & Bever, 1967). Here the underlying concept has been acquired late in infancy. When the verbal tests are first given, there has not been enough time for the initial discovery to have been sufficiently specified for the child to be incapable of applying the discovery to other situations. With older children, however, the initial discovery has been made highly specific, and the relation between the initial problem and the new problem is therefore obscured. They must dredge the initial discovery from their memory, erring until they do, and they will seem to repeat an earlier phase of their cognitive development.

I am proposing that in development, perception is initially a process whereby infants attain representations of the events occurring in the world around them. These representations are initially highly abstract. With development, they become more and more specific, more and more detailed. According to this view, the acquisition of perceptual meaning is a process of differentiation and specification. I must emphasize that I consider this a perceptual process, a change in the perceptual system rather than in some "higher" center.

Consider some recent, although tentative, data on how the perceptual system can respond to abstract, higher-order or -level information and how it changes with development. The research is on intersensory substitutability. For some years I have been examining the ability of young blind infants to use the information provided by an ultrasonic detection system (Fig. 8.1). The essence of this system, for our present purposes, is that it is wholly man-made. Despite this, young babies have no problem using it (Bower, 1977, 1978b). What does this imply about the perceptual system of the infant? It seems to me to imply that the system is set to respond to very abstract properties of stimulation, such as the form of the change in stimulation produced by an

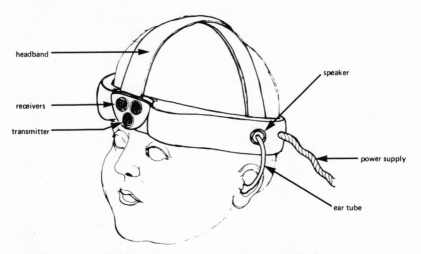

DISTANCE is signalled by the PITCH of the signal. Low pitch means near, high pitch means distant.
SIZE is signalled by the AMPLITUDE of the signal. Low volume means small object, high volume means far away.
TEXTURE is signalled by the CLARITY of the signal. Clear sound means hard object, fuzzy sound means soft object.
RIGHT—LEFT POSITION is given by TIME—OF—ARRIVAL difference of a signal at the two ears.
UP—DOWN POSITION is not given directly but can be ascertained by HEAD—MOVEMENTS.

FIG. 8.1. The sonic guide: This device continuously irradiates the environment with ultrasound. This reflects off any object within range and is then converted by the device into audible sound. As indicated in the figure, information as to distance, size, texture, and direction of the object can be obtained from this signal.

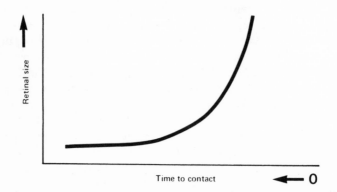

FIG. 8.2. As an object approaches, retinal size increases as time to contact decreases.

event. Figure 8.2 shows the form of the change produced by an object approaching the eye. This form can be produced via the ear using devices like the sonic guide. It could be produced via the skin using an interface like that devised by Bach-y-Rita (Bach-y-Rita, Collins, Saunders, White, & Scadden, 1969). It is the form that seems to be important, however. All the young blind infants studied have been able to make use of the information provided by the guide. This implies that the sounds produced by the guide are heard in a very different way by infants and adults. The infants do not hear the sounds as sounds, still less as properties of an object; indeed the sound is no more experienced by them than light is by us when we survey a scene. I emphasize the word *young,* because it appears that by about 13 months, this early facility may have disappeared. One blind infant of this age, taught over 3 days to use the guide for reaching, persistently acted as if she thought the sound she heard must be a property of objects. After grasping any object that had been placed in the field of the guide, she persistently took it to her ear. She did not seem to be responding to sound in the same abstract way as younger babies. Processes of differentiation seemed to have brought her to a Type I description of the situation. However, Type I responses are not typical of younger babies.

Thus far I have concentrated on the directly given, although the studies by Bryant et al. (1972), Day and McKenzie (1973), and Wishart and Bower (1978) referred to earlier have clear implications for a theory of representation. All three imply that representation itself is as abstract as the percepts it mirrors. Piaget (1967) reported some experiments that indicate that representation—and possibly perception—continue in this abstract fashion for some years. These experiments were extremely simple. Children of various ages were shown various displays and asked to reproduce the displays after a variety of time intervals, ranging from a few hours to a few months. The display shown in Fig. 8.3A was reproduced by preoperational children in ways that suggest verbal storage. Their reproductions (Fig. 8.3B) suggested storage of the form, "a tilted glass with water in it." Not "knowing" how water behaves, preoperational children reproduced the display as shown. The paradoxical finding was that as children who had been preoperational when shown the display became operational, their "memory" improved, and their reproductions became accurate. This could hardly be improvement in a memory image. It must rather have been a change in their interpretation of their symbolically encoded memory. From this and many similar experiments it can be argued that children at this level are not all able to form images of displays, but rather they rely on symbolic descriptions for memory.

It follows that perceptual development is a process in which representations of the world are made more precise. That process can account for a great deal of what is commonly called cognitive development. Our use of the word *cognition* reflects, I feel, associationist presumptions about the nature

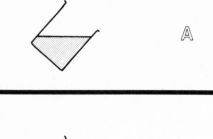

FIG. 8.3. When asked to re-produce from memory the display shown in (A), preoperational children produce displays such as those shown in (B).

of perceptual experience—presumptions that force the postulation of some system to convert low-order givens into higher-order principles.

I shall not now discuss the mechanisms of differentiation. However, I will discuss briefly what it is that is differentiated. It will be obvious that I have retained a very precise linkage between perception and representation in the account already given. We have abstract representations because we have abstract perceptions. As perception differentiates, the representations created by it likewise differentiate. What then happens to the abstract representations created by the formerly abstract perceptual system? I propose that they persist in their original abstract form, thus creating a hierarchy of knowledge that remains active throughout life and that functions to condition the *possible* differentiated perceptions and representations we can form. Consider again the blind child: It is well known that sight-restoration surgery must not be delayed too long if it is to have any possibility of success. If there has been some vision prior to the onset of blindness, this condition does not necessarily apply (Gregory, 1974; Von Senden, 1932/1960). It is likewise known that the congenitally blind child has a very poor comprehension of the three-dimensional structure of the world, even when compared with children who became blind around 2 years of age—a difference that persists throughout adulthood. If we examine the behavior of these two groups, there is often little discernible difference. The congenitally blind and the late blind may be equally mobile, equally dextrous. However, the former seem to have no comprehension whatsoever of the three-dimensional structure of the world. Where does the difference come from? I argued earlier that the young infant will respond to the formal characteristics of stimulation that specify tridimensional order regardless of the modality of stimulation. The representations laid down by these inputs must likewise be rather abstract statements about the tridimensional order of the world—the very kind of statement that in later years is easily elicited from sighted or late-blinded children but not from the congenitally blinded. I would argue that the latter group never receive any abstract three-dimensional input from the world; they thus have no abstract representations of three-dimensional order to use in the appropriate task situations. Rather, they have abstract representations of a temporally ordered world, a world without spatial properties.

It seems to me, then, that the representations established in infancy function as "spectacles" of a sort, conditioning the way we register events. The sighted infant learns to register the world in three-dimensional terms; the blind infant learns to register the world in one-dimensional, temporal terms. Later changes in input characteristics—the result of blinding or sight restoration—will have no effect on these early "spectacles"; in the latter case, three-dimensional visual input will be sorted into a one-dimensional frame.

Before closing, I would like to make some comments on the acquisition of word meaning. The view presented here—that perceptual development is a process of differentiation and specification—has its counterpart in theories of the growth of word meaning. There, too, one can find theories that insist on the opposite—that the acquisition of meaning is a process of abstraction. Anglin (1977), in a recent review, has argued that evidence exists for both views. It seems to me that the result one obtains in studies of the acquisition of word meaning depends on the state of the child's perceptual development and the task in question. The growth of word meaning for me is a process in which perceptual representations are made public. The representations that will be made public are those that are demanded by the communicational network of which the child is a part. However, I would propose that the representations that can be most easily made public are those that have been most recently acquired. If these are early, undifferentiated, abstract representations, then word use will reflect that; as the representations become more specific, so will word use. If, however, the perceptual system has reached a state in which representations are specific, then the word use will begin as specific. It may stay specific, as color words do, for example; or it may be forced by the communicational demand system to become more abstract, so that the child must search through the preexisting representational hierarchy to find an appropriate public level of meaning. As I have indicated elsewhere (Bower, 1978a), the best evidence for such a process is the U-shaped developmental curves that are becoming increasingly easy to find (e.g., Nathan & Bever, in press). These curves are constructed from cross-sectional data. The youngest children are still perceiving the event in question in an abstract, undifferentiated way; their word use reflects this abstract perception of the situation. The perceptions of the intermediate and oldest children will be specified; the word use of the intermediate child will reflect this specification; the word use of the oldest children will reflect this and the communicational demands of their culture and may thus have returned to the early, abstract representation of the event in question. This might be seen as a process of association; I consider it to be a process in which private representations are specified in public form—another example of the universal process of differentiation and specification.

ACKNOWLEDGMENTS

The research reported in this paper was supported by Medical Research Council Grant Nos. G969/559/C and G972/186/N.

REFERENCES

Alegria, J., & Noirot, E. Neonate orientation behaviour towards the human voice. *International Journal of Behavioral Development*, 1979, in press.

Anglin, J. M. *Word, object and conceptual development*. New York: Norton, 1977.

Bach-y-Rita, P., Collins, C. C., Saunders, F., White, B. W., & Scadden, L. Vision substitution by tactile image projection. *Nature*, 1969, *221*, 963–964.

Bateson, G. *Steps toward an ecology of mind*. New York: Ballantine Books, 1972.

Bechtold, A. G., & Salapatek, P. Research reported in Annual Report of the Institute of Child Development, University of Minnesota, 1976–1977.

Bower, T. G. R. *Development in infancy*. San Francisco: Freeman, 1974.

Bower, T. G. R. Blind babies see with their ears. *New Scientist*, 1977, *73*, 255–257.

Bower, T. G. R. *Concepts of development*. Paper presented at the 21st International Congress of Psychology, Paris, July 1976. Paris: Presses Universitaires de France, 1978, in press. (a)

Bower, T. G. R. Visual development in the blind child. In A. Macfarlane (Ed.) *Clinic in developmental medicine on vision*. London: Spastics International Medical Publications, 1978, in press. (b)

Bower, T. G. R., Broughton, J. M., & Moore, M. K. The coordination of visual and tactual input in infancy. *Perception & Psychophysics*, 1970, *8*, 51–53.

Bower, T. G. R., Dunkeld, J., & Wishart, J. G. Infant perception of visually presented objects. *Science*, 1979, in press.

Bruner, J. S. On cognitive growth. In J. S. Bruner, R. R. Olver, P. M. Greenfield et al., In *Studies in cognitive growth*. New York: Wiley, 1966.

Bryant, P. E., Jones, P., Claxton, V., & Perkins, G. M. Recognition of shapes across modalities by infants. *Nature*, 1972, *240*, 303–304.

Caron, A. J., Caron, R. F., & Carlson, V. R. *Do infants see objects or retinal images? Shape constancy revisited*. Paper presented at the meeting of the Society for Research in Child Development, New Orleans, March 1977.

Day, R. H., & McKenzie, B. E.   Perceptual shape constancy in early infancy. *Perception*, 1973, *2*, 315–321.

Dodwell, P. C., Muir, D., & DiFranco, D.   Response of infants to visually presented objects. *Science*, 1976, *194*, 209–210.

Field, J.   Coordination of vision and prehension in young infants. *Child Development*, 1977, *48*, 97–103.

Fodor, J. A., Bever, T. G., & Garrett, M. F.   *The psychology of language. An introduction to psycholinguistics and generative grammar.* New York: McGraw-Hill, 1974.

Freedman, D. G.   Smiling in blind infants and the issue of innate versus acquired. *Journal of Child Psychology and Psychiatry and Allied Disciplines*, 1964, *5*, 171–184.

Gibson, J. J.   *The perception of the visual world.* Boston: Houghton Mifflin, 1950.

Gordon, R. F., & Yonas, A.   Sensitivity to binocular depth information in infants. *Journal of Experimental Child Psychology*, 1976, *22*, 413–422.

Gregory, R. L.   *Concepts and mechanisms of perception.* London: Duckworth, 1974.

Macfarlane, A.   *The psychology of childbirth.* London and Cambridge, Mass.: Open Books and Harvard University Press, 1977.

Maratsos, M. P.   Decrease in the understanding of the word "Big" in pre-school children. *Child Development*, 1973, *44*, 747–752.

McGurk, H., Turnure, C., & Creighton, S. J.   Auditory–visual coordination in neonates. *Child Development*, 1977, *48*, 138–143.

Mehler, J., & Bever, T.   Cognitive capacity of very young children. *Science*, 1967, *158*, 141–142.

Mendelson, M. J., & Haith, M. M.   The relation between audition and vision in the human newborn. *Monographs for Society for Research in Child Development*, 1978, *167*.

Nathan, H., & Bever, T. (Eds.).   *Dips in learning: Proceedings of the OECD Conference on dips in learning and development curves, St. Paul-de-Vence, March 1975.* Hillsdale, N.J.: Lawrence Erlbaum Associates, in press.

Piaget, J.   *On the development of memory and identity: Heinz Werner lectures, Clark University, Worcester* (Vol. 2). Barre, Mass.: Barre Publishers, 1967.

Schaffer, H. R., & Parry, M. H.   Perceptual–motor behavior in infancy as a function of age and stimulus familiarity. *British Journal of Psychology*, 1969, *60*, 1–9.

Schaffer, H. R., & Parry, M. H.   The effects of short-term familiarisation of infants' perceptual–motor coordination in a simultaneous discrimination situation. *British Journal of Psychology*, 1970, *61*, 559–569.

Turkewitz, G., Birch, H. B., Moreau, T., Levy, L., & Cornwell, A. C.   Effect of intensity of auditory stimulation on directional eye movements in the human neonate. *Animal Behaviour*, 1966, *14*, 93–101.

Urwin, C.   *The development of a blind baby.* Unpublished manuscript presented at Edinburgh University, 1973.

Von Senden, M.   *Space and sight.* London: Methuen, 1960 (Originally published, 1932.)

Ward, J.   *Psychological principals.* Cambridge: Cambridge University Press, 1918.

Wertheimer, M.   Psycho-motor coordination of auditory–visual space at birth. *Science*, 1961, *134*, 1692.

Wishart, J. G., & Bower, T. G. R.   *Comprehension of spatial relations in the development of the object concept.* Manuscript in preparation, 1978.

Wishart, J. G., Bower, T. G. R., & Dunkeld, J.   Reaching in the dark. *Perception*, 1978, *7*, 507–512.

Yonas, A., & Pick, H. L.   An approach to the study of infant space perception. In L. B. Cohen & P. Salapatek (Eds.), *Infant perception: From sensation to cognition* (Vol. II). New York: Academic Press, 1975.

V EXPLORATION AND SELECTIVITY IN PERCEPTUAL DEVELOPMENT

9 The Control of Information Pickup in Selective Looking

Ulric Neisser
Cornell University

Perception is the activity by which we pick up information about environmental objects and events. As Eleanor Gibson has pointed out, that information exists at several levels: Skilled perceivers make use of higher-order structure where infants and novices may have to depend on simpler features. In addition, perception is selective.The fact that a perceiver is capable of picking up a certain kind of information does not mean that she will do so in every case. We refer to this selectivity when we say that she *attends* to one or another subset of the information available. The terms *perception* and *attention* refer to different aspects of the same activity.

Perceiving and attending can be studied from various points of view. One approach, which has been especially dominant in the study of attention, emphasizes the discovery of the mental mechanisms involved. It is to this approach that we owe such concepts as filtering (Broadbent, 1958), late selection (Deutsch & Deutsch, 1963), capacity allocation (Kahneman, 1973), and encoding (Posner, 1973). As Gibson (1978) has suggested, however, concepts like these may be of little lasting value. They lead to a rapid proliferation of speculative models and of experimental paradigms in which the models can be tested, but they produce few insights about ordinary perceiving or its development. Such insight is more likely to follow from a detailed analysis of the perceptual information itself. One principal goal of Gibsonian research is to discover the types of structures to which perceivers are actually sensitive; another is to find out just how skills of information pickup develop and mature.

These two approaches may not be entirely irreconcilable. It is possible to combine a healthy respect for perceptual information with a continued interest in the prepared mental structures that accept it. These structures must undergo continuous change and reorganization, even in a single perceptual act. Perceiving is not instantaneous but occurs over time. It is a cyclic activity, the outcome of which depends both on the information available and on the cognitive structures, or schemata, that perceivers bring to bear on it. Since I have summarized this approach to perception elsewhere (Neisser, 1976), I do not elaborate it here. Instead, I describe a series of experiments that have some relevance for all three theoretical positions. All the studies make use of a procedure called "selective looking," which was originally designed to illustrate the inadequacies of the filter theory of attention. Because this procedure involves the subject deeply in a well-defined perceptual cycle, it offers an excellent opportunity to explore the manner in which that cycle controls the pickup of information. And because it is based on an easy and natural kind of perceptual activity, it has also allowed us to examine the role of different levels of structure—featural and kinetic information—in event perception. In addition, we have conducted several studies that explore the development of perceptual selectivity in infancy and childhood.

The first two experiments described here (Neisser & Becklen, 1975; Littman & Becklen, 1976) were designed primarily with filter theory in mind. The third (Becklen, Neisser, & Littman, 1979) occupies an ambiguous position. It can be seen as a further test of the filter theory, as an essentially Gibsonian study of the information on which selective looking depends, or as an illustration of the power of the perceptual cycle in controlling information pickup. The fourth is a study of selective looking in infants; it extends the argument along developmental lines using techniques developed in Eleanor Gibson's laboratory by Elizabeth Spelke (1976), somewhat modified for our own purposes (Bahrick, Walker, & Neisser, 1979). The remaining experiments are less theoretical. They explore the conditions that lead people to notice unexpected events. In two of them, the subjects were adults (Neisser & Dube, 1978; Neisser, Dube, Karis, & Bahrick, 1979), whereas in the third, they were school-age children (Neisser & Rooney, 1979). The theory of the perceptual cycle is used here to interpret their results, but it is clear that we are only beginning to explore the problems they raise.

SELECTIVE LOOKING: THE EARLY STUDIES

A large part of the data base for information-processing theories of attention comes from studies of selective listening. In these studies, subjects are presented with two independent speech events—two voices reading separate texts aloud, for example—and must follow one of them while ignoring the other. The first and most fundamental finding of the research is that selective listening is easy. Subjects have no difficulty in following the experimenter's instructions and report being aware only of the attended message. To theorists like Cherry and Broadbent and Treisman (see Neisser, 1967, for a review of this work), the remarkable simplicity of the task required a theoretical explanation. Given the assumption that information reaching the receptors is generally "processed" to successively higher stages of the nervous system, some special mechanism seemed necessary to prevent the irrelevant message from being processed just as thoroughly as the relevant one. Broadbent called this hypothetical mechanism a "filter" and the name has stuck. It was an attractive idea, though alternative information-processing accounts of the experimental findings have since been proposed by other theorists. Presumably, human beings were thought to have filters for speech because they are often in situations that demand selective listening; either evolution or past experience has established a particular mechanism to cope with such situations.

A different interpretation is possible, however. The need for a filter arises in these theories only because perception is conceived as essentially passive. They assume that information will force its way into the organism if it is not somehow kept out. Such an assumption is by no means necessary. When perceiving is thought of as a constructive process (as I described it in 1967) or as information pickup guided by specific anticipatory schemata (as I would prefer to describe it now), no filter is required at all. The perceiver ignores information simply by not doing anything with it. Such information is just not perceived, in the same sense that objects currently lying on my desk are not being grasped and my pipe is currently not being smoked.

If this latter approach is the correct one, the phenomena observed in selective listening experiments reflect the properties of perception in general, not those of a particular mechanism. They should manifest themselves in every perceptual activity, even where the situation is so unfamiliar that neither evolution nor experience can have prepared a selective device to deal with it. To make this point, Robert Becklen and I deliberately devised a situation that lacked ecological validity. Although we presented our subjects with two rather ordinary events, the information that specified them was confounded in a way that never occurs in the normal environment. The events were two rather familiar kinds of games. Each was easy to keep track of when it was shown by itself, but we superimposed the two on the same television screen. One episode was a "ballgame" in which three men passed a basketball around while moving haphazardly around the room; the other was a "handgame" in which two players tried to slap one another's hands with irregular movements. Figure 9.1 suggests what the superimposed display looked like. On some trials, subjects demonstrated their attentiveness to the ballgame by pressing a response key every time the ball was thrown. In this condition, they were to ignore the handgame entirely. On trials where the handgame was the target, they ignored the ballgame while pressing a key at every slap. The results have been reported elsewhere (Neisser & Becklen, 1975). They mimicked those of the selective listening studies rather well: It is just as easy to follow one of two overlapped visual episodes as to listen to one of the two simultaneous conversations. No special practice is required. Our subjects reported that they simply did not see the unattended episode, just as one does not hear unattended voices.

Because our subjects' eye movements were not constrained in this experiment, they probably tracked the attended episode visually. If the tracking was successful, the target game must have been imaged on the foveae of the subjects' eyes most of the time, whereas the unattended one was often peripheral. This suggests a theoretical possibility: Could the relatively poor acuity of peripheral vision have served as a filtering device, with the effect that less information about the unattended game reached higher processing centers? This could hardly be a complete explanation of perceptual selection, since a subject would have to be following the target on some other basis to make the right eye movements in the first place. Nevertheless, we decided to test it explicitly. Littman and Becklen (1976) compromised ecological validity still further: New subjects were asked to fixate a dot in the center of the television screen while still following one of the two superimposed games. They did so successfully. Perception is selective whether it involves eye movements or not, and even in situations where no special filtering mechanism has been established by experience.

THE SIMILARITY EXPERIMENT

The subject of a selective looking experiment must pick up information that is specific to her task so she can follow the target episode successfully. Some of this information refers to permanent characteristics of the target objects (the three men who play the ballgame, for example, and the ball with which they are playing). This is featural information (i.e., the ball is small and round; the players have hands and feet and other human attributes). Featural information is available not only in our kinetic video display but in any single frame of that display as well. Indeed, it is not difficult to pick up the ballgame from a static drawing like Fig. 9.1. In addition to features of this sort, however, selective looking displays also present kinetic information. This information, not represented in Fig. 9.1, is based on the flow of action as the game proceeds. The trajectory of the ball specifies where it is to be found a moment later, and the movements of the players indicate which of them will be in a position to catch it. This movement-based information may also be useful in selective looking, enabling the perceiver to continue following the game once she has begun to do so. The design of our first experiments did not

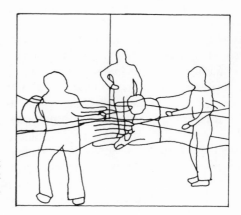

FIG. 9.1. A selective looking display involving two different games. (From Neisser & Becklen, 1975.)

permit us to determine the relative importance of featural and kinetic information in the conduct of the task.

The distinction between these two kinds of information is relevant to all three of the theoretical approaches described earlier. The filter mechanisms of information-processing theory are usually described as sensitive to stimulus features. In Broadbent's original theory of selective listening, for example, the filter might be tuned to pass only voices that came from a particular spatial location, or that had a particular fundamental pitch. A similar theory applied to selective looking would suggest that the perceiver relies on featural information to distinguish between the relevant and irrelevant games. If the filter is doing its job, information about ball-like objects should be passed on to higher centers whereas information about hands is not. This argument leads to a rather specific prediction. If the relevant and irrelevant games are made increasingly similar, selection should become increasingly difficult: The filter will tend to admit information about the wrong game as well as the right one. When no feature serves to distinguish the two episodes, selection should be impossible.

If perception is based on continuously changing and structured antici-pations, however, a different possibility suggests itself. Although some of the perceiver's schemata are relatively permanent, others are continuously restructured by new information. Kinetic information that she has already picked up creates a readiness for what will be perceivable next, which will in turn establish new anticipations. Thus it should be possible to follow the target game regardless of the properties of the irrelevant one, as long as adequate kinetic information remains available. Selective looking may become somewhat more difficult if the perceiver has been relying partly on featural information, but there is no reason to believe that it should become impossible.

Although I have presented the distinction between featural and kinetic information as a way of distinguishing schemata from filters, it is by no means irrelevant to a Gibsonian analysis of the same situation. Indeed, it *is* a Gibsonian analysis, correspondingly closely to Eleanor Gibson's distinction between simple features and higher-order structure. Thus, an experiment undertaken to see which kind of information subjects actually use in selective looking is of more than passing interest for Gibsonian theory. Whatever "processing" hypothesis it may support, such a study will at least tell us something more about how complex naturalistic events are perceived.

When Becklen, Littman, and I (1979) designed our study, these theoretical alternatives were not as clear to us as they now seem. We had a more crudely empirical ambition: to find out whether selective looking depended on the similarity between the two visible episodes. Our first problem, then, was to find some operational criterion of similarity. This problem seemed insuperable as long as we considered unrelated pairs of activities like the ballgame and the handgame, because there is no metric on which their similarity can be defined. Therefore we decided to work with displays in which both episodes had the same basic structure. Our subjects had to follow one ballgame while ignoring another ballgame on which it was superimposed, with differences in the players' appearance serving to create varying degrees of similarity between the relevant and irrelevant events.

All the videotapes made for this experiment showed the same three players (in fact, the three experimenters) moving around haphazardly in a large room and throwing a basketball back and forth at irregular intervals. They made about 30 passes per minute. When two such videotapes had been electronically superimposed to make a stimulus tape, both "teams" (six persons and two balls) were easily visible as in Fig. 9.2. If two players happened to occupy the same region on the screen (one originally from one game and one from the other), they seemed to pass through one another in a "ghostly" manner.

We introduced two stimulus features by which the simultaneously visible teams might be distinguished. In some conditions the three players in one game all wore dark shirts, while those in the other game all wore light shirts. This attribute was highly salient, as Fig. 9.2 illustrates. The other distinguishing feature was the presence or absence of sunglasses, which were worn by all members of a given team or by none. By choosing appropriate episodes of these kinds to superimpose on one another, we defined four experimental conditions that we hoped would form an ascending scale of similarity. In the *two-cue* condition, the superimposed teams were distinguished both by the color of their shirts and by the presence or absence of sunglasses. In the *shirt-cue* condition, one team wore dark shirts while the

FIG. 9.2.   A selective looking display from the *shirt-cue* condition.

other wore light shirts, but both wore (or both didn't wear) the glasses. In the *glasses-cue* condition, both teams wore shirts of the same color, but one had sunglasses and the other did not. In the *no-cue* condition, neither shirts nor glasses distinguished the teams: Two episodes of exactly the same kind were superimposed. In all these videotapes, the target team first appeared alone for a few seconds before the irrelevant episode was faded in electronically. There was also a *one-game* condition, in which a single team was visible without superposition for the entire trial. Many videotapes were made for each condition; no subject saw any tape more than once.

Twenty-four adult subjects (13 females and 11 males) participated in our experiment. All were given twelve 1-minute trials in the five conditions just listed, in the following order: On the first day (after a brief practice trial), a *one-game* trial was followed by *two-cue, shirt-cue, glasses-cue,* and two *no-cue* trials; on the second day, two more *no-cue* trials were followed by *glasses-cue, shirt-cue, two-cue,* and *one-game* trials in that order. (Certain other kinds of trials were also given at the end of the second session, but are not described here.) The subject was seated at a comfortable distance from the black-and-white television screen and given a response key, which she was to press whenever one player on the target team passed the ball to another. (Half the subjects were also asked to indicate in which direction the throw had gone, but since this additional task had no effect on the results, it is not discussed further here. The data have been collapsed across this variable.) The target team was defined for the subject as the one that appeared on the screen first.

She was always told what kind of trial was coming, i.e., what features(s), if any, would distinguish the target game from the irrelevant one. In the *no-cue* condition, she was further instructed that if she "lost track" of the target game at any point, she should choose one of the two teams at random and start following again.

If the visual selection depends primarily on featural information (as a filter theory would have to predict, I think), one might expect that even the *two-cue* condition would be difficult. The players of the two teams are distinguished by two attributes in this condition, but they still have many features in common; indeed, they are the same people. Moreover, no feature distinguished the two balls from each other. One would further expect that the conditions with fewer cues would pose even greater difficulty, and that following one game would be entirely impossible in the *no-cue* condition, when no featural information distinguished the two episodes at all.

In fact, our subjects found the *two-cue* condition very easy. The average hit rate, which was about 97% in *one-game,* only dropped to 93% in the two-cue case. (A "hit" is defined as a response made within a 1-second criterial interval around a pass in the target game.) By treating hits as evidence that the subject is on target and analogously defined "misses" and "false alarms" as evidence that she is not, it is possible to calculate her "on time": the fraction of each trial during which she was following the target game. (See Becklen, Neisser, & Littman, 1979, for details of this method of scoring.) This raw on-time (ROT) proportion averaged .96 for *one-game* and .91 for *two-cue.* The difference was statistically significant (by analysis of variance followed by *t* test) but hardly impressive.

The presence or absence of the sunglasses made rather little difference to our subjects. In retrospect, this should have been obvious; it was rather difficult to see the sunglasses on the television screen. For this reason, *shirt-cue* produced only a slightly and insignificantly lower ROT than *two-cue* (.87). But what seems at first to be an enormous effect of similarity appeared at the next level, in conditions where all players wore shirts of the same color. Whether the teams were distinguished by sunglasses or not, it was difficult to stay with the target episode in these conditions. The ROT scores dropped, very significantly, to .66 in *glasses-cue* and .67 in *no-cue.* The same pattern of results appeared on both days of the experiment, though there was a slight overall practice effect.

The low ROT scores in the *no-cue* condition (or in the essentially equivalent *glasses-cue* condition) might be taken to imply that perceptual selection depends critically on featural information. They seem to confirm a prediction of filter theory: People cannot reject undesired stimuli unless there is some feature to which the filter can be tuned. Such a conclusion would be premature, however. The subjects themselves claimed that for the most part they had no difficulty in following one team and ignoring the other. The trouble arose only at occasional points in the action when they could not determine which of the visible balls was the one they had just been watching. When they started to follow one team again, they had no way of knowing whether it was still the right one. The ambiguous points are in the videotape itself. In his doctoral dissertation, Littman (1976) verified that most subjects who "lose" the target team and start following the wrong one do so at the same places.

Inspection of the stimulus tapes reveals the objective basis of these ambiguities. In one common case, the two balls (one being used by each team) happen to be in the same region of the screen and are momentarily obscured by the players. When they become visible again, the viewer cannot know which one she had been following before, and so has an even chance of "switching" to the previously ignored team. One or two such points of ambiguity occurred in most of our *no-cue* trials. At these moments kinetic information is genuinely inadequate, and *no* mechanism could enable the subject to stay on target. The rest of the time, selective looking can continue normally.

If this interpretation is correct, the ROT score does not give an accurate picture of the perceiver's achievements in the *no-cue* case. When she is not following the originally specified team and is scored as being off target, a subject may very well be following the other one instead. Unfortunately a simple total of the times spent following *either* game would also be an unsatisfactory measure, because of the probability of being scored on target by chance alone. This probability turns out to be rather high. For statistical purposes, a subject can be treated as if she were responding about half the time (30 responses per minute, with a criterial interval of 1 second) to targets that are also present about half the time. If she responds at random she is equally likely to get a hit, a miss, or a false alarm (intervals with neither a target nor a response do not affect this calculation), and therefore has an expected ROT of .33. Empirical tests indicate that the chance ROT is indeed close to this value. (See Becklen et al., 1979, for details of these estimates.)

Isolated hits can occur frequently by chance, but long periods of following a single game (i.e., of making no misses or false alarms) are much less likely. Similar calculations show that runs of 6 or more seconds on target have a probability of only .048. In an extended test sample, they actually occurred with an empirical frequency of .042. (Again, see Becklen, et al., 1979 for details.) On this basis we devised a Corrected On-Time index (COT) to show how well a subject had followed one game or the other without capitalizing on chance. In computing the COT index, subjects are scored as *on* during all runs of 6 seconds or longer with respect to either game, and as off target otherwise. The difference between COT and the ROT was very slight for the shirt-cue condition, as might be expected: COT was .82 where ROT had been .87. (The small drop means that a correspondingly small portion of the original time on target had occurred in bursts of less than 6 seconds.) In the *no-cue* case, however, the difference was very large. Where the mean ROT score had been .67, the COT mean was .81. When time spent following either game is counted as correct—scoring only runs that cannot easily be attributed to chance—subjects can follow superimposed games almost as well without a distinguishing feature as when one is present.

The argument warrants further discussion, as it has a peculiarly Gibsonian moral. Perceivers can follow the action of a natural event with kinetic information alone. When they do, their perception is inherently selective. It is not disturbed even by the presence of another event with exactly the same features (e.g., our subjects could follow one game for long periods of time). No theory based on featural information can explain this achievement. It must be described in terms of the pickup of higher-order information (as Eleanor Gibson would put it) or in terms of the perceptual cycle of anticipations and confirmations. When subjects do falter in this task, it is not because some mental mechanism has failed but simply because the objective data that would make it possible are not available. To paraphrase J. J. Gibson, the necessary information is not in the light. At such points—but only at such points—selection must break down. As long as distinguishing information is available (whether kinetic or featural), the perceiver can tune herself to it and will perceive selectively.

SELECTIVE LOOKING IN INFANTS

If the selectivity of perception is an intrinsic aspect of the activity itself, it should be observable in every situation and at every age. This conclusion follows easily from a Gibsonian perspective but contrasts sharply with the predictions of information-processing theory. Since that theory attributes selection to the activity of special mechanisms of attention, it suggests that inexperienced perceivers may be less selective than sophisticated ones. Indeed, the notion that children are more distractible and less focused than adults has been repeatedly proposed in recent years. I do not believe it. In my view, the apparently greater distractibility of young children appears because they do not have the same interests as adults, and tend to turn away from tasks with which an adult would continue. They can attend closely and continuously to events that genuinely interest them. When they do, their perception should be no less selective than ours.

If this hypothesis is correct, it should be possible to demonstrate selective looking at any age, even in early infancy. Infants are probably less skilled in picking up kinetic information than adults and may be sensitive to different features of objects and events, but as long as they can pick up *some* information they should do so in a selective way. A demonstration of this point would have some theoretical value. More important, it might provide new insight into the perceptual abilities of early infancy. Despite the work of Eleanor Gibson and a few others, there is still relatively little solid knowledge of what infant perceivers can and cannot do. We need to know much more before we can flesh out the details of an adequate theory of perceptual development.

These considerations led Lorraine Bahrick, Arlene Walker, and me to undertake a selective looking study with 4-month-old infants. (Eleanor Gibson was kind enough to let us use the facilities of her infant laboratory for this purpose.) Such a study involves more than presenting superimposed visual events to babies. There must also be some way of ensuring that the subject actually follows one of the events as distinguished from the other. Fortunately, a technique was available that controls infants' selection of visual episodes rather effectively. The method is that devised by Elizabeth Spelke to study intermodal perception and exploration (Spelke, 1976; see also Chapter 10 of this volume). When a baby is shown two films side by side on a split screen and hears the sound track that goes with one of them, she tends to look at the film that goes with the sound. As Spelke pointed out, this behavior shows a remarkable sensitivity to the amodal, temporal structure of the information available to the eye and to the ear. What would happen if we superimposed the films, instead of showing them side by side, while playing one of the appropriate sound tracks? We hoped for exactly the same outcome—that the baby would follow the event that went with the sound she heard, ignoring the other event. In other words, she would exhibit selective looking.

Two additional steps were necessary before we could actually conduct such an experiment. First, we had to make sound films that would produce the strongest possible Spelke effect. Infants had displayed about a two-to-one preference for the sound film in her first study (where one film was of a woman playing peekaboo and the other of percussion instruments being hit), but in subsequent experiments with less natural events the effect had been substantially weaker. Spelke went on to demonstrate intermodal perception in these later experiments with another technique, but for our purposes the simple preference effect had to be compelling. This required events that were intrinsically interesting, making sounds that were uniquely characteristic of them.

To solve this problem, we made a number of color films and pilot-tested them in Spelke's paradigm. Finally we selected three that seemed to work well. The "Pattycake" film shows the hands and forearms of two people playing a rhythmic game of pattycake that involves regular banging on a visible surface as well as mutual handclaps. The "Slinky" film shows two colorfully gloved hands manipulating a spiral Slinky toy back and forth as it makes its characteristic metallic clashing sound. The "Xylophone" film shows two color-wrapped sticks banging out a simple repetitive tune on a toy xylophone. These events have several desirable features. Each has a rich, complexly nested visual structure and a correspondingly complex auditory one; they are interesting and offer a lot to the viewer. Moreover, they are distinct from one another both visually and acoustically. Each of the sound tracks goes very well with its own visual display and is suitably uncorrelated with either of the others. Finally, they are surely all new to 4-month-old babies. Infants of that age have had little opportunity to watch Slinkies, xylophones, or people playing pattycake. Any Spelke effect observed with such materials cannot readily be attributed to past experience; it would suggest that infants can detect sight–sound correspondences directly.

Because this last point had some theoretical importance in its own right, we decided to conduct a formal replication of Spelke's experiment before using our materials to study selective looking. The replication was straightforward. Using all three possible pairs of our films (with eight subjects seeing each pair), we showed two films side by side while playing the sound track that went with one of them through a central loudspeaker. The 4-month-old subjects sat in an infant seat at a comfortable distance from the split screen, and a hidden observer monitored their eye movements. The results confirmed Spelke's findings completely: The infants watched the sound-appropriate film 67% of the time (See Bahrick et al., 1979, for details). It is evident that babies can detect the common temporal structure of auditory and visual sequences even in complex and unfamiliar naturalistic displays. It is also evident that our films produce the strong visual preferences that a demonstration of selective looking requires.

The other prerequisite for that demonstration is a methodological one: The infants must have some way to indicate that they are selectively attending to one of the events as opposed to the other. In Spelke's method, the subject demonstrates this simply by looking to the right or to the left. Her eye position then shows which film she is watching. Though it might seem that such an indicator cannot be used when the films are superimposed on one screen, a slight modification makes this possible after all. This modification (originally suggested to us by Frank Keil) requires momentary "de-superimposition" of the visual information. On half a dozen occasions during a 2-minute presentation of fully superimposed films, the projectors are briefly moved apart and then moved together again. The effect is to slide the two images apart on the screen, one to the right and the other to the left. The sound track is cut off as soon as the separation begins, so that the audiovisual consistency, which is to control selective looking, is only available during full superimposition. Infants who have been following the sound-appropriate film might manifest this in either of two ways as the images separate. They may continue to look at the previously attended film, but they may also prefer the previously silent one (which they are essentially seeing for the first time). If we observe a marked tendency in either direction, it will provide evidence that selective looking has been taking place.

At the time of this writing, we have only collected pilot data with the image-separation method. So far, it appears that most infants look at the previously silent film. If the final results are consistent with the pilot data, we will have demonstrated that perception is selective even at 4 months of age, and even with unfamiliar and superimposed displays. If the final data are not in agreement with the earlier results, we may conclude that our subjects lacked the skill to perceive these aspects of the sound-appropriate event necessary for selective looking. Failure to perceive is common enough. Failure to be distracted by things to which one is not attending requires neither a mechanism nor an explanation.

PREATTENTIVE PICKUP

All the studies described so far demonstrate the successful pickup of information about a target event despite superimposed information about an irrelevant one. Strictly speaking, they do not prove that the irrelevant episode was ignored but only that it created very little interference with the subjects' main task. In fact, however, most subjects say that they don't see it at all. My own introspections confirm theirs. Although the irrelevant game never "vanishes," I do not see it when I follow the target game closely (see Neisser & Becklen, 1975, for a discussion of the phenomenology of selective looking). The theory of the perceptual cycle predicts just this outcome. Perceiving is a matter of picking up information over time. Things are seen only when the information they offer is incorporated in the cycle of anticipation, pickup, and further anticipation; otherwise they are not seen.

My argument does not imply that unattended or unexpected events can never be noticed but that seeing them requires the initiation of a new perceptual cycle. There are several ways in which this can happen. First, the nervous system is innately responsive to certain kinds of signals (loud noises, for example). These signals automatically trigger orienting responses that allow new perceptual cycles to begin. Information of this kind constitutes a kind of exception to the principle stated earlier. It does "force itself" on the perceiver in a sense, because she cannot help being prepared for it. Such information pickup may be called "preattentive," to distinguish it from genuine perception.

A second type of preattentive pickup occurs as a result of experience rather than as innate endowment. People can come to be more or less permanently ready for certain kinds of information, which then triggers orienting responses when it occurs.[1] Information obtained preattentively is meager and fragmentary, however, because it has no temporal dimension. It can lead to an orienting response, but by itself it cannot specify the identity or the meaning of events and has no phenomenal impact. It makes a difference only when it initiates a perceptual cycle. Under what conditions does that take place?

Relatively few researchers have addressed this question. It does not fit comfortably into a Gibsonian framework, because it concerns not only the available information and the individual's perceptual skill but also the conditions under which she does (or doesn't) use that skill. It sometimes crops up in experiments on attention (as when Moray [1959] discovered that people may respond to their own names in unattended messages), but has not been treated systematically. It is most often discussed in context of the psychology of testimony (e.g., Buckhout, 1974; Stern, 1904) but without an adequate experimental paradigm. The method of selective looking seems excellently suited to meet that need.

To begin the study of the pickup of unexpected information, we made a selective looking tape with an unexpected event in it. About halfway through the 1-minute ballgame, a young woman carrying an open umbrella sauntered across the playing area from one side to the other. She appeared on the television screen for about 4 seconds. This tape was electronically blended with another ballgame in the usual way, as the unattended game in a *two-cue* trial. Figure 9.3 shows roughly what it looked like.

In our first explorations with this tape, we showed it to casual visitors in the laboratory. They were not warned of anything unusual but simply given the standard selective looking instructions: Press the key whenever the team in the dark shirts passes the ball. These occasional subjects never saw the umbrella woman. They had no idea what we were talking about when we asked about her, and they expressed real surprise when the tape was subsequently replayed. Occasionally, however, we had two visitors; one served as the subject while the other simply watched. The one who did not have to respond always noticed the unexpected event immediately.

To examine the matter further, we showed the tape as a last trial to some of the subjects of the 2-day similarity experiment described earlier. We expected that they, too, would fail to notice the umbrella woman. To our surprise, most of them (7 of 9) saw her right away and commented on her presence. In retrospect, however, it is not difficult to explain both aspects of these preliminary findings. A subject who is new to the selective looking task and highly committed to it does not want to give up the cycle in which she is

---

[1]One can even learn to conduct several independent perceptual cycles at the same time. For discussions of that ability, see Hirst, Neisser, and Spelke (1978); Hirst, Spelke, Reaves, Caharack, and Neisser (1979); Spelke, Hirst, and Neisser (1976).

FIG. 9.3.   The umbrella woman.

engaged. She believes that the task requires undivided attention, that if she engages in any other activity she may miss a throw in the target game. Even if she picks up some fragment of information about the umbrella woman preattentively (a flash of white from the surface of the umbrella, for example), she does not allow a new perceptual cycle to begin. Nonparticipants are much more likely to see the umbrella woman, because they do not have to restrict themselves in this way. Skilled subjects are also freer to undertake new cycles but for a very different reason. They have learned that the task is not so hard in the first place, and have acquired skills of looking that make it easier still.

To test these hypotheses, Fred Dube and I showed the experimental tape to new subjects in various conditions (Neisser & Dube, 1978). Twenty-eight were treated just like our laboratory visitors; that is, the selective looking task was explained to them, and the critical tape was then shown on the very first trial. Most of these subjects completely failed to see the umbrella woman. She was noticed by only six of them (21%). This is a remarkably small proportion when one considers how prolonged, odd, and obvious her appearance on the screen actually is.

We used four criteria to determine whether a subject had noticed the umbrella woman. First, we just watched. This turned out to be a rather good measure, because for some reason most people smile as soon as they see her. Second, we interrogated the subject as thoroughly as we could after the trial without giving anything away: "Were there any particularly difficult places? Did anything happen that is especially worth mentioning?" Third, we used an imagery technique to look for any unconscious residue that the stimulus might have left behind. This involved administering Slee's (1976) *Visual Elaboration Scale*, in which the subject is told to think of various objects ("a cup and a box on a table," for example) and then asked whether certain other aspects of the imagined scene had also been present in her thought (say, the composition of the table's surface). At the end of the scale we told the subject to "think of a person walking with an umbrella," and then asked about the sex of the person, the color of the umbrella, and so on. The results were negative: No subject who had previously failed to report the umbrella woman produced a relevant image. Finally, we replayed the tape, pointed out the critical event, and asked the subject whether she had noticed it in the earlier presentation. The people whom we have classified as nonnoticers failed all these tests.

In the second condition of our experiment, the critical tape was not shown on the first trial. It was presented only on the third, after two other *two-cue* trials. This more than doubled the frequency of noticing the umbrella woman: 48% (12/25) of the subjects saw her. In another condition, the critical tape was again used as the third trial, but the just-previous (second) trial had involved a *no-cue* rather than a *two-cue* task. We hoped that the subjects would find the critical (*two-cue*) trial relatively easy compared with the one that had just preceded it, and that this might make them feel less constrained to follow the action very closely. Indeed 63% (17/27) of these subjects noticed the umbrella woman. These three proportions of noticers (6/28, 12/25, 17/27) are significantly different from one another at the .001 level by a chi-square test.

We also explored several other conditions with varying instructions; the critical tape always appeared on the first trial. Ten subjects were told not to press the response key but just to watch the screen; they all saw the umbrella woman immediately. Other subjects were required to respond but were given instructions that de-emphasized the task; some were told that it was "just a practice trial" and others that they would "find it very easy." This had a positive effect: 47% (8/17) of these subjects noticed her. Overall, then, our hypotheses were supported. People fail to notice unexpected events when they are deeply engaged in a task that they believe to be difficult. The easier the task becomes or seems to become, the more likely they are to notice other things.

We have conducted a few further studies of noticing in the selective looking paradigm. Because it seemed important to vary the stimulus conditions as well as the subject's set, we made a number of new unexpected-event tapes. In some of these, the umbrella woman wears a light shirt like the unattended team; in others, a dark shirt like the attended team. In some, she simply walks across the scene as before; in others, she does a little dance number for several seconds in the middle of the action. In still others, the unexpected person is a 10-year-old boy drinking a can of soda instead of a woman carrying an umbrella. Demetrios Karis and Lorraine Bahrick ran 80 subjects with these tapes (Neisser et al., 1979). Again only a quarter of the subjects (10/40) noticed the umbrella woman (on the first trial) when she walked through the game; the color of her shirt seemed to make no difference. The proportion of noticers went up to 70% (14/20) in the dance condition and down to 5% (1/20) when the child was the unexpected person. These variations are surely due to differences in stimulus information. The dance involved a different and more extensive pattern of movement; the child took up less space on the screen.

Because of the widely held view that children are more distractible than adults, we decided to repeat some of these experiments with younger subjects. If young children have less efficient filters than adults do, they should be more likely to notice the umbrella woman or the boy with the soda. Our own prediction was quite different. As long as the children are interested in the principal task and believe it to be within their capability, they should be no more likely to notice unexpected events than anyone else.

With this in mind, Patrick Rooney and I (Neisser & Rooney, 1979) tested some fourth and first graders at a local elementary school. (We are grateful to Eleanor Gibson for allowing us to use research facilities at the school that she had established.) The fourth graders accepted the selective looking task eagerly and performed it well. As a result, their pattern of noticing was very similar to that of the college students we had tested before. When the umbrella woman appeared (on the first trial), only 22% (4/19) of the fourth graders noticed her. The boy with the soda fared slightly worse: He was noticed by only 17% (3/18) of the subjects to whom he was shown.

The results with the first graders were different. Our selective looking task turns out to be difficult at this age. The subjects rarely responded to throws of the ball; when they did respond, their latencies were so great that other throws had occurred in the meantime. Mostly they just looked helplessly at the screen. As a result (we think), most of them did notice the critical events: 75% (15/20) saw the umbrella woman, and 76% (13/17) saw the boy. We do not interpret these data as indicating that younger children cannot perceive selectively, of course, since we think that selective looking occurs even in infants. Rather, we attribute the high proportion of noticing among first graders to their lack of involvement with the primary task. We hope soon to devise a task more appropriate to their abilities and to use it to conduct a more appropriate test of the probability that they notice unexpected events.

UNANSWERED QUESTIONS

The selective looking technique was originally devised to demonstrate the inadequacy of the filter theory of attention and its variants. I think this goal has been achieved. Perception is selective even with novel and ecologically impossible displays, even when no consistent feature distinguishes the relevant events from the irrelevant and apparently even in 4-month-old infants. Most reviews of experiments end with a call for further research, but I do not think any more is needed to make this central point.

That does not mean, however, that there is nothing more to do. The second line of research described here, dealing with the noticing (or nonnoticing) of unexpected events, has only begun. It is "still in its infancy," as we developmental psychologists like to say. So far, we do not know what preattentively noted fragements of information lead to noticing, in what sort of people, of what ages, under what conditions. We do not know what a perceiver must bring to a situation if she is to notice what another equally skilled perceiver would overlook. These are difficult questions, and their solution will require a collaborative effort in which we all learn from each other—developmental and nondevelopmental psychologists, Gibsonians and non-Gibsonians. In my experience, this kind of collaboration has been fruitful and rewarding indeed. It leads to a constructive blurring of theoretical identities and a consequent ability to focus on the important questions—on "How Perception Really Develops," as Eleanor Gibson (1978) has put it, and on how it really works.

ACKNOWLEDGMENTS

Most of the research reported in this paper was supported by the National Science Foundation through research Grant No. 75-10965.

REFERENCES

Bahrick, L., Walker, A., & Neisser, U. *Infants' perception of multimodal information in novel events*. Manuscript submitted for publication. 1979.

Becklen, R., Neisser, U., & Littman, D. *Selective looking as a function of similarity between events*. Manuscript in preparation, 1979.

Broadbent, D. E. *Perception and communication*. New York: Pergamon, 1958.

Buckhout, R. Eyewitness testimony. *Scientific American*, 1974, *231*(Dec.), 23–31.

Deutsch, J. A., & Deutsch, D. Attention: Some theoretical considerations. *Psychological Review*, 1963, *70*, 80–90.

Gibson, E. J. How perception really develops: A view from outside the network. In D. LaBerge & S. J. Samuels (Eds.), *Basic processes in reading*. Hillsdale, N.J.: Lawrence Erlbaum Associates, 1978.

Hirst, W. C., Neisser, U., & Spelke, E. S. Divided attention. *Human Nature*, 1978, *1*(June), 54–61.

Hirst, W. C., Spelke, E. S., Reaves, C. C., Caharack, G., & Neisser, U. Dividing attention without alternation or automaticity. *Journal of Experimental Psychology (General)*, 1979, in press.

Kahneman, D. *Attention and effort*. Englewood Cliffs, N.J.: Prentice-Hall, 1973.

Littman, D. *The effects of stimulus continuity and concurrent sound on selective looking.* Unpublished doctoral dissertation, Cornell University, 1976.

Littman, D., & Becklen, R. Selective looking with minimal eye movements. *Perception & Psychophysics*, 1976, *20*, 77–79.

Moray, N. Attention in dichotic listening: Affective cues and the influence of instructions. *Quarterly Journal of Experimental Psychology*, 1959, *11*, 56–60.

Neisser, U. *Cognitive psychology.* Englewood Cliffs, N.J.: Prentice-Hall, 1967.

Neisser, U. *Cognition and reality.* San Francisco: Freeman, 1976.

Neisser, U., & Becklen, R. Selective looking: Attending to visually specified events. *Cognitive Psychology*, 1975, *7*, 480–494.

Neisser, U., & Dube, E. F. *Interrupting the perceptual cycle: When do we notice unexpected events?* Paper presented at the meeting of the Eastern Psychological Association, Washington, D.C., March 1978.

Neisser, U., Dube, E. F., Karis, D., & Bahrick, L. *Noticing unexpected events.* Manuscript in preparation, 1979.

Neisser, U., & Rooney, P. *A developmental study of noticing unexpected events.* Manuscript in preparation, 1979.

Posner, M. I. Coordination of internal codes. In W. G. Chase (Ed.), *Visual information processing.* New York: Academic Press, 1973.

Slee, J. A. *The perceptual nature of visual imagery.* Unpublished doctoral dissertation. Australian National University, 1976.

Spelke, E. S. Infants' intermodal perception of events. *Cognitive Psychology*, 1976, *4*, 553–560.

Spelke, E. S., Hirst, W. C., & Neisser, U. Skills of divided attention. *Cognition*, 1976, *4*, 215–230.

Stern, W. Wirklichkeitsversuche. *Beitrage zur Psychologie der Aussage*, 1904, *2*, 1–31.

10 Exploring Audible and Visible Events in Infancy

Elizabeth S. Spelke
University of Pennsylvania

EXPLORING AND KNOWING

Young perceivers face the formidable task of discovering and making sense of their surroundings. Each individual must learn about nonliving objects and happenings, about people and social encounters, about actions and their consequences. Human infants appear to approach this task by investigating events capably and persistently. Exploration may be an infant's principal endeavor. By the end of the 1st year, a baby seeks and obtains information by looking, listening, touching, locomoting, and acting on the world. Eleanor Gibson has emphasized that perception develops as young creatures actively search for stimulus information specifying the significant properties of things. Human infancy thus may be a time of rapid perceptual change.

I am intrigued by the infant's explorations because of the intimate relation of exploring to knowing. Knowledge guides exploration in two respects. First, perceivers must seek to extend their knowledge of the things they investigate. By definition, they must have questions to ask. Second, perceivers must already know something about an event in order to investigate it. Exploration would be highly inefficient—and perhaps impossible—for those who knew nothing about when, where, and how to seek relevant information. The very nature of exploration gives promise to studies of information-seeking in infancy. Observations of an exploring infant may reveal both the knowledge on which the earliest investigations depend and the knowledge to which they lead.

I focus on infants' explorations of events that they see and hear. Mature perceivers know a great deal about the audible and visible characteristics of things. When adults look and listen to an event at once, they recognize that they are following a single episode. When they look at one event while listening to another, they perceive that the object they see is not that which they hear. Furthermore, an adult who only hears an episode can often imagine how it looks, whereas one who only sees an object may anticipate the sounds it will produce. These abilities reflect the adult's knowledge of auditory–visual relations. This knowledge increases the economy of perception. Human adults can detect objects with manifold properties from a glance or a brief sound. Knowledge also increases the effectiveness of auditory–visual exploration. When adults hear an event, for example, they can use what they know of its visible properties to look for it directly. The effects of the adult's knowledge are clear, but its origins are obscure. Studies of exploration in infancy may help to reveal those origins.

I have investigated some of the knowledge permitting young perceivers to explore bimodally specified events and some of the knowledge that they gain by exploring. A series of experiments has been conducted with 4-month-old infants. The studies reported in the next section focused on one capacity underlying exploration: the ability to detect a relation between optic and acoustic stimulation specifying an event. Infants were found to be capable of perceiving auditory–visual relations when sounds occurred in synchrony with the visible movements of objects. The experiments described in the following section focused on some of the knowledge that an exploring infant acquired. Infants who were presented with certain bimodally specified events were able to learn something about them. Infants revealed what they learned by engaging in futher exploration. Acquired knowledge permitted them to explore even when no immediately given information united what they saw with what they heard.

These experiments suggest that infants can perceive unitary, bimodally specified events. As they explore by looking and listening, infants appear to gain knowledge of the events' distinctive properties. Thus they become capable of further exploration. An adult's knowledge of audible and visible episodes may derive from a cycle of exploring and knowing that begins early in life.

A BASIS FOR EXPLORATION: SENSITIVITY TO AUDITORY-VISUAL RELATIONS

Young infants tend to look at times and in places where sounds occur. Newborns may open their eyes in a dark room if a ringing bell is played (Haith, 1968), and they may scan simple displays in a more controlled manner if the displays are accompanied by human speech (Mendelson & Haith, 1976). Newborn infants sometimes move their eyes in the spatial direction of a voice or a click (Mendelson & Haith, 1976; Wertheimer, 1961), and 2-month-old infants increase their attention to a checkerboard pattern if they detect changes in the speech or music that accompanies it (Horowitz, 1974). These observations indicate that young infants can explore visual and auditory episodes sharing no internal structure and specifying no unitary event. The studies do not reveal, however, if infants perceive a relation between the displays they see and hear. In order to explore events effectively, perceivers must be able to distinguish sights and sounds that specify a single episode from those that occur together by chance. They must perceive the *unity* of a bimodally specified event and the separateness of unrelated sights and sounds. According to traditional associationist theories of perception (e.g., Berkeley, 1709/1910; Mill, 1829), very young infants are not capable of this. For naive perceivers, sights and sounds are not yet associated, and so are experienced as unrelated visual and auditory sensations. A different expectation arises from the perspective of Eleanor and James Gibson, who propose that there are amodal invariants in stimulus information. Eleanor Gibson (1969) has suggested that perceivers of any age should be able to discover intermodal relations if they can detect information that is available in more than one stimulus modality. I began by asking whether infants can perceive auditory-visual relations, and if so, on what basis.

In these studies, infants revealed their capacity for biomodal perception by their patterns of exploration. They viewed two events, side by side, while hearing sounds appropriate to one event through a central speaker. We judged when the babies looked to the acoustically specified and nonspecified episodes. In some of the experiments, a "visual preference" procedure was used to investigate the exploratory activity of following an event by looking and listening. A sound accompaniment was played for several minutes, and total looking time to each event was assessed. Infants were expected to look more to the sounding object if they could detect the intermodal relationship. In some studies, a "visual search" procedure was used to focus on the activity of looking for the source of a sound. An auditory accompaniment was played briefly while infants looked between two events, and subsequent looking toward each event was recorded. If a baby was aware of the auditory–visual relation he or she was expected to search for the acoustically specified episode.

In an initial study, part of which was reported in Spelke (1976), the preference method was used. Four-month-old infants viewed two natural and possibly familiar events. One event was game of "peekaboo" played by a woman they did not know. The other was a sequence of percussion music played with a tambourine, a wood block, and a moving wooden baton. Both episodes were filmed in sound, and each sound track was temporally synchronized with the movements of the appropriate visible object. While the films were shown side by side, an experimental group of infants heard each sound track in succession for several minutes. The sounds were played through a speaker placed behind the projection screen and centered between the films. A control group of infants watched the same events projected silently. The measure of interest was the proportion of total looking time that was devoted to the acoustically specified episode.

Infants in the experimental group directed 64% of their looking time to whichever event was projected in sound [$t(21) = 5.60$, $p < .001$]. A comparison of the experimental and control groups revealed that infants responded to the sound of the percussion sequence (see Table 10.1). They looked longer to the percussion film when it was projected in sound than when it was projected with no sound accompaniment; the peekaboo sound track had no comparable effect on looking. Infants explored the musical episode by looking and listening.

In a more recent preference experiment by Bahrick, Walker, and Neisser (1978), auditory–visual exploration of other natural events was investigated. Four-month-old infants were shown a game of pattycake, a musical sequence played on a xylophone, and the movements of a Slinky toy that repeatedly opened and closed as it was held by two hands. Each infant viewed two of these events, accompanied by sounds appropriate to one of them. The subjects devoted two-thirds of their looking time to the member of the pair that was acoustically specified.

The young perceivers in these initial experiments looked primarily at events they heard. They did not simply look at times or in places where sounds occurred, since each sound was concurrent with two events and was played between them. Knowledge of intermodal relations guided looking. The babies in these studies were able to discover a relation between the optic and acoustic stimulation that specified each episode.

Infants might discover such auditory–visual relations in either of two ways. First, they might be able to detect certain familiar objects by looking and listening. For example, the infants studied by Bahrick et al. (1978) might have seen and heard the pattycake sequence to involve clapping hands, an event not depicted in the other films. Learned associations between the sight and

TABLE 10.1
Proportion of Looking Time to Acoustically Specified
and Nonspecified Natural Events

	Peekaboo	Percussion
Event projected in sound ($n = 22$)	.72	.56
Both events projected silently ($n = 16$)	.65	.35
$t(36)$	0.74	2.20*

*$p < .05$.

sound of this event might have guided exploration. Alternatively, infants might be able to detect the common temporal structure of optic and acoustic stimulation. Every sound in the filmed events was synchronized with the visible movements of an object. The subjects might have responded to this temporal synchrony. By 7 months, infants are known to detect the invariance of a temporal pattern over visual and auditory modalities (Allen, Walker, Symonds, & Marcell, 1977). It seems possible that infants use this ability to discover intermodal relations.

In three experiments reported in Spelke (1978), this possibility was tested. I investigated infants' sensitivity to the temporal synchrony of the sounds and visible movements of objects. In the first experiment, two objects moved and sounded in synchrony, each at a distinctive rate. Sixteen 4-month-old infants were presented with two films, each depicting a toy animal—a kangaroo or a donkey—that was lifted by invisible strings into the air and dropped to the ground. A percussion sound accompanied each landing: a "thump" for one animal and a "gong" for the other. One animal bounced approximately once every 2 sec, whereas the other bounced about four times as rapidly. The animals moved out of phase with each other. When the two films were shown with one auditory accompaniment, the sounds were synchronized with only one event. The pairing of sounds and objects was arbitrary and counter-balanced. Infants could respond to the intermodal relations only by detecting the temporal synchrony of sound and movement.

The experiment consisted of a visual preference episode followed by a visual search episode. During the preference episode, each infant viewed one film of the kangaroo and one of the donkey. One animal moved in time to each percussion sound. The films were projected side by side as the sound tracks were heard in succession through a centrally placed speaker. Looking time was recorded and coded as in the previous preference studies.

The visual search episode followed 5 minutes after the preference episode. Each infant viewed the same events in the same locations. While the films were projected silently, a flashing light attracted the baby's gaze between the events and heralded the onset of a sound. The synchronized sound of one event was played for 5 sec through the central speaker while the filmed objects continued to move as before. The infant's looking to the events was recorded during that brief period. This procedure was repeated up to 12 times with each sound track, producing as many as 24 search trials. Coders eliminated all trials on which an infant was already looking at one of the events when the sound began. An average of 9 trials remained for analysis. The coders calculated the number of trials on which an infant looked first to the acoustically synchronized event after the onset of a sound, and the number of trials on which he or she looked first to the nonsynchronized event.

The principal results appear on the first three lines of Table 10.2(a). Infants tended to look to the acoustically synchronized event during the search

TABLE 10.2
Visual Exploration of Acoustically Synchronized Events

	Synchronized Event	Nonsynchronized Event	$t(15)$
(a) Sounds temporally synchronized with objects moving at two tempos			
Preference Session 1	52.9	32.6	1.87*
Preference Session 2	35.5	41.4	< 1
Search (Experimental Group)	4.44	3.50	2.34*
Search (Control Group)	3.12	1.62	3.83**
(b) Nonsynchronized sounds and movements at two tempos			
Preference Session 1	37.9	41.1	< 1
Preference Session 2	36.5	32.5	< 1
Search	5.00	3.50	2.14*
(c) Sounds temporally synchronized with objects moving at one tempo			
Preference Session 1	47.0	32.7	1.53†
Preference Session 2	54.6	33.1	< 1
Search	4.12	3.06	1.93*

*$p < .05$.
**$p < .01$.
†$p < .10$.

episode but not during the preference episode. The babies looked longer to the appropriate object during the first preference session only, and the overall tendency to prefer the acoustically specified event was not strong. During the search episode, infants looked first to the synchronized object on reliably more trials. When a sound was played, they tended to look for the object that moved in concert with it.

Since every infant participated in the search test after the preference test, the earlier episode served as a period of familiarization with these events. A subsidiary study revealed that visual search would occur even without this period of familiarization. Sixteen additional 4-month-old infants participated in the same search test with the kangaroo and donkey events. This test was preceded by a familiarization period with completely different events: the peekaboo and percussion sequences. The experiment was otherwise identical to the main study. An average of six usable search trials was administered to each infant. The results of the search test appear on the fourth line of Table 10.2(a). Infants again looked first on more trials to the event synchronized with each brief sound. An analysis comparing the two experimental conditions confirmed that infants tended to look to the synchronized object [$F(1, 30) = 18.64$, $p < .001$], irrespective of their familiarization condition

($F < 1$). The infants were able to search for sounding objects by detecting the synchrony of sound and movement during the search test itself, even if they had never seen the objects previously.

The results of these experimental conditions provide evidence that infants are sensitive to the synchrony of sound and movement. Babies can use this temporal relation to guide exploration of unfamiliar events. A young perceiver does not need to learn that the particular sight and particular sound of an object belong together through a long and laborious process of association. He or she can detect this relation in events never before witnessed, provided that the sounds and visible movements are temporally synchronized.

Infants in this experiment could have detected either of two aspects of the temporal relation. First, since the objects moved at different rates, infants may have responded to the common tempo of sound and movement. They may have discovered that one object moved at the same speed as the auditory accompaniment. Second, since each object contacted the ground at the time that the appropriate sound occurred, infants may have responded to the simultaneity of sounds and moments of impact. The next two studies revealed that young perceivers can do both these things. They detect both the common tempo and the simultaneity of sounds and visible impacts.

In the second experiment of this series, infants were presented with two objects moving at different speeds, accompanied by sounds that occurred in the rhythm of one object's movement, but not at the time of either object's impacts. The films and procedure of the preceding study were used with one modification—each accompanying sound was played out of phase with the event that it specified. Tape recordings of the sound tracks from the kangaroo and donkey films were played as the films were shown. The films and recordings were begun at haphazard locations so that sounds did not systematically accompany either object's impacts. Furthermore, the speeds of each machine varied slightly and changed the phase relations of sounds and movement. Sounds did not always occur at the same point in the cycle of movement of either object. Since each auditory accompaniment occurred at the same rate as the movements of one filmed object, an infant could perceive an auditory–visual relation by detecting this common tempo. The events were shown to sixteen 4-month-old infants during a preference episode followed by a search episode. The search episode provided an average of 10 usable trials.

Infants once again perceived the auditory–visual relations, as indicated in Table 10.2(b). They showed no tendency to look to the acoustically specified events during either preference episode, but they looked for those events reliably during the search test. By their searching, infants revealed their ability to detect the common rate of sound and visible movement. Objects need not make contact at the time that sounds occur in order for a baby to perceive that the sounds and objects go together.

In the third temporal synchrony experiment, infants' sensitivity to the simultaneity of sounds and visible impacts was investigated. Infants viewed films of the kangaroo and donkey, each moving at the identical rate of one bounce per 2 sec. A sound was produced whenever the appropriate object made contact with the ground. One event was synchronized with the "thump" sound and one with the "gong." The films were begun at haphazard times, and the exact speed of the projectors varied slightly. Therefore, the objects rarely moved in phase with each other, and their phase relation changed over the course of a session. The simultaneity of sounds and impacts consistently tied each sound with one visible event, whereas the tempo of an auditory accompaniment was equally compatible with both events. Sixteen 4-month-old infants participated in a preference episode followed by a search episode. The procedure followed that of the preceding studies. An average of nine usable search trials was administered.

The results of the experiment appear in Table 10.2(c). Although infants showed no clear visual preference for the synchronized events, they searched reliably for an object when the appropriate sound was played. Infants were able to detect the simultaneity of sounds and impacts, even when the tempo of impacts could not be used to discriminate the acoustically specified event from the nonspecified event.

These experiments reveal that human infants can discover and explore unitary events by detecting a temporal pattern in light and sound. Infants are sensitive both to the common tempo and to the simultaneity of sounds and visible impacts. They should therefore be able to detect bimodal relations when sounding objects move in a variety of rhythms. This ability should serve them well, since many sounds are produced by visibly moving objects.

It is puzzling that such weak visual preferences were exhibited in the last three experiments, in view of the results of the earlier preference studies. I suspect that infants looked proportionately less to the sounding animals because of the extreme redundancy of these events. Babies may have attempted to follow both events during the preference episode, not just the event that they heard. A similar pattern of results has now been obtained with adult observers. College students were shown the kangaroo and donkey films under conditions like those of the infant preference studies. They viewed two films with one sound track on each of 4 trials (16 subjects) or 10 trials (12 subjects). Different sounds, films, and film positions were used on different trials. On each trial, the students were asked which event, if either, was projected in sound and where the sound had come from. These observers were clearly aware of the auditory–visual relations. They reported that the sound "went with" the synchronously moving animal on every trial. They also tended to localize the sound in the direction of the synchronized event. Although the sound track was always played from a central speaker, the subjects judged that the sound came from between the films on only 41% of the trials. They judged that the sound came from a speaker on the side of the synchronized object on 44% of the trials and from a speaker on the opposite side on 15% of the trials. The students nevertheless showed no visual preference for the synchronized events. Looking times were vicariously recorded on the first trial. Only 50.3% of the total looking time was devoted to the synchronized event. Clearly, neither infants nor adults always look and listen to the bimodally specified events they perceive. Infants nevertheless demonstrated their ability to detect auditory–visual relations by looking to an object at the time that its sound began.

In summary, 4-month-old infants consistently attempted to explore by listening and looking. Their searching revealed an ability to perceive the unity of certain events. They perceived an auditory-visual relation when sounds accompanied the visible contacts of an object with the ground. Infants probably detected the synchrony of sound and movment in the more natural events studied by Spelke (1976) and by Bahrick et al. (1978) as well. They appear to perceive the unity of a variety of audible and visible episodes.

The present findings complement those of research on exploring by sight and touch. Babies consistently seek to manipulate the objects that they see. Furthermore, their reaching, grasping, and precursory activities are noticeably accommodated to an object's visually specified distance (Bower, 1972; Field, 1976; von Hofsten, 1976), size (Bower, 1972; Bruner & Koslowski, 1972), and shape (Bower, 1972; Bryant, Jones, Claxton, & Perkins, 1972; Gottfield, Rose, & Bridger, 1977). Although the age of emergence of these activities has been debated, all appear within the first year of life. Young perceivers use knowledge about a variety of intermodal relations to guide their investigations of objects.

THE FRUITS OF EXPLORATION:
LEARNING ABOUT AUDITORY–VISUAL RELATIONS

I have focused so far on the perceptual knowledge that makes exploration possible. I consider now the further knowledge to which exploration may lead. As adults, we possess knowledge about many of the objects that we see and hear. We know, for example, that telephones have a characteristic look and sound, and that people gesture and speak in certain ways. When an infant perceives a bimodally specified event and investigates it by looking and listening, does he or she begin to learn about its properties? In two experiments, I sought to determine whether infants can acquire knowledge about the audible and visible properties of events.

These experiments have a precedent in Lyons-Ruth's (1977) recent study of infants' ability to learn about a moving, sounding object. She familiarized 4-month-old infants with a toy by waving it in front of them and producing its sound. The sound was heard in the toy's direction. Lyons-Ruth tested learning by presenting the sound to the baby's side, where the original or a different toy could be seen. Infants looked less to the novel than to the familiar toy. This difference was taken to reflect "gaze aversion" from the novel object, a conflict reaction to the unexpected juxtaposition of the sound and object. Whether or not her subjects were really in conflict, they evidently learned something about the sight and sound of the toy.

In the present experiments, I investigated whether acquired knowledge of an object could guide auditory–visual exploration. Infants were shown two familiar sounding objects, presented in such a way that optic and acoustic stimulation were spatially and temporally unrelated. The babies participated in a visual search test. I expected that infants who encountered a familiar sound would look for the object that it specified.

The first experiment, conducted with Cynthia Owsley, confirmed that $3\frac{1}{2}$- to $7\frac{1}{2}$-month-old infants know about the audible and visible characteristics of their parents. We used a variant of the visual search method. Each infant sat facing between the mother and father, who faced their baby. After a toy was waved between the parents to attract the baby's attention, one parent was heard to speak for several seconds. The parent's voice was played from a tape recording made prior to the experimental episode. It was heard between the two adults, who remained motionless. Thus, faces and voices were neither spatially coincident nor temporally synchronized. Only an infant who knew about the audible and visible characterisitics of the parents could search appropriately. The procedure otherwise followed that of the previous search experiments. Thirteen usable trials, on average, were administered to each baby. (For more information, see Spelke & Owsley, 1979.)

Infants tended to search visually for the parent whose voice was played (Table 10.3). They looked to the "speaking" parent on more trials than to the "silent" parent [$F(1,24) = 10.22, p < .01$]. This tendency did not interact with the age of the subject ($F < 1$). Although searching was most consistent at the oldest age, a separate replication confirmed that the youngest infants searched as well. Since no spatial or temporal information united a parent's

TABLE 10.3
Visual Search for a Parent Who Is Heard to Speak

Age	"Speaking" Parent	"Silent" Parent	$F(1,24)$
$3\frac{1}{2}$	6.67	4.43	5.48*
$5\frac{1}{2}$	6.56	5.67	1.36
$7\frac{1}{2}$	7.44	4.89	5.98*

*$p < .05$.

face and voice, knowledge must have guided looking. By four months, infants possess and use such knowledge.

The mother and father are surely among the most well-known objects in the child's environment, but they are not the only ones that a baby comes to know. A final experiment indicated that babies can learn rapidly about the audible and visible characteristics of less familiar things. Infants were introduced to two new sounding objects. Their learning about the objects was revealed through a subsequent search test.

In this experiment, I used the films and sound tracks of the last temporal synchrony study: the kangaroo and donkey, each bouncing at the same tempo. Sixteen infants viewed these events in two visual preference sessions. During each session, the objects moved out of phase with each other, and a sound occurred whenever one of them hit the ground. The infants subsequently participated in a search test in which sounds and movements were not synchronized. As in the mother–father study, the sound tracks were played from a tape recording. Since the objects moved at the same rate, no temporal information united either sound with either object during the test. Infants could search for the object that was previously synchronized with each sound only if they had learned about the auditory–visual relations.

The results are given in Table 10.4. Infants did not consistently prefer the acoustically synchronized event during the familiarization period, but they learned something about it. During the search test, they looked first reliably more often to the event that had previously been synchronized with each sound. Infants searched despite the absence of any temporal information uniting what they saw and heard. They evidently acquired knowledge during the preference episode that guided their looking.

In summary, a baby can develop knowledge about temporally synchronized sounds and objects. He or she can use this knowledge to explore in the absence of any spatial or temporal information. Infants successfully searched for their parents in the study by Spelke and Owsley (1979) and for new objects in the last experiment. A child seems to learn rapidly about auditory–visual

TABLE 10.4
The Effect of Knowledge on Visual Search for Aurally Specified Events

	Acoustically Specified Event	Non- Specified Event	$t(15)$
Preference Session 1	48.6	31.2	1.04
Preference Session 2	29.7	40.9	< 1
Search	4.94	3.88	2.72*

*$p < .01$.

relations. Knowledge derived from prior investigations leads to further investigations.

ISSUES AND QUESTIONS

The findings that I have discussed lead to several questions. First, in what sense can infants perceive a bimodally specified event? Do they experience a direct association of visual and auditory patterns, or do they perceive these sources of information to specify an object not tied to stimulation in any particular modality? For example, do infants perceive that the mother's speaking face "goes with" her voice, or do they perceive that the mother's face and voice are two specifiers of a single, "amodal" object? The experiments described so far certainly do not resolve this difficult issue. Studies of the child's ability to learn about objects that can be seen, heard, and felt may do so. Suppose, for example, that infants were familiarized first with an event specified visually and tactually, and then with the same event specified aurally and tactually. Would these infants grasp the relation between the sight and sound of that event? If infants could learn about intermodal relations under these circumstances, it would seem that they are learning about objects, not simply about auditory–visual correspondences. Experiments to test this possibility are getting under way.

The second question concerns the nature of the child's acquired knowledge. What is learned by infants who search for an object that is spatially and temporally unrelated to its sound? Do they learn to look for the object, or do they learn that the object can be brought to view by executing a particular response, such as a leftward turn of the head? If babies look for an object, do they identify it by its location or by certain of its internal characteristics? Preliminary research on these questions suggests that babies acquire knowledge about objects with particular visible characteristics, not about places or responses. Infants were familiarized with two sounding objects and then were given a search test. During the test, the lateral positions of the objects were reversed. Infants nevertheless tended to search for the object that each sound specified, looking in a new direction and toward a new place in order to do so.

A final question concerns the kinds of intermodal relations that babies can detect. Optic and acoustic stimulation from an event are usually related in three general ways. First, the visible impacts of surfaces are synchronized with any sounds that they produce. Second, sounds and their visible sources can be perceived in the same place. Third, objects tend to be audible and visible at the same time. We have seen that infants are sensitive to the temporal synchrony of sound and movement. Do they detect the other auditory–visual relations as well? Babies were not able to respond to those relations in my studies, since each sound accompaniment occurred at the same time as two visible events and was centered between them. Further research could compare infants' sensitivity to the three kinds of auditory–visual relations directly. Such comparisons may reveal which relations are detected first, and whether infants' appreciation of one serves as a basis for their discovery of the others.

CONCLUSIONS AND SPECULATIONS

My experiments have focused on the infant's ability to explore bimodally specified events. Their findings suggest that infants engage in a cycle of perceiving, exploring, and knowing. Exploration of events, guided by an ability to perceive their unity, may bring the infant knowledge, and this knowledge may make further investigations possible. A mature perceiver's awareness of the visible and audible properties of objects may ultimately derive from this cycle of exploratory activity.

In discussing these studies, I have so far bypassed two issues that dominate most investigations of intermodal coordination in infancy. I will conclude by considering: (1) the roles of nature and nurture in the development of auditory–visual perception; and (2) the qualitative or quantitative nature of of developmental changes in intersensory functioning. These comments are speculative. My ideas evolved as I considered the role of exploration in learning and development.

Although many earlier psychologists have credited the newborn infant with little knowledge about the world, it is now clear that babies arrive with a host of capacities (cf. Cohen & Salapatek, 1975; Gibson, 1977). Empiricist assumptions are yielding to a growing appreciation of the infant's considerable native endowment. Quite paradoxically, this new respect for the innate competence of humans may ultimately provide new ground for empiricism. Infants appear blessed primarily with the ability to explore and learn. They know how to find out about their environment. They are able to investigate objects and events in order to begin developing the rich perceptual capacities that will support them as adults.

To focus on the infant's intermodal exploration is to bridge the nativist–empiricist controversy in a special way. In order to explore a visible and audible event, the infant must be able to relate information from different sensory systems and perceive a unitary episode. However, babies may begin with little knowledge of the characteristic sights and sounds of most objects. They may use their capacity to explore audible and visible events primarily in order to gain knowledge. As knowledge accrues, this capacity will grow.

What happens to the child's perceptual abilities as he or she develops? Do the abilities undergo qualitative change? According to some descriptions of intersensory development, young infants perceive events in fundamentally different ways from adults, and their perceptions often deceive them. Infants are thought either to experience unrelated modality-specific sensations or to perceive at any moment all sights, sounds, smells, and other feelings as one unique and indivisible whole. In either case, perception must undergo a particularly dramatic developmental change. Infants must shed false perceptions for true ones as they come to appreciate that information in different stimulus modalities sometimes specifies a unitary event and sometimes does not. Similar developments have been proposed in other realms: The child progresses from experiences of fleeting images to the awareness of permanent objects, from amorphous bodily sensations to the differentiation of self from world, from egocentrism to social reciprocity.

If infants are viewed as seekers of information, they will appear to suffer not from perceptions that are misguided but from knowledge that is insufficiently precise. Infants, like adults, recognize that patterns of light and sound are sometimes related and sometimes not. They may begin with some ability to perceive bimodally specified events. But infants know vastly less about these events than an adult, and their means for exploring them are few. As they grow, infants gain knowledge that permits them to perceive and explore ever more effectively the things they see and hear.

One who views infants as explorers will be impressed both with their native abilities and with the enormity of what they must learn, both with the adaptiveness and with the poverty of early perception. Such a person will affirm, with Eleanor Gibson, that perception, exploration, and knowledge of an event are nearly always adapted to the event's real properties but that this correspondence becomes increasingly specific and differentiated with development. He or she might turn to research on human infancy, as Gibson herself has done, in order to discover the initial capacities for exploring, perceiving, and knowing that allow this development to begin.

REFERENCES

Allen, T. W., Walker, K., Symonds, L., & Marcell, M. Intrasensory and intersensory perception of temporal sequences during infancy. *Developmental Psychology,* 1977, *13,* 225–229.

Bahrick, L., Walker, A., & Neisser, U. *Infants' perception of multimodal information in novel events.* Paper presented at the meeting of the Eastern Psychological Association, Washington, D.C., March 1978.

Berkeley, G. An essay towards a new theory of vision, 1709. In A. C. Fraser (Ed.), *Selections from Berkeley.* Oxford: Clarendon, 1910.

Bower, T. G. R. Object perception in infants. *Perception,* 1972, *1,* 15–30.

Bruner, J. S., & Koslowski, B. Visually preadapted constituents of manipulatory action. *Perception,* 1972, *1,* 3–14.

Bryant, P. E., Jones, P., Claxton, V. C., & Perkins, G. M. Recognition of shapes across modalities by infants. *Nature,* 1972, *240,* 303–304.

Cohen, L. B., & Salapatek, P. *Infant perception: From sensation to cognition.* New York: Academic Press, 1975.

Field, J. Relation of young infants' reaching behavior to stimulus distance and solidity. *Developmental Psychology,* 1976, *12,* 444–448.

Gibson, E. J. *Principles of perceptual learning and development.* Englewood Cliffs, N.J.: Prentice-Hall, 1969.

Gibson, E. J. *The ecological optics of infancy: The differentiation of invariants given by optical motion.* Presidential Address to Division 3 of the Annual Convention of the American Psychological Association, San Francisco, August 1977.

Gottfried, A. W., Rose, S. A., & Bridger, W. H. Cross-modal transfer in human infants. *Child Development,* 1977, *48,* 118–123.

Haith, M. *Visual scanning in infants.* Paper presented at the regional meeting of the Society for Research in Child Development, Worcester, Mass., March 1968.

von Hofsten, C. Binocular convergence as a determinant of reaching behavior in infancy. *Perception,* 1976, *6,* 139–144.

Horowitz, F. C. (Ed.). Visual attention, auditory stimulation, and language discrimination in young infants. *Monographs of the Society for Research in Child Development,* 1974, *39,*(5–6, Serial No. 158).

Lyons-Ruth, K. Bimodal perception in infancy: response to auditory–visual incongruity. *Child Development,* 1977, *48,* 820–827.

Mendelson, M. J., & Haith, M. M. The relation between audition and vision in the human newborn. *Monographs of the Society for Research in Child Development,* 1976, *41*(1, Serial No. 167).

Mill, J. *Analysis of the phenomena of the human mind.* London: Longman & Dyer, 1829.

Spelke, E. Infants' intermodal perception of events. *Cognitive Psychology,* 1976, *8,* 553–560.

Spelke, E. *Intermodal exploration by four-month-old infants: Perception and knowledge of auditory–visual events.* Unpublished doctoral dissertation, Cornell University, 1978.

Spelke, E., & Owsley, C. Intermodal exploration and knowledge in infancy. *Infant Behavior and Development,* 1979, *2,* 13–27.

Wertheimer, M. Psychomotor co-ordination of auditory–visual space at birth. *Science,* 1961, *134,* 1962.

Afterword

Eleanor J. Gibson
Cornell University

Harry Levin
Harvard University

Festschriften seem to me to put the emphasis the wrong way about. The person being honored has the least distinct voice in the volume. Of course, the contributors have admired and been influenced by Eleanor Gibson, but the readers must decide what she herself thinks by inference from the various chapters. When the editor asked me to do a personal afterword I decided that the readers would be more interested and better served by Jackie Gibson telling us about her intellectual life in psychology. Who influenced her? How have her ideas changed during her career? What have been the theoretical consistencies in her own research? Where has psychology gone astray, in her opinion, and what directions look promising for the future?

We had serveral hours, not of interviews, but of conversations attended by a tape recorder. The version here is much condensed. I have only juxtaposed a small amount of material when I thought that later comments helped expand points we had talked about earlier. I kept the vernacular style rather than try to convert conversations to a literary voice. Besides, as you will see when you read, Jackie Gibson talks in remarkably well-formed sentences. As I listened to the tapes, I regret that I did not ask her to talk more about her present research on infants' development of perception.

HARRY LEVIN
Cambridge, Mass.

237

L: As a beginning, would you talk about people you have known during your career in psychology: people who have influenced you, or people you have known to be interesting as psychologists, or in other ways?

G: The people who had an opportunity to influence me at Smith included Koffka, of course, who was the most illustrious psychologist there at the time. And I suppose he did, as I think back on it now, because I went to Yale finding myself pretty much outside the S/R climate that was characteristic of Yale at that time; S/R learning theory was going to solve everything, across the board. I had to stay within the limits of it somehow in order to get a degree there, but you can think your own thoughts in the meantime and translate back and forth, luckily.

L: How much contact did you have with Koffka?

G: He taught a course in Gestalt psychology which was taken by seniors and the graduate students. It was the basis of his book, *The Principles of Gestalt Psychology.* He taught the course, in fact, by writing his lecture for the day—a piece of a chapter—wherever he was in the book. He would bring it to class and read it from his longhand manuscript—literally read it to the class. We all wrote it down as best we could. And then, the next day, some student was assigned at the beginning of the hour to give a 5 or 10 minute précis of what he had read us the day before. Afterward, he would go on with the new pages.

L: It sounds terribly dull—no discussion?

G: He did not invite questions. Once in a while people would ask questions, but he would deal with them very summarily. The substitute for it was supposed to be this précis that somebody would do. When it contained ideas that he considered wrong, or mispresentations, he would correct them.

To continue about Koffka—there wasn't only that class. If it had been the only contact I had with him, I don't think I would have been influenced except to think that he was a bore as a lecturer. But he also gave a seminar, year after year. The seminar was attended by members of the department faculty and whatever graduate students there were. In that seminar—run as a regular seminar—people would give reports on various things, and since there were faculty members there, there was discussion. That's when I suppose I really got some grip on what he was thinking.

L: What intrigued you about his theories?

G: I suppose it was the breadth of the theory as much as anything; also it seemed closer to life and the way people really perceived things and thought than anything that was going on at Yale then, where the research was done with rats and you didn't talk about how people perceived the world at all.

L: Who else influenced you?

G: I suppose everybody who becomes a good friend, that you spend a lot of time talking to, has an influence on you, but I find it impossible to say that I owe what I am to specific people. I believe, maybe incorrectly, that there have been a lot of people I've listened to and learned from, but I've tried to put it together for myself. I would find it very difficult to say that one person was my prime influence, that what I am today I owe to my dear old mentor so and so. I believe I owe more to Jimmy (James J. Gibson) than to anyone else because we've talked to each other a lot longer, or rather we've read each other a lot longer—when we talk together we argue because it's so important to both of us.

I wouldn't name Hull as a major influence; not that I didn't have a lot of respect for him—I did. I felt that he was a man of huge integrity, that he felt the importance of his goals almost in the way that a minister would. In fact, he was very ministerial. What he was doing was almost like a religion to him. You can't help admiring someone who takes his work so seriously. Also I admired him because, unlike many people, he was able to switch his research to another angle many times. And he did it well. He would sit down and learn things—study a new kind of mathematics, or read the logical positivists—and start out on a whole new tack. When you recall that his first book was a book on testing, the next one on hypnosis, and that he wound up being the major learning theoriest in the country, that's pretty unusual. I have a great admiration for people who don't get stuck in one channel, sing the same song over and over again. I think a mark of a good scholar is the ability to change one's act when circumstances make it appropriate.

L: So, Hull's influence was indirect, like Koffka's?

G: I certainly got something from him, but when I came to Yale I came with other things in mind. The place that I was heading for then was really comparative psychology—I was interested in animal behavior, and I did not get that from either Koffka or Hull. I went to Yale hoping to work with Yerkes. At the time Yale seemed to be the place where most was going on in comparative psychology. I got that interest from a course I took on animal behavior with a psychologist at Smith named Margaret Curti, whom you probably know nothing about. I was fascinated by the subject. When I met Jimmy I got very interested in experimental psychology and that's what really stuck in the end, but I was eager to study animal behavior when I went to Yale. At Yale, there was an opportunity to work with animals besides rats. I thought that I could work with other animals and look at the whole subject from a broad comparative view. It turned out that I couldn't.

L: Do you trace your emphasis on adaptive behavior to your early interests in comparative?

G: Yes. And possibly I've had an influence on Jimmy's point of view in that respect. Mostly he's influenced me, but I think in that way I may have influenced him, too. I think that he became more concerned with evolution and with adaptive aspects of behavior and perception than he would have if we hadn't had many discussions together when I was working with animals, at the Behavior Farm and with the visual cliff.

L: What influences have you and Jimmy had on each other?

G: Well, he has taught me all I know about perception, of course, except what I learned from Koffka, but that was far less than I ever learned from Jimmy; much less, because I keep on learning from him all the time. But also, his emphasis on ecology has been very important to me. As I said, I may have influenced him to some extent, toward an ethological emphasis. He doesn't use that word much; he talks about ecology instead, but nevertheless it's there. His notion of affordance, for instance, is very much related to ethological concepts, to the notion of adaptation.

L: What do you mean by an ethological concept?

G: It's hard to say clearly; the derivation of the word doesn't tell you. The people that we think of as starting ethology (if you think of it as a discipline) were people who worked in the first place with birds, studying their behavior in relation to the natural habitat. You can trace it back farther than Lorenz to people like Craig and Spalding, who had simiar points of view—they wanted to study animal behavior in relation to the animal's habitat and what was adaptive for its survival in that habitat. That's what I think of basically as an ethological point of view. Lorenz had that, but he also invented a lot of concepts that are not essential for an ethological point of view, like critical periods and innate releasers. To me, the important thing about ethology is the idea that you must consider the behavior of a creature in relation to its habitat and consider how its behavior or its perception, either one, is relevant for surviving in its particular niche and being a successful species.

L: Your own work has always been in the laboratory.

G: I see no reason why an ethologist shouldn't work in a laboratory, and lots of them do. They make themselves aware of the animal's habitat and try to watch objectively, with good observational methods, how it behaves in that habitat. Since it turned out that I couldn't work with animals, and instead found myself working with human beings, I suppose you could say I had the option of becoming an anthropologist and going around looking at people here and there, but that wasn't what I was trained to do. One can try to look at how people behave adaptively in relation to their habitats much as one can with animals. But I want, in doing that, to keep in mind a comparative point of view. I think if you lose that, you begin to do what so-called human ethologists have been doing. There's a group of them—mostly child psychologists and psychiatrists. The ideas that they have borrowed from ethology often seem to me to be the irrelevant ones. They are interested in critical periods, in innate releasers (the smile is often cited as one), and so on. The borrowed concepts sometimes seem more emphasized than the adaptive features of the behavior vis-a-vis the human animal's world.

L: What's happened to comparative psychology, in your opinion?

G: There was very little in this country for quite a while during the heyday of behaviorism. People were concentrating on a white rat and thought they could get the answers for all mammalian learning by doing that, so there weren't many comparative psychologists around. There were a few at the Museum of Natural History, but they didn't enjoy great popularity—there was Schneirla who was principally interested in ants. But there was a real hole there. People like Lorenz and Tinbergen came along and filled the hole. Psychology lost a field, and it was gained by people with a different kind of training.

L: So you don't think that comparative psychology has much of a future in psychology?

G: I think it could, but I think that it's been preempted by the ethologists and I doubt that they are going to let it go back to psychology departments, in terms of institutional arrangements.

L: Let's talk a bit more about Hull. It seems to me that at the time of *Principles of Behavior,* there were a number of people like Guthrie and Tolman, who were building big theories—theories of behavior. And that doesn't seem to be done very much any more. People are theorizing about small areas in which they are working.

G: Maybe they are afraid to do it because they look back at Guthrie and find that he had one simple-minded idea which he wished to apply across the board, and it looks ridiculous to them. Perhaps the same thing is true of Hull, less so because Hull tried much harder to show how he was going to apply his principles broadly. I think Hull aspired to have a grand theory—he always hoped to come full circle, back to his Ph.D. thesis—he was going to finish with concepts. But of course he didn't.

L: Do you think that psychologists work on grand theories now?

G: I think that most psychologists have some kind of theory in the back of their minds, which is for them a sort of framework for what they are doing, and then they have circles within that that get gradually smaller until they get down to what they are actually doing research on at the moment.

L: In psychology, whose theorizing do you admire?

G: What's stylish at the moment, of course, is information processing and constructivism and I suppose that the person in psychology who has the grandest theory is Piaget. I can think of no one at present who aspires to as much grandness of theory as he does. Would you agree with that? He wants to cover everything from reflexes to epistemology.

L: The constructivist notion is one that you have argued with for a long time. Why is it appealing to most of psychology? And I wonder why it has taken so long, or been so hard, for American psychology to give up the S/R model?

G: Do you think it's really prevalent still?

L: I think so.

G: Well, there's been a shift to information processing, but as you imply it's not really very different from an S/R approach. The difference seems to be mainly a willingness to talk about mentalistic things like memory, sensory input, and then some kind of transduction to other inferred processes. But it's still associationistic.

L: You began to work on a few information-processing studies, and I gather you became disenchanted with that approach.

G: Yes. I did that when I was first reading research of Dick Neisser's, and I thought he had some nice methods—especially the search task—that would be good for studying perceptual development. I proceeded to try it for a while, but when I found myself getting stuck in the bog of parallel or sequential processing, I felt that it was leading nowhere and I stopped.

L: What do you find dissatisfying about information processing?

G: I don't find anything satisfying about it. It seems to me that information processors do not, in the first place, analyze the stimulus information at all. They just talk about input. The emphasis is on a series of transductions or "codings." There is input that arrives at some kind of processor (a little man of some kind) and then moves on through a chain of inferred processes. It seems to me that it's full of mythical processes that no one has found a counterpart for in a nervous system, that it deals with trivial kinds of information extraction and doesn't start with anything real. It's a new way of talking about sensation-based perception in the context of a construction theory. It certainly never considers the adaptive functions of perceiving.

L: Do you think that information processing is going anywhere?

G: No, I don't think so. I don't think it has much longer to survive (probably wishful thinking).

L: What do you make of Chomsky's influence on American psychology?

G: I am not sure that its's had much influence on psychology, except for psycholinguistics. In psycholinguistics, it has had an influence, and I think to some extent it's still there. One of my students was writing about meaning— the meaning of language as it relates to the real world, and she had a splendid example showing the relation between the two. She wound up her paper by saying that although she finds that pragmatics and experience are very important in language development in young children, nevertheless, when it comes right down to it, language is a separate mode from the rest of cognition—it remains apart, it has its own rules, and they cannot be rooted in perception.

As far as Chomsky's nativism goes, I think, on the whole, that psychology at the moment is happily free of arguments about nativism–empiricism. I think at the moment we are enjoying the climate of knowing that an organism only survives in an environment and in fact has evolved in it, so the controversy isn't cluttering things up. Of course there's the IQ controversy. Maybe we can never get rid of it.

L: Let's think about your own work. What are the consistent ideas that run through your work?

G: When I was doing my thesis with Hull, I had to use what were the conventional rubrics of the time—all terms taken from conditioning. I talked about stimulus generalization and response generalization, but the main concept that I found useful was differentiation. And although I talked about differential inhibition, I didn't think of it in terms of inhibition in a Pavlovian sense at all. I think that the concept I had in my head was differentiation much as I think of it now, as a process that could take the place of association, which was central at that time. That concept has stuck with me ever since. It was somewhat disguised in my thesis because, in order to get a degree at Yale, it was essential to use the lingo that was conventional at that time.

L: I think most of the people who read those papers know that you were using the lingo but you weren't quite saying the same thing. You were telling Hull something about generalization.

G: Or differentiation, which I though of as the central concept, and still do. I think that I had the notion of perceptual learning in the back of my head then. I think of development, too, as being a process of differentiation. I have come farther than that, because in the experiments that we are doing now I am still concerned with differentiation as a process in the perceptual development of infants; but I am also much concerned with the development of a child's ability to pick up invariants over transformations. That idea has intrigued me more in recent years. When I wrote the book on perceptual learning and development, I was thinking of what was differentiated chiefly as being distinctive features of sets of things. First the sets get differentiated, then distinctive features within the sets, and so on. Perhaps the reason that was such a central idea for me at the time was because I was working on reading, and I had been thinking about perceptual differentiation of letters—of things drawn on paper—and there aren't invariants in the sense that there are real things happening over time in three dimensions. Distinctive features is a very useful concept for pictures, letters, that kind of thing. And it is to some extent for objects, like vases and faces, though it's less useful for faces than I thought at one time. If you try to think what distinctive features of a face are, you get awfully muddled because as well we know, it's nothing like eyes, and nose, and hair. Those vary, yes, but we don't recognize a face by recognizing the shape of the nose or eye color. There is something that is invariant, that is somehow a characteristic or a property of a person's face. I have a lot of samples that I have cut out of newspapers of pictures of the same person sitting up, giving an interview, and lying on a sofa thinking. Sometimes you wouldn't know it's the same person, because they are all static snapshots. But if you had seen that person while he was giving you the interview, you would know perfectly well that they were all the same person, because you would have detected some kind of invariant over all those changing perspectives.

L: In displays as complex as faces, what are the levels of these invariants?

G: I don't know—and I don't think anybody does. But I recall attempts like the one made by Harmon, for instance, who worked from an information-processing point of view. He had a set of 39 features (like nose shape and width of face), each one with three levels, and he had people sort photographs until they came down to the photograph they thought fitted the feature description they had been given. They were right about 50% of the time, and even then it was a limited set that they had to deal with; the exericse bore little relation to what happens in real life. You don't very often make a mistake in recognizing a person by his appearance—even when it's someone you haven't seen for 25 years.

L: Are there other ideas like differentiation that you can trace through your research?

G: I think that my interest in comparative psycholgy has led me to take an evolutionary point of view always; that goes for my interest in development as well.

L: Do you think of development as periods in the life of the organism that you can use for comparative purposes, or do you see it as a methodology?

G: You can think of it either way. Some people like to think of developmental research as being a way of studying a problem. They might think of perception as being the problem, and development as an approach you can take to studying perception. That's O.K.—I would agree with that. But I think also, that development is worth looking at in its own right. It seems to me that there are changes going on that are themselves very interesting. My ideas about comparative development in the sense of species development, and development of an individual are coming together. I have come to feel that the inheritance of the species is much more important than I used to think. I believe a lot of development is accounted for by species development and that the role of the environment in individual development is to realize what the possibilities are, to provide the sustenance for the potentials.

L: Then, do you think the genetic component of development is selective?

G: It's been selected by the time an organism begins. It's been selected for the species, and to some extent for individual members of the species, though less so. The basic selection is for the species, it seems to me. I also like Piaget's distinction between two aspects of experience that affect development. One is provided by the environment that is common to the species, like the physical layout of the world, and the other is the idiosyncratic environment peculiar to particular individuals—some people grow up in a home where there are lots of books and some don't, for example. It seems to me that's a simple, useful distinction. So many people get involved in battles over heredity and environment and forget that we are prepared as a species to develop and grow if we have certain very fundamental surroundings. Those fundamental surroundings include parents, enough to eat, opportunities to learn about the physical environment, and so on, and presumably they aren't going to be very different for different members of the species, but once in a while they are. That's when there's real trouble. The other aspect—the idiosyncratic one—probably accounts for a certain amount of variance, like which people achieve best in school. But on the whole, in terms of natural selection, that wouldn't have been very important.

L: What problems in developmental intrigue you now? What does the next decade in developmental research look like to you—what do you think is important?

G: A question that is intriguing a lot of people right now is a question that no one asked for a long time—that is, What moves development along? The answer, in terms of traditional American child psychology, was simply that there was an accumulation—you added up the associations. I was just looking at one of the articles that I used to give my students to read—an article by Sheldon White—about learning theory and development. The American child psychologist's view of development was traditionally based on learning theory and that's all. The article is very useful because it brings out so well what you get when you look at development that way—just one thing piled on another and nothing related to anything else.

Developmental psychologists have finally gotten back to the question that was asked 75 years ago by James Mark Baldwin—What is the nature of development? It's unfortunate for the history of developmental psychology that the person who made the big mark in this country was not Baldwin, but instead, G. Stanley Hall.

Baldwin was much influenced by the theory of evolution. Just before him there had been the rage for baby biographies; lots were written, as you know. There was, therefore, a kind of data base. Some of them weren't very good, but some were. Some are as interesting today as they were when they were written, like Preyer's "Mind of the Child." So, there was material about development, but no one tried to make a discipline of it, to say how we account for it. Hall said that "Ontogeny recapitulates phylogeny," a kind of theory I suppose, but Baldwin was really interested in a theory of development. His book *Mental Development in the Child and the Race* was an attempt. Unfortunately, his writing is academic and labored and awfully hard to read, but worth the trouble. Piaget apparently got many of his ideas (assimilation and accommodation for example) from Baldwin.

To return to your question, psychologists now are taking an interest in development as a process and what makes it move along. Piaget's notion is equilibration, but I never understood exactly what he means by it. He has just written a new book on it, so I bought it, but it hasn't clarified things for me.

L: What would be an example of a productive idea on the question, "What is development?"?

G: A few people would like to think of development as a dialectic process, in which there is conflict and then some sort of resolution of the conflict, when things reach an equilibrium, and a new conflict can arise. That may be the way

Piaget thinks of it, that that's what equilibration is all about. I think that the essential processes are the discovery of invariants in the world and the detection of affordances of things and events.

L: You don't think this is a stage process?

G: No, I don't think it's a stage process—only in the sense that some invariants cannot be discovered until other ones have been discovered before them. But that would not be stages in the sense that new faculties mature. I don't think that man is genetically built so that he goes through a sensorimotor stage that stops at 2 years, a preoperational stage that lasts until 7, and then another one until 11 and so on. It's a very old idea though. Rousseau had such a notion.

L: We talked a little bit about learning theory. What happened to learning theory?

G: That's a good question. There are still people who are doing conditioning experiments and comparing classical conditioning with operant conditioning, but they sound awfully out-of-date when you hear them talk. I don't think that there is a new learning theory. I think, instead, that information processing has substituted memory. Hardly anyone talks about a learning process. Even in developmental psychology, it's more stylish to talk about memory ("metacognition" is an in-word).

L: Of your own studies, over the years, can you think of one that pleases you the most—one that you really enjoyed doing, the results are important, one that you are particularly proud of?

G: It's really hard to choose. I guess I had more fun with the visual cliff than anything else. But. that may have been because it was the first time I worked with babies. I enjoy what we are doing with infants now as much as anything I've ever done, maybe more.

Author Index

Italicized page numbers denote pages with complete bibliographic information.

A

Abrams, M., 131, 140, *144*
Adamson, L., 99, *106*
Ai, J. W., 171, 172, *181*
Alegria, J., 187, 188, *196*
Allen, T. W., 225, *234*
Ames, A., 100, 102, 104, *106*
Anderson, G. G., 97, *106*
Anderson, I. H., 169, 174, 176, 179, 180, *181*
Anderson, R. C., 156, *165*
Anglin, J. M., 185, 195, *196*
Aslin, R., 95, *107*
Aslin, R. N., 91, *106*
Attneave, F., 147, *164*
Avin, E., 25, *36*

B

Bach-y-Rita, P., 193, *196*
Bahrick, L., 202, 212, 217, *218, 219,* 224, 229, *234*
Baker, J., 74, *86*
Ball, W. A., 98, *106*
Bamber, D., 132, 140, *143*
Bass, M. J., 9, *36*

Bateson, G., 186, *196*
Bean, K. L., 162, *164*
Bechtold, A. G., 96, 98, *107,* 188, *196*
Beck, L. F., 90, 93, *107*
Becklen, R., 202, 204, 205, 206, 208, 209, 213, *218, 219*
Benson, K., 101, *106*
Berkeley, G., 223, *234*
Bever, T., 191, 195, *197*
Bever, T. G., 183, *197*
Bindra, D., 131, *143*
Birch, H. B., 187, *197*
Blough, D. S., 17, 19, 20, 23, 24, 27, 28, 29, 33, 34, 35, *36*
Blyler, D., 157, *164*
Bond, G. L., 170, *181*
Boneau, C. A., 13, 17, 18, 19, 23, 25, *36*
Boswell, S. L., 101, *107*
Bouma, H., 177, *181*
Bower, G. H., 39, *60*
Bower, T. G. R., 90, 92, 98, 99, 101, *106, 188, 189, 190, 191, 193, 195, *196, 197,* 229, *234*
Bradley, D. R., 83, *86*
Bridger, W. H., 229, *235*
Broadbent, D. E., 201, *218*
Broughton, J. M., 91, 92, 98, *106,* 188, *196*
Brown, C. H., 179, *182*

247

Subject Index